Finding Virginia

Adventures Along the Rocky Trail of Life

By David Eilers

Copyright © 2011 David Eilers & eWillys

All rights reserved.

Version 1.0

ISBN: **1468079182**
ISBN-13: **978-1468079180**

This is a true story of love, loss, life, jeeps and me.

1. MAY 12TH, 2011

May 12, 2011 – 10:14 AM

David,

"Your dad fell down again in the dining room trying to carry a salad plate back to the kitchen and pushing the walker with one hand. Not a good idea and, of course, I had told him that, but he needs to do it 'my way'. It was complicated by his sciatic nerve thing which made getting him back up almost impossible. I decided to call the fire dept and they were here shortly and got him back up. He is not having any fun with this affliction."

Mom's email fills the screen of my Apple laptop, an appendage that dogs me in a love/hate manner. I read the words with a painful realization: Dad's body is breaking down, unable to support itself with certainty. A father bigger than life, stronger than most, my seventy-seven-year-old dad never wanted to be feeble, helpless, dependent. As a man who could fix anything, the inability to fix himself grates on his independence. Despite the daily knee bends in the living room, which has become his sleeping quarters, his emergency potty, and his convalescence room, my father's walk weakens and balance worsens. Unwilling to give in easily, along with his knee bends, he utilizes the two, five and ten pound weights I carried upstairs for him from his basement workout room of thirty years. He asked for heavier weights, but the doctor wouldn't allow it, so he makes do with the lighter weights. All this work fuels his hope that he can fix himself, if he just keeps at it. In his mind, if he can just get a little stronger, he will overcome the physical damage done by a stroke he suffered ten years ago, which stole much of the coordination and strength from his right side, and be whole once more.

His approach to life demands that positive attitude. To think otherwise acquiesces to the inevitable, forcing him to acknowledge his weakening abilities. His hope has been to die quickly, or at least that is what he told my only sister Kim. Dad would never say that to me. We never speak that way, never that emotionally, never that intimately. He and I are not friends, but not enemies either. Our relationship is best described as classic or old school, which differs from my relationship with my kids, where I am part father and part friend, a relic of divorce. In our case, Dad is the father, a kind, good, honest soul, and I am the son, following his moral legacy while finding my own way.

This morning's fall is the third one. He fell for the first time just two weeks ago, while walking in the narrow hall that leads from my parents' bathroom to their bedroom in the house they have lived in for forty-seven years. The sound of his 6' 2" 210lb body falling on the floor of the old house echoed loud enough that no yelling was necessary to notify Mom he had a problem. Mom, my aunt Marilyn and her longtime partner Phil, who happened to be visiting, easily heard the noise. Fortunately, Phil is similar in size to my father and still in good health, so he wrapped a bed sheet around Dad's waist, a strategy learned from the hospital staff during Dad's recovery from his stroke, and pulled my father upward to a standing position.

The second fall occurred last week close to the bathroom, again within a narrow hallway of the old house. This time my mom and dad were alone. Though five-foot seven and physically strong for a seventy-year-old woman, Mom's replacement hip doesn't allow her to bend all that well anymore, so she couldn't help lift him from the ground. Luckily, he fell close to the bathroom, allowing Dad to drag/crawl his tired body to the white, cast-iron bathtub. Because he wore his usual outfit, a plaid long-sleeved shirt and jeans, he could slide along the wooden floors.

Once at the tub, Dad, employing years of chest presses, pushed his body upward from the tub, while Mom acted as ballast to enhance his stability, their trust of forty-seven years of marriage guiding the effort. Though Dad has a great deal of strength after lifting weights for so long, that muscle has become more anchor than attribute. Regardless, that day they conquered gravity together, but time and gravity continue to plague their later years.

This recent fall, the third in three weeks, was in the dining room, too far from the bathroom to crawl there. As usual, he had the will to get up, but the physical coordination on his right side can no longer direct the muscles necessary to help him to his feet. His heart muscle, the very symbol of his kind nature and the best and strongest muscle on his body, was unable to pump the energy to lift him. Without the necessary strength, Mom and Dad were helpless for the first time in their lives. Unable to turn to my sister and me for help, because we live too far away, my mom called 911. She told me she felt humiliated as she dialed the number, calling just to get her husband off the floor.

I can imagine Dad feeling humiliated too. My father and I are enough alike, both tall, big shouldered and slim with blue eyes, and our personalities similar enough — quiet, stubborn, thoughtful — that in him I see my own mortality, the curtains thrust aside and the complete truth revealed. The differences appear purely cosmetic, such as he is left handed and I right handed, he has no hair and I still have plenty, he likes the rain and I'm more of a desert guy.

As the family historian, I can tell you that over the last five generations each male has lived into their seventies, but never into their eighties. The longest living male was my great-great-grandfather, who lived seventy-eight years and three months. Dad is at seventy-seven years and eight months. His goal is to hit eighty. At the moment, I'm not confident he will make it.

Will I make it any further? The odds appear against me based on the family timelines, even with, by all appearances, my excellent health. This means my life will be over in three and a half decades, a sobering fact. When young, the distant end is too far away for any worry, but as a forty-five-year-old, twice-divorced, three-time father, who will be forty-six in twenty days and lives five hundred miles away from my father, unable to help him when he falls, the end seems all too near.

Not only am I in the middle age-wise, but also geographically, for home is Boise, Idaho, halfway between my kids' world in Salt Lake City and my parents, who live in Renton, Washington, a suburb of Seattle, still in the same house where I was born. I'm also halfway from the beginning of my adult life at age twenty-one, venturing off on my own, and the age of seventy, when Dad had his stroke and when I fear my own physical decline could begin in earnest. However, I try not to fear the end, believing I can outwit it, at least for a little while, which explains the large number of books on food and health that fill my bookshelves.

So, as Dad fights for his last few years, I feel a great urge to spend the remainder of my life in the most fulfilling ways possible. Thwarting my opportunities is an economy that I find unrecognizable, which seems unsatisfied with wiping out my company, the value of the home where I live, available jobs and even my goals. Yet, I seek no pity for my circumstances nor for what I have lost, because others have lost too; Instead, I will keep struggling through this crazy economy until opportunity present themselves. And I need look no further for the inspiration to keep trying then to observe my father, for he has never sought pity for his diminished speaking, seeing, and physical abilities due to his stroke in 2002. When he falls down and is helped back to his feet, he soldiers forward fighting as best he can against his scythed enemy. He keeps fighting because, as he will proudly tell any who asks in his halting speech, he has one more goal in life: he wants to reach the age of eighty. That leaves me wondering, what goals should I chase as age chases me?

• • • •

Prior to this latest fall, my father was on my mind, but for a different reason. For three and a half years I have run a website for classic jeeps, eWillys.com, linking buyers and sellers and entertaining lovers of classic jeeps, such as those seen in movies of World War II. I think of it as a hobby I work like a job and a job that pays me like a hobby.

Why launch and maintain a website about classic jeeps that provides little income? Readers have emailed me with that question many times. The answer is complicated. It involves the relationship with my father and watching him build a wrecked jeep in the cold, detached, two-car garage adjacent to my parents' house. It involves several generations of my family who have spent much of their lives exploring and moving around the West since the civil war. It involves a peculiar passion for old jeeps, or as others call them old Willys ("Willys Sickness" is a favorite phrase among my website readers), a passion I put aside for fifteen years after getting married, finishing college and a MBA degree, moving, working, and fathering children. It involves the crash of my financial world as the economy imploded. It involves my own self-fulfillment.

However, after reading Mom's email, I found myself questioning my efforts with the site. Well, I was questioning life itself. Dad's predicament made me wonder if I would look back on my work helping and entertaining people with eWillys and ask myself if it was time well spent. When reaching the age of seventy-seven and one half, would I tell myself I had lived my life in the right way, made a difference in my own way? After all, running a classic jeep site will hardly cure cancer, feed hungry people, or solve our pollution issues; but what it does provide is an opportunity to distract people from those more serious issues for a little while. Besides, I had already tried once to 'make the world a better place' by attempting to create a public education and information utility online. I worked long hours, exhausted my credit, and gave everything to help raise twenty million dollars hoping to build the "PBS of the Web". Despite great intentions and great effort from many people, the flames from the crash of that company burned me badly, leaving financial scars that are still healing. Dad always said I should go into business for myself. Losing everything, however, made me pause and question: perhaps I chose the wrong business.

Am I choosing the right business this time? Or, perhaps, the right hobby is a better perspective. I think the pre-stroke version of Dad might approve.

The old Dad might even have read and followed the website. After all, jeeps, jeeping, and jeep clubs run throughout my family's DNA, with lots of great memories buried deep within our chromosomes. I started life riding on my mother's lap in the front passenger seat of their blue-green 1959 stock CJ-5 jeep, bouncing over trails before the age of one. As Dad drove, Mom's arms snuggled me safely asleep while we three explored the trails of Western Washington. Mom says the moment Dad stopped the jeep I would pop awake, wondering why my slumber had been disturbed. Yes, I was born into a jeep and my family members were jeepers.

When I was two, my sister arrived. I moved to the bench seat in the rear of the jeep and my sister replaced me in Mom's lap until she was big enough to ride back with me. Those were good times filled with camping, socializing and playing in the vast forests of the Cascade Mountains, participating in local parades, volunteering to plant trees, attending jeep club meetings, and watching Dad fix the jeep in our garage. I was awed at his ability to fix anything.

When my own life needed some fixing in 2007, as the economic storm began to rain on the sunny times of the mid 2000s, my soul wanted to retreat, to find comfort in the familiar. Tired of the virtual world the 2000s represented, I sought a tactile passion, something to touch, hold and build. For me the world of jeeps means more than just a vehicle. Therefore, my re-entry into the world of jeeps just made sense, because little else did. Jeeps are simple, utilitarian, and inexpensive compared to the complex cars of today. That's what I needed, something simple to restart my life, gain back some confidence, and place my focus upon a new project to distract me from other forces in my life.

So, in 2007, for the second time in my life, I began building a jeep that I have named Lost Biscuit, a name I borrowed from my youngest child, who'd made up the name for his xBox Live online video game account. I love the name, because getting lost in a jeep is part of the fun and because I love to cook and biscuits are a simple dish. Biscuit is a simple jeep, so simple that it doesn't need a key; instead, I jump in and push a button to start it. I built Biscuit to be a better version of 'The Great Escape', a jeep I built back in 1984, the jeep that helped me mature from a teenager into a man.

Lost Biscuit, built between 2007 & 2009, was my second jeep. I am driving with my daughter in the passenger seat and sons in the back.

As part of this second build, Biscuit would be better designed, smoothing out the rough edges of my low budget racing/trail/road jeep of two decades ago. When I created my first jeep, I gained confidence and learned about life by undertaking the project. It transformed my life. This second jeep was less about transformation and more about recovery from all I had been through — divorce, financial loss, stress, business crashes, moves, friendships lost, and more — over the last seven years.

As I gathered the parts to build Biscuit, it occurred to me that the website I needed — a site that specialized in old school builds, parts for sale, and old Willys for sale — didn't exist. After pondering how I'd approach a site, what content to use and the utility to potential readers, I tiptoed back into the virtual world, launching eWillys in 2008.

The website began with a poor design and even worse logo. Rather than launch a perfect site, I decided to employ the revision strategy I'd learned building software. Version one of the site was intended to be a functioning site. After a year of running the site, version two revisited the design, addressed bugs, and added functionality. At year two, version three was released, finalizing the logo — a scripted eWillys with black text on a white background, something simple and elegant —, the design, the color scheme and the layout. At least, it is final until the next version, which remains unscheduled. As the years have passed, I have also re-written content, to improve readers' experiences.

In fact, before Mom's email arrived today, I was rewriting my biography for the website, which I hadn't touched in three years. I wanted to explain more thoroughly to readers how jeeps played one role or another throughout my life into adulthood, knowing that once I shared my stories, readers would understand how I literally grew up 'jeep'.

One of my favorite stories involved being named 'Jeep Dave'. How much more 'jeep' can a person become? This happened during the summer of 1986, when I was twenty-one, after moving from the Seattle area to the San Juan Islands, where I landed a summer job as a cook. But describing that summer, the most formative experience of my life, would take more than a webpage. Too much happened to me while I was at the remote resort of Roche Harbor.

At a time prior to the internet and cell phones, when Alf and the A-Team ruled TV and Top Gun blasted into theatres, Roche was an old-school resort, an oasis that felt far away from anything else. Roche Harbor and the Roche Harbor Resort are located at the northern tip of San Juan Island, the most populous island in the San Juan Islands, a group of islands that sits between Bellingham, Washington, to the east and Canada's

Vancouver Island to the West. Offering the Pacific Northwest's first boating resort, it opened in 1956, offering docks for visiting boats, a three-story hotel, a restaurant, a grocery store, a church and more. When I arrived in 1986, it was a place unknown to many people outside the Puget Sound area.

Roche was the perfect place for me at the time. The resort had an innocence about it and, I suppose, that is a word that described me too. I lived a sheltered life, void of drama and heartache; there was no divorce in my family and no fighting between my parents. No one close to me had died, other than my grandfathers. I was free to roam my neighborhood any time of day or night without fear. My childhood was simple and easy. For me, Roche was the first time I faced the world on my own, away from family, forging my own way. It was a perfect stepping stone, leading to a summer full of fond memories. I became a man in many ways, making good friends, plunging into adventures, working hard and saving money. Through trial-by-fire, literally, my blossoming cooking skills matured, expanding both my knowledge and passion for food. And, for the first time, I flirted with love. Her name was Virginia and for a couple of weeks our lives intertwined.

Virginia . . .

What became of the woman who wandered into my life at the beginning of August 1986? She'd opened the door, walked quickly inside, settling next to my heart for several weeks. Then, as quickly as she had entered, she was gone again, leaving me only with fond memories, a letter on a note card and some pictures I have inexplicably kept to this day.

Thinking about her always makes me wonder, is she happy now? Where is she? Is she even alive? For twenty-five years I have occasionally thought about her. Why hadn't I searched for her?

I suppose wondering about the meaning of life and one's purpose always forces one to look at past choices, ponder them, evaluate them, and consider the mistakes made. Was it my father's situation or was it my own that has brought Virginia to the surface? Whatever the reason, once again she's on my mind.

Unlike what people might expect, at least how the movies might portray it, this wasn't some torrid love affair. Since then, I have had torrid love affairs. They tend to burn hot, then chill. Even with the freedom to do as we pleased, Virginia and I weren't tearing each other's clothes off and bedding at a moment's notice. Though we slept next to each other for several nights, we never consummated the relationship. She asked that we not, because she was just completing a divorce. Sexually, she needed to close one door completely, before opening another. I respected her for that; she was a beautiful creature of her convictions.

Instead of a wild, passionate experience, it was gentle, tender, warm, and touching. Tenderness. That is the word that comes to mind these days. I remember the tenderness, from the warmth of her smile as she greeted me, broad and full of love and happiness, to the thoughtful conversations we had, our time together was peaceful and beautiful. I remember the joy as she gently brushed her brown curly hair from her face when flirting with me. Even on a windless day her unruly hair was much like her spirit, gentle yet untamable. But, most amazing was the energy we felt when we touched, natural and honest. Just to hold her hand, caress her neck, or smooth her hair would ignite my senses.

Even twenty-five years later I savor that experience, storing it and compartmentalizing it for myself and only myself. I never shared the story with others, lovers, friends or family. Amazingly, in total, we might have spent fourteen days together in August. Had it been that short of time?

I can't think about Virginia without thinking of our last point of contact, a letter written from her on a lavender note card still stored in my temporary filing cabinet, better known as a cardboard box, just another of my easily movable items that has survived many moves. Saving it all this time, along with some pictures of us with silly captions on the back authored by her, I wished at least one picture had us both, but none did. It's the only letter or card I kept from any of my relationships.

For me to still possess her note is unusual, because my many moves from house to house and state to state have forced me to throw away other keepsakes like this, to live lean. In fact, 1986 marked the beginning of a wanderlust that pushed and pulled me from place to place. My latest stay in Boise of three and a half years is the longest I have remained in one spot in twenty-five years, but that was only due to complications caused by the market crash. Five years ago on my fortieth birthday I listed all the places I had lived for longer than a month. The list totaled twenty-five moves in twenty years. An array of reasons continued to push me in new directions. Sometimes moves were relationship oriented, sometimes opportunity oriented, and sometimes they were just adventures I needed to pursue. Yet, I would love to find peace, that one place that feels like mine, a place where I can store my center, my thoughts, my keepsakes and being. Until then, my stay will always feel temporary, no matter the length.

Along my journeys, I started and ended relationships, started and ended jobs, and started and closed businesses. I learned how to live light. For example, for four months, from November of 1999 to March 2000, at age thirty-five, I lived in my law school office at the University of Utah, where I worked as a web developer and faculty computer manager. I moved there during my divorce from my wife of ten years and mother to my three children. As most know, divorce is rarely a simple process. At the end of much discussion and frustration, I was the one to leave. When that time arrived, having no other options, I moved into my office. Then, I handed over all my paychecks for several months while trying to get extra work to cover my own expenses, such as food for starters.

Living in an office wasn't all that bad at the turn of 2000, though the drab off-white concrete walls, thin carpet, and metal shelves hardly made for a beautiful space. The lack of windows did provide complete privacy and the building was kept warm, so I stayed cozy. I had a comfortable high-back blue chair when I wanted to relax or my computer chair when wanting to stay busy. Because it was a university campus, I could go workout and shower at any of the gyms, so the benefits were nice. I had

Internet and broadband connectivity galore, so I kept in touch with the outside world. As the law school's web manager and faculty support person, I had master keys that allowed me to access most of the law school. Thus, my freedom within the building was vast. I never felt sorry for myself there; instead, I felt fortunate, as many other people in the world had much worse lives. I knew I would bounce back . . . somehow.

To keep a low profile, I kept a couple days worth of clothes neatly folded in a box hidden behind my office door, consisting of socks, underwear, two sets of blue jeans, one set of brown pants, a few long sleeve shirts, and t-shirts. There was nothing fancy, just enough to last a week and a half. Any clothes not in the office were stored in a second box I kept in the back of my 1989 Nissan Maxima.

I maintained a regular routine. Each evening around eleven o'clock at night I shut my office door, unrolled my sleeping bag, an old, hardy, soft, down sleeping bag with a fuzzy animal motif on the inside lining, and fell asleep on it, not in it. The room was warm, while the floor was hard. Sometimes I would throw a jacket over myself if I needed to feel some weight on top of me. I still own the sleeping bag, just in case the need for it arises again. In the morning I awoke at six o'clock, which is the time the janitors arrived (the last thing I needed was to have the janitors open the door and find me sleeping on the floor). After waking, I changed clothes, rolled up my bag, and stored it behind the door atop my clothes box, ready to pretend I had just arrived at the law school for work that day. The routine worked smoothly.

For most of the faculty and staff at the school, it appeared I was a hard worker. In reality, I had nowhere else to go. Frankly, the school benefited, as I was more than happy to help faculty at all hours, which seemed a reasonable trade for sleeping there. If their computer stopped working at 7am, I fixed it. If a change needed to be made to the website late at night, I could fix that. There was always plenty of work to keep me busy, so no one questioned my constant presence there. After a while, I confided in a secretary that the law school was my home. A few others eventually learned the truth, too.

The biggest challenge I had was what to do with my kids. When broke and living in an office, what does a person do with their kids three times a week? And, when I mean broke, I mean one week I had ten dollars to buy food for the entire week! The answer was that our playground was the University. I quickly learned that the campus historical museum was free from four o'clock in the afternoon to closing time at five o'clock. My kids were young, so we didn't need much more time than that anyway. Free buses downtown were another path to adventure and entertainment. Best of all, while I had no TV, I did have access to the school's VCR and projector. So, I would roll the combo into the rarely used and private faculty break room, cook up some macaroni and cheese (thank goodness there was a stove in there) or some soup, and shine whatever movie I could find onto the wall, filling it from floor to ceiling. The room became our own big screen adventure. Occasionally a faculty member would walk into the room, smile, get what they needed and walk out. The law faculty and staff were wonderful.

Living light became my mantra, especially in the early 2000s. Selling and dumping stuff became easier for me, too. If money was tight I sold my tools on Craigslist, had a garage sale, or called friends about buying things. I owned so little at the time that everything I had fit in the back of my car, including my table saw, which fit snuggly in my trunk (next to the box that contained my spare clothes). With that background, it should be easy to understand that throwing away invaluable papers and documents wasn't all that difficult for me.

This constant restlessness was far from a life I had imagined or lived in my childhood. The house in which I was raised differs little from my childhood, only the mismatched floors are a little more worn and the countless trees and bushes that fill my parents' one-acre property have reached new heights. As a child I roamed the tree lined property, climbing pine and cedar trees and getting sticky pitch on my hands. Another favorite past time was digging in the dirt and building elaborate garages for my Tonka Toys, which back then were metal and indestructible.

Animals were a constant throughout my childhood, first cats and dogs, guinea pigs and hamsters, and then horses. When my sister and I were young, if one of our cats had had kittens it was a major event. When the kittens got old enough for us to handle, we would line them up and have mini cat races, where the kittens would have to travel a foot or so to win. We were always good to the kittens though or we would get into trouble.

One area of my parents' property was devoted to the garden Mom annually cultivated. Eating fresh fruit off trees and bushes — raspberries, strawberries, apples, peaches, red huckleberries, cherries, blueberries — was an annual experience. The garden seemed to fit our location, because during the late 1960s and into the 1970s we lived in the country. The closest McDonalds restaurant was more than a half hour away at the northwest end of Renton, at a time when the french fries were cooked in beef fat. I can still taste that yummy flavor, a taste unfamiliar to today's kids. However, it didn't take long for the country feel to be washed away by the incoming tide of houses and people. By the 1980s, there were three McDonalds within ten minutes of my parents' home. Their acre of country living is now an island in a sea of suburbia.

It was a fine life, as I never went hungry and there was little family discord. I remember asking Dad once if we were middle class. I was in middle school at the time and asked the question in Dad's man-cave, our cob-webby basement that became his workout center. As he stood there pondering the question, wearing his blue cotton sweats with his employer's name, BOEING, written down one side and a hole ripped in one knee, he said we were lower middle class. I found his answer confusing, because we had plenty. But, through subsequent family research, I now understand he knew what being wealthy meant, but as a country boy growing up in Renton I knew no better.

Because of my childhood, I assumed I would marry, have kids, get a college education and enjoy an adult life similar to my parents. In fact, by 1999, I was married, had kids, bought a house at the north end of the Harvard-Yale area of Salt Lake City, which is a nice area, and even obtained an advanced degree (MBA). But my life as I expected it was not to be. Instead, one year later, in 2000, I became the very first of my lineage to divorce. It turns out, there isn't much of a road map for divorce, which is partly why I landed homeless, living in an office. Following my divorce, for complex reasons, I threw my hands up at the world and charted my own course, taking that path Robert Frost metaphorically describes as the one less traveled.

Yet, despite my office stay, various relationships, and misadventures, I never threw away the note card from Virginia and never felt tempted to do so. Not once. Instead, every year or so I flipped through my personal files stored in a file box I kept to make sure her note card was still there.

With thoughts of Virginia on my mind it doesn't take long before I find myself digging into my files to find it. I leaf past my passport, past my PADI (Professional Association of Diving Instructors) certificate, certifying me for open water diving (which I earned the hard way, by diving in the cold murky waters of Puget Sound). Next to the PADI certificate sits the cover of an old Truck and Trader magazine from 1992 with the picture of my original custom fiberglass flatfender jeep, a jeep I built in 1984 and sold in 1992 to fund a move to Wisconsin. I was always thrilled it made the front cover. Next to that is a newspaper clipping that shows me helping a ten-year-old kid with a computer, recording my time as a volunteer for a science camp at the Pacific Science Center near the Space Needle.

After the newspaper clipping appears a photo of Tesh, my former boss, and me. The photograph was taken as we peered over the back porch of the BurgerWorks, the place at age eighteen where I started my cooking career. The photo shows my dark blonde hair, curly and thick, partly hiding the ends of the glasses I wore. I am not smiling in the photo, but rather have a purposeful look, slightly tough-guy as I lean forward on the railing of the small porch with a cooking spatula in my hand. However, it is hard to pull off a tough-guy look when wielding a cooking spatula, even if I was six-feet tall. No, my baby face has never looked particularly mean or tough.

*Tesh (left) and me, age twenty, at the BurgerWorks,
my first cooking job in 1985.*

Finally, my search yields the note card and eight pictures Virginia mailed me in September of 1986. Plucking it from the file folder I open it. The photos remain nestled inside. On the back of each photo she wrote something cute and loving. The lavender note card with its handwritten script looks so old fashioned, nearly a museum piece in these days of email. On the inside it reads:

September 16, 1986

Dear Dave,

I'm sorry it has taken me so long to return your letter. I've been so busy and have been thru so much in the last week. I made <u>almost</u> every life change possible. I finished my dissolution of marriage, talked to my priest, found an apt, got my phone for my new place, opened my own checking account (again), and I finally decided to look for a salary job. That is a lot of changes!

I also prepared my resume and had it typeset. My resume looks great! I start serious job hunting tomorrow, so I need to find a job fast. I'm not worried, but I am excited. I've really cut some strings and started over.

The day I received your letter I was just walking out to go to the attorney's office. It was an extremely <u>welcome</u> letter. Thank you so much! I was also glad for your invitation to visit. I'd like to, but as you can see I need to do things here, but I want to for sure. I hope you'll visit me too.

Love and Kisses, Virginia

Strangely, opening the card feels different this time than in previous years. For some reason, this time I *have* to know what happened to her. Maybe it is the twenty-five year mark, an anniversary of sorts, which compels me to want to find her; or, it is my personal struggles — lack of employment, the house foreclosure, Dad's illness, my relationship, the crash of my company, so many struggles in the last few years — facing me. Whatever the motivation, I have to know . . . is she good? Is she well? Is she happy? One time in 2001, after reading her note, I searched for her on the web, most likely using AltaVista. But nothing appeared, so I put the card away, assuming she was lost forever.

Now, armed with a more powerful search engine, Google, I decide to search for her one more time. Sitting back down at my desk I reach for my laptop. I launch Firefox and type in her full name, hoping it hasn't changed due to marriage.

Unfortunately, too many results yield what seems to be the wrong Virginia. Some women are too old, some too young, and some professionals in jobs I can't imagine her doing, such as accounting, municipal water management, and day care.

I poke through possibilities and chase dead ends. Finally, my diligence and patience reveals a clue. Someone named Virginia left a comment on a blog post. In the comment, the writer lent support to the cast of "Sex in the City 2", telling them to ignore criticism and keep making their movies. She said she was a big fan and hoped to see another movie soon.

"Never Give Up", she wrote conclusively. Is this a cosmic sign for me not to give up, to keep searching for her?

I love the post. It is rambling, yet powered with energy and excitement. I can imagine the Virginia who captivated me during the summer of 1986 so bound with enthusiasm her message literally burst from her and, in her excitement, made a few mistakes while writing her comment. In addition, remembering she loved movies, design and color, I figure she still has an interest in them. This has to be her. This has to be the Virginia from twenty-five years ago. But, can I find her using the information in the blog post?

Well, if there is one thing I do well, it is research effectively on the internet. Employing a few nuggets of information found in the comment, I complete more searches. Eventually, my additional detective work yields a small site with her name on it. On the site is a hotmail address. And, the best part, there she is, a picture of her. IT IS HER!

Amazing. After twenty-five years, she looks about the same. It must be a picture from her late thirties, because she doesn't look nearly fifty at all.

The suddenness of this situation hits me. Fifteen minutes ago the note card I am holding in my hands was a memento from my youthful past, marking the end of my teen years and an entrance into adulthood. It was my first taste of love and flirtation on an adult level. Up to that point, I'd never had a long-term relationship. A late bloomer, I was slow to understand the finer points of how to treat women. That's not to say I treated women badly, but rather my shyness, goofiness and kindness seemed to lead to friendships rather than loves. Before that summer, I lacked real confidence, the confidence to approach a woman and know what to say, the confidence to grab her when the time was right and kiss her, and the confidence to take the lead when necessary. By late July 1986, in the midst of the most transformative summer of my life, my confidence bloomed. The timing for meeting her couldn't have been more perfect.

But, that was then. What do I write to her now? Will she remember me? How will I feel if she doesn't respond? How should I phrase the email? After considering these questions and more, making the letter short and to the point seems a priority. Most importantly, I want to know if she is *the* Virginia I had known?

On Thursday, May 12th, 2011, keeping it short and casual just in case I don't have the right Virginia, I send my email:

May 12th, 2011 – 12:02 PM

Hi Virginia,

In August of 1986 I met a Virginia Anderson, a beautiful and sweet 26-year-old woman. I was 21, cooking at the Roche Harbor Restaurant and generally living life one day at a time. We met in Roche Harbor and shared some fond memories that I cherish to this day. I was going through some of my things and ran across the last note she, well I think you, wrote me. So, I thought I'd do a search and see if I came across anyone.

If this isn't the same Virginia in the attached image, then my apologies.

If it is you, lets catch up sometime, because I always wanted to know what happened to you :-)

- David Eilers

As the email states, I also attach a picture, the only one she sent of herself. The photo was taken at the McMillin family mausoleum, one of the most unusual sites at Roche Harbor. Set back far away from the main part of the resort, to get there we walked up a dirt road in the woods. Normally, it was a little spooky even during the day, due to the nearby cemetery and the whisper of the trees as the wind gently blew through them. One could easily imagine the dead quietly conversing. However, on the afternoon day of the picture, in August of 1986, rather than spooky, the sun shone on Virginia, making a scene that could not be more beautiful.

The photo I attach to the email shows Virginia sitting in the center of the mausoleum's table, hands behind her, feet extended straight. The limestone table is big enough, six feet in diameter that her five foot four frame fits comfortably atop it. Brown hair falls to her shoulders in tight, natural curls. Along with her big smile, she wears a white t-shirt with a collection of green and red flowers that reads, "Artists Do It Colorfully". Around the table are limestone chairs. Surrounding the chairs are tall doric columns that support a circular crown open in the center. Designed with masonic elements in mind, everything is symbolic, especially the side with a 'broken' column and missing chair.

Prior to taking the picture, I remember describing to her how the broken column refers to the inability of a person to complete everything he or she sets out to do in life. I also explained that when the mausoleum was built it had views in all directions, but the passing of time and growth of trees transformed the experience from an open and airy one to a nestled and quiet one.

With picture attached, sending the email is cathartic for me, because I have finally made a real attempt to contact her. Would it take an hour for her to respond? A day? A week? Would she respond at all? All I can do is wait . . . impatiently.

2. MAY 15TH, 2011

A few days have passed since emailing Virginia. My inbox still contains no letter from her; my hope for a quick response fades. Perhaps she will remain lost to time. In the absence of concrete reasons, possible ones percolate in my mind. Maybe she read the email and didn't remember me. Could her spam filter have efficiently moved it into a junk folder? It is possible the email sailed into the electronic ether and never made it to its destination. Since I have used email for almost two decades, I know technology is not a perfect medium, so I will remain patient for now and send a follow up email in a few days just in case.

Besides, I have more important issues to worry about then a missing email. Foremost on my mind, as he has been all week, is Dad. His back still hurts from moving the mower after it broke down in late April. This led to the problem with his sciatic nerve, making it extremely uncomfortable to walk, sit, or sleep, which also led to his third and most recent fall a few days ago, prompting my mother's email. Even worse, the pain from the nerve plus his fear of falling has, according to my mother when I spoke with her this morning, shattered his confidence, making him take tiny steps when walking, small and uncertain, rather than his more confident post-stroke half stride. He has also begun using a walker full-time rather than his cane. To discourage him from walking any more than necessary, Mom has become more and more a twenty-four-hour-a-day caregiver. Her phone calls, like the one this morning, are tinged with exhaustion and heavy sighs. As the patient enduring all this, Dad is miserable and unable to sleep well, constantly shifting in bed. This is not the best of times for them.

Luckily for Dad, Mom has the time to care for him because it is almost summer. During winter and spring my mother is often away from home, traveling all over Western Washington judging junior high and high school gymnastic meets. An accidental judge, she originally took judging classes to help coach middle school gymnasts. With a few judging classes behind her, someone asked her to judge a meet, where she judged terribly, according to her. She didn't want to go back, but the school programs desperately needed judges, so she reluctantly tried again. The second chance was all she needed, because now, thirty years later, she is judging some of the children of kids she judged at the beginning of her career.

However, regardless of the fact she doesn't have a job during the summer, she keeps extremely busy maintaining their one-acre property, annually preparing her garden, picking weeds, cooking, killing slugs and managing all the issues with the house. Because my father can't do as much around the property anymore, Mom has expanded her role, but there is only so much she can do. Yet, because the property is worth more to developers than to a single homebuyer, she wants to limit her investment of time and money on the property. She understands that all her work could disappear to make way for six houses, years of naturally grown and cultivated fruit and vegetables destroyed. While I can understand the financial rationality of a developer altering the land, destroying all my mother's work is a legacy that saddens her.

Since it is mid May, Mom has been busy managing Dad's issues, along with planting the garden and cleaning up after the long rainy winter. When I call my mother on the afternoon of May 15th to talk about Dad's situation, in her usual stoic manner she won't admit to needing help, but it is clear after talking with her that Dad's increasing struggles have dampened her normal chipper attitude. She sounds stressed and tired. So, instead of asking, I tell her to expect me in a few days and I will stay a week. She says she is happy to have me visit.

• • • •

Fortunately for my parents, I lead a life full of flexibility. For example, if I decide to make a last minute trip to Seattle and stay a week, I do not have to re-arrange my schedule. There is no need to ask for time off. No meetings are cancelled and no one will miss me at work. But, I am employed; well, more like a contract. Actually, it isn't exactly a contract, as nothing is signed. Yet I get paid. More like, I get a stipend for doing nothing. I receive enough to make expenses — child support, my half of the house payment, food — but not enough to thrive. While grateful for the money, it feels I am not earning it and that rubs me wrong. The money is a gift to keep me afloat, a gift from the company that invited me to Idaho to build an online payday loan company. Because only a month after my move to Idaho in November of 2006, internal conflicts unrelated to me altered the project's trajectory, sending it into the ground. I was disappointed, but not surprised; by the end of 2006, all my businesses and investments were crumbling.

It all started in April of 2001, when I quit my web-development job at the University of Utah's College of Law to become an entrepreneur. There were four reasons why I chose to abandon the certainty of a paycheck for the uncertainty of entrepreneurial life. First, while I was in college, Dad once told me that being self-employed was a good idea. He approved of it for me, but never sought it for himself, something I never understood. Second, while working for a business bank between 1992-1994 in Madison, Wisconsin, I reviewed the tax returns from a variety of successful business people. Very few received a paycheck; instead, most made money by owning their own businesses, by earning income through real estate (rental homes for example), and by keeping their cars and similar assets attached to their business, so they could expense the assets through their business taxes, which saved them additional money. I learned that having a little bite of earnings from a variety of businesses could improve my livelihood and reduce my financial risk. The recipes for success varied only by the type of ingredients, but not the strategy. I thought the strategy was a good one, so I pledged to use it when I got the chance. Third, my family research exemplified the upside of entrepreneurship, because just a few generations back my family's entrepreneurial efforts in mining, smelting, and refining created an enormous fortune, much of which was wiped out during the Great Depression.

The final reason to become an entrepreneur was rooted in my experience as a finance student at the University of Puget Sound during the 1990-1991 Recession. I watched jobs like my father's – a mid level manager who distributed electrical test equipment among the Seattle area Boeing plants, a job that made enough money to support a wife and kids, allowed him to enjoy his weekends jeeping with our family, gave us great healthcare, and provided him with a significant retirement package – disappear. I believed that the elimination of middle management jobs was caused by leaps in technology, improving the capability of high-level management to direct and monitor lower level employees. The loss of middle management was also caused by price competition from abroad, forcing American companies to cut costs.

Finally, I felt strongly that maturing financial theory had caused businesses to shift from an arithmetic concept of profit, revenue minus expenses equals successful profit, to a geometric concept of profit, where net profit had to grow at an ever increasing rate each year. Under this new type of financial model concepts like Net Present Value and Internal Rate of Return were used by companies to show, and for third parties to evaluate, success. Therefore, profit was no longer enough. Instead, if business revenue didn't grow at a fast enough pace, expenses had to be cut, with salaries becoming the principal relief valve.

As a result, I recognized that jobs similar to my father's were being eliminated, reducing the available career ladders to executive level positions, where people were making more money, rewarded in part for taking over the duties of the eliminated middle management. I concluded, if climbing my way to the top of a company had become more difficult, then starting at the top by creating my own company made the most sense. This also convinced me to obtain my MBA, a business graduate degree I felt improved my ability to either jump to the executive corporate ladder or give me the skills to better build a company.

By 2001, having received my MBA in 1998, but forced to get a job quickly to deal with bills, I found myself hanging on the highest rung of the University of Utah College of Law's computer department, unable to climb any higher or improve my salary. There were no more rungs to climb. I decided it was time to jump off the ladder and start building my own business. This was not without significant financial risk, for I had child support payments, graduate loans, undergraduate loans, and living expenses I had to cover. I could fail and destroy my financial life, or succeed and meet my financial goals.

So, in April of 2001 a friend of mine, Jon Firmage, and I launched a company specializing in online Barter called BarterFarm. Users of the site could create a list of items they had and a list of items they wanted and our system would match people with like wants and haves, first locally, then regionally, and then nationally. Themes of farming, self-sufficiency, and interdependent success were part of our approach. We pitched the idea to potential investors as a locally focused, globally interconnected framework. Even while raising funds, we encouraged investors to view themselves as part of the business, as if this was a true farming cooperative, and to be actively involved.

To launch the company, we had some funding, few assets and big dreams, a perfect recipe for difficult times. Sure enough, after quitting my job to start BarterFarm, the funding didn't materialize as we were told it would, so we hit the road armed with a business plan to drum up funding with gas money made from garage sales. Those were lean times, with me sleeping on the couch of Jon's two-bedroom apartment in May and June of 2001, while Jon, his wife and two kids used the bedrooms. Jon's wife even pawned her wedding ring to help fund our business. My credit was obliterated. We were all in it together, for better or worse.

From that bleak start, in fits and gasps, BarterFarm grew slowly until we combined it with internet legend Joe Firmage's OneCosmos venture, creating ManyOne Networks in 2002. Jon's older brother, Joe, had co-founded USWeb in 1995, which quickly grew to become the largest internet consulting company in the world, serving a variety of Fortune 500 companies. Joe left USWeb in 1998 to blend his two passions, science and technology, in a way that would help the world, leading to the launch of OneCosmos in 2000.

From 2002 - 2005, I employed my strategy for financial success. First and foremost was a regular paycheck, which ManyOne Networks finally started providing in late 2003. I also was owed a significant amount of back pay and owned five million shares of stock, so if ManyOne worked, I would be rich. During 2002, Jon left ManyOne to rebuild BarterFarm, which later became Matchbin. I was able to help the company by providing time and resources, earning one hundred thousand shares. During this time I also did some consulting work for large companies and small companies, which generated extra income.

By 2005, I had money, was paying down back debt, catching up on child support, and felt confident that my financial strategy was working. However, I wasn't going to let up, I wanted to do more, so in early 2006 I helped a friend launch a coffee shop franchise aimed at business people who needed meeting places a little more professional than Starbucks. We called the company Vagabonds, envisioning it as a meeting solution for mobile professionals like us. By March 2006 we had a concept shop open, raised some capital, and owned a nice condo that an investor traded for stock. We were ready to expand, awaiting the injection of a 'guaranteed' investment by a large copy and print company in April of 2006.

I felt successful, with my touch making things work everywhere I went. I even had a backup nest egg buried in my ex-wife's home, which I would realize once it sold. I just knew that all the work I had invested in my education along with the vacation-less, money-tight life I had led so far was maturing. I had executed the plan forged years earlier: create multiple income streams to reduce my risk and bury money in different types of investments. I stood on a financial peak, seeing a wonderful and interesting future in front of me.

At least, that was the case until an economic earthquake knocked me off that peak, undoing all the work I had done.

It started in mid-2006. First, the funding expected for the Vagabonds concept didn't materialize. Unable to continue supporting the prototype café, due to a drop in foot traffic, the business crashed. At the same time, ManyOne ran into funding issues, which was holding up payroll and threatening my main source of cash. Executives in the company started leaving due to the lack of consistent paychecks. I was worried too and, because as co-founder my name was on the bank accounts, removed my name from them. As the situation at ManyOne worsened, and my frustrations increased, I chose to leave the headquarters in California and move to Idaho, where I could still provide remote services, such as web development, to ManyOne. Importantly, moving to Idaho reduced my living expenses, allowing me to survive longer with the infrequent nature of payroll.

The other reason to move to Idaho was that my friend and his business partners opened a new business that offered online payday loans and they needed help building it. I felt this supplemental income would support me if ManyOne crashed. Critical to my decision was that the Idaho partners had the funding to support the business internally, because they owned several successful businesses. So, I felt my risk was low on the payday loan project. It seemed like a smart move.

However, by the end of 2006, the Idaho partners had a disagreement over ownership, causing one of them to leave the company. With the driver of the project gone, the venture wilted, and I had neither the position nor the authority to take it over and drive it myself. Thus, my move to Idaho professionally was a bust. But, I wasn't worried, as there were plenty of good things happening in the Boise economy.

In fact, I felt so confident financially that when my girlfriend and I wanted to buy the house we were renting in May 2007, we did it; or, more importantly, she bought it and I rented. It seemed like a smart purchase, because at $320,000 it was much less than the median and average home values of $500,000 in the area. The house was in a new subdivision with few homes for sale, a brand new bike park was being built nearby, and the economy of Boise appeared strong. The downsides were few, so that if something happened between us, at least she would have an asset she could keep or sell.

But fast forward to January 2011 where Idaho ranked as the fifth highest state per capita in foreclosures. Any optimism I had about investing in the house evaporated as its value plummeted, dropping from the 2007 appraisal of $330,000 to a value of $180,000 by January of 2011. Meanwhile, ManyOne would turn to partial payroll payments and then none, sliding into bankruptcy in 2009 and halting any chance for unemployment benefits. In addition, my contracting work disappeared. Even Matchbin, which was growing quite well (and continues to grow as of 2011), had to perform a 10-to-1 split, meaning my hundred thousand shares turned into ten thousand shares, a decision I understood, but none-the-less, was just another unexpected financial change.

In other words, I had built multiple revenue and asset streams per my strategy to reduce my risk. I expected one or two would disappear, but to have all my streams disappear was a complete shock! And it's not that I was spending too much, rather I kept my expenses low. No, it was that revenue just disappeared, completely. What made it worse, and perhaps tinged my feelings with hopelessness, was that I could see the same things happening to my friends. Whether entrepreneurs or long time company employees, we were all getting knocked around. None of us had ever experienced anything like it. No matter how hard we worked, no projects seemed to get the successful steam they needed to work, unlike they did just a few years earlier.

Not only had my girlfriend's mortgage fallen far below the house value, through no fault of our own, but I was also living in a state whose high tech workforce had been decimated due to substantial layoffs between 2007 and 2009. Even worse, I wanted to separate from my girlfriend, but could not do it because if I did, the bank would foreclose on her house. If that happened, the bank that financed her loan would haunt her for she had no assets to cover the underwater portion of the mortgage. I was hemmed in by a moral dilemma. Because I had promised nothing nor implied any contract in terms of the house and could leave at any time, do I stay and prolong the relationship to save her financially or do I leave? I chose the former, as I could not let the financial wolves eviscerate her. She was too nice a person for that.

Finally, my ex-wife lost her Salt Lake City house, losing the nest egg I thought was my safest investment. In fact, her house wasn't actually underwater. Instead, Wells Fargo saw a chance to foreclose at a profit, due to the 35% equity in the house, and went after it with zeal, auctioning the house in December of 2009. Of course, my ex wasn't blameless, but Wells played dirty, telling her they were working with her while simultaneously readying the house for auction. Their "Together we will go far" slogan rings hollow. I guess seeing my kids get kicked out of their house twenty days before Christmas forces me to view Wells Fargo's remorseless efficiency with complete disgust.

By the winter of 2010-2011 my only financial lifeline was the monthly gift I received from the Idaho business partners, for whom I started doing consulting in mid-2009. Though they ran low on work a few months later, they kept paying me whether I did actual work or not, a situation that made me feel very uncomfortable. I guess they felt bad they had let me down with the payday loan project, so they did their best to help me survive until something real appeared on the horizon.

Fortunately, my fourteen-year-old car was paid off and I had no credit card debt, but that's because I had no credit cards. I paid off my undergraduate loans, but most of my grad loans still loomed. My taxes were muddled, in part because I paid taxes to California rather than Idaho. Child support continued to be a monthly drain, but they are my children, so I support them. After falling behind in support through 2003, because of my entrepreneurial activities, by 2007 I had finally made up the gap, and began paying ahead so that I would never fall behind again.

So, celebrating New Years at 2011 was tough, because my financial cupboard was bare and the falling value of the house depressed me. I applied for jobs, but no one would respond, not that I blamed them for my resume isn't structured well for the corporate world. Though I ran eWillys still, it made little money, but at least provided a passion and made me feel as if I was contributing to the world and to peoples' lives. I could make a difference, even if I was in financial hell.

Finally, in January of 2011, the first rays of financial hope appeared. We discovered a program called HAFA (Home Affordable Foreclosure Alternatives Program) launched by the federal government in 2010. Created by Congress, we learned that homes sold under HAFA had the balance of the outstanding mortgage reduced to the amount covered by the sale of the house, releasing the homeowner from future liability for the amount of debt underwater. In other words, under such a program the bank could no longer go after my girlfriend for the remainder of the debt above the home sale price. Although this might seem unfair to the banks, it turns out the banks had insurance to cover loans, so they wouldn't necessarily lose. In fact, they were collecting both the insurance and going after homeowners, which improved their bottom line, but also made some in Congress angry, which inspired the HAFA legislation in the first place.

By May 2011 the house had been readied for a short-sale within the HAFA program, leaving me confident my girlfriend would escape the financial disaster that that seemed inevitable in January. This also freed me up to exit the relationship. Though we still had a couple weeks to go before the house would be listed for sale, I finally felt hope after all. I believed this meant my life was turning around, that I could start climbing out of my hole and begin feeling like a normal person, that I could begin paying down my graduate loan debt, fix my taxes, and live a normal life. Maybe, I could even get a credit card again.

Until I live the dream and have my very own credit card, I face reality's cold stare and manage with my monthly 'gift'. Though I do handle an occasional consulting emergency for them — write a press release, draft a post card, build a website — most of the time I am on call. To fill the dead time over the past few years, I focused on two areas, family research and eWillys. I needed both of these long-term projects to help me keep my sanity, by keeping me busy and productive.

While eWillys was started only a few years ago, my family research has been an ongoing project for more than twenty years, but for much of that time work and family life has kept me from exploring and gathering family information in a serious way, in the way necessary to write a book. However, having plenty of time over the last few years, I made an effort to research, collect, organize and publish my findings through my personal website. I felt doing this would allow me to use my research to attract other people who are searching for my ancestors. That way, I could improve my ability to gather information by encouraging people to find me, instead of me always finding them. In the past few years that strategy has proven very successful, allowing me to reconnect with family on the East Coast who have family documents and items of historical interest.

Just as the research into my family history is personal, so is my effort with eWillys, but for a different reason. The idea for eWillys occurred to me in late 2007 as a project that I could build myself. At the time I was tired of partnering with people. Instead, I wanted something I could do myself, something that would succeed or fail on my own efforts. I also wanted a project that had legs, one that could potentially turn into a long-term business: a jeep museum. By late 2007, I was also in the midst of building Lost Biscuit and had seen a need for the type of jeep-related website I wanted to build. So, during the last two weeks of 2007, I built the first rendition of eWillys.

Admittedly, the 2008 launch of eWillys was pretty weak. No guards were hired to restrain the excited crowds, no parades were held in its honor, no grand speeches were crafted to announce it and, likely, not even the two people I offhandedly mentioned my intentions to days before the site launched even dropped by to see it. I admit I'm more builder than marketer. I'm a doer, generally letting my work speak for itself.

Even without marketing it, readers slowly discovered the site. Perhaps it was the daily updates that attracted readers, or the deals on jeeps for sale I found all over the US, or simply the excitement about not knowing what item of interest would appear each successive day (truth be told, I often don't know what feature post will appear on any given day). It was likely a combination of all of those attributes. My goal has been to publish what I find interesting or entertaining and share good deals on classic jeeps whenever possible. I felt if I kept the focus on those aspects, people would find utility with the site. And if there is one thing I have learned over the past ten years building internet-focused companies, it is that no website succeeds without some level of utility, something people find useful, whether financially or emotionally.

So, I was both surprised and grateful when, on occasion, over successive months in 2008, I would receive an email from someone I had never met, someone from a different state, or even a different country. They would write me, asking my opinion about a jeep, thanking me for publishing eWillys, wondering if I would like to know more about their jeep, or asking some obscure question, such as why some models of old jeeps had tailgates and some did not. The funny thing is, I didn't know many of the answers — I thought I knew a lot about jeeps, but it turns out there was much, much more to know.

Luckily, many of the answers exist at other jeep related sites. So, when I didn't have the answer, I could quickly find it and reply to the reader. Not only was this useful for the reader, but doing this often leads to the development of posts related to the topic brought up by the reader. Sure, it is some work on my part, or sometimes a ton of work, but I believe it has been a win-win-win for everyone.

Even more importantly, all the stress I felt over the collapse of my personal economy was abated by my involvement with the website. eWillys was something I could control. It cost little financially to operate, though did require plenty of time. Yet, time I had and money I didn't, so burying myself in the site proved, or better yet re-proved, I could build something from scratch and make it successful.

The results of this hard work are most evident by the responses from readers. Here are some examples of recent comments:

> *I must say I love your web site and thank you for all the effort you spend to provide this info to the general public. Since I found your site a few months ago I look at it every day with great anticipation of what might show up next. Keep up the good work.*

> *I want to say that you really do an amazing job with your blog — your bulletin boards are by far the best I've seen, and I get an amazing education every time I read a page. Yours is the kind of website that I can't wait to log into, even if it's just to check out the new listings.*

> *I wanted to send you a thank you!!! I was able to sell the jeep yesterday ... out of the many forums I posted with you were the only one to respond and quickly at that! I will recommend my jeepn' friends check out your website. Again, I Thank you!*

> *Thanks a million for your information! It was enough to get me pointed in the right direction & buy the part I was looking for. Honestly, this website has quickly become an invaluable tool in restoring this CJ2A. I'll be around a lot.*

My mother thought I was a bit on the loony side when launching the site, though she thinks that a lot about me. She has asked the "How-will-you-make-money-from-all-the-work-you-do" question more than once. My friends said that as well, "You need to monetize it". I have heard this over and over again and again. But, once Mom read the types of comments readers sent me her resistance slowly faded. She's even a regular reader of the website now.

Besides, the site itself was never intended to directly generate a living for me. In fact, I didn't think it could, because it is too niche focused for advertising to be successful and there are too many existing players in the field of parts sales for me to enter that arena. In late 2007, when I concluded there was little money in this project, I rejected all the common sense and monetary financial leanings I learned while obtaining my MBA. Instead, the more eWillys grew, the more I felt the need to follow this path, pursue this passion, and just see where this trip into the wilderness took me. Even if it was just a lifeline through a frustrating period of time it would prove invaluable.

Yet, from its very beginning I knew eWillys was more than just a lifeline. Since I wanted to build a jeep museum, I had to start somewhere. However, rather than just start building one, I felt eWillys could act as a giant research project to determine if there was a large enough demographic to make a museum successful. It could also be used to calculate the cost of gathering the jeeps, to seek out people who had large collections (if there were any at all – turns out there are) and, finally, to determine what types of jeeps would be necessary for a museum.

What I have learned about the jeep and its role in history, in small and large ways, has exceeded my expectations. For example, not many people know that the first five generations of Zamboni Ice Resurfacers® were jeeps or built on the jeep platform. Most have never seen the many lightweight prototype jeeps designed for the Military. Few know the true story behind the jeep and how American Bantam, a car company scratching for survival, created the original jeep, the Bantam Reconnaissance Car (BRC). Despite all my years of jeeping, I didn't know how the jeep was invented.

The story of the jeep begins with American Bantam. In June of 1940, the company's future looking bleak and most of the workers already gone, Bantam bet its future on obtaining a contract from the Army to make a reconnaissance vehicle, a mechanized horse of sorts. The company met with the Army and worked through ideas and specifications. Even with these meetings, in July of 1940 the Army still insisted that Bantam, along with 134 other companies, submit a bid for a contract to build seventy total jeeps, one of which had to be constructed and delivered in forty-nine days.

Fortunately for Bantam, the only other company to respond to the bid was Willys-Overland Motors, whose bid ignored the requirement to deliver a pilot vehicle in forty-nine days, a time frame they thought too short.

This allowed Bantam to win the Army contract on July 25, 1940, despite being so broke their plant was shut down. By accepting the it, Bantam assured the Army they could build and deliver the pilot jeep within the forty-nine day period or face a $100-per-day fine, something the cash strapped company could not afford. With everything at risk the Bantam team raced to design and build a part-time four wheel drive vehicle with high and low range, a vehicle that had never before existed. An engineering mountain faced the company, but somehow, by the forty-eighth day, Bantam had reached the summit, constructing a running pilot vehicle. The only distance left to travel on their road to success was literally a road, the 230 miles of road that separated American Bantam's Butler, Pa, headquarters from the Army's vehicle testing facility in Camp Holabird.

On the 49th day, with a deadline of 5:00pm, plant manager Henry Christ and Designer Karl Probst began their trip to Maryland early in the morning traveling on slow roads at a slow pace, driving an untested, wildly unusual vehicle. When the pair arrived at Holabird, beating the contract deadline by half an hour, they were immediately surrounded by crowds of soldiers who stared at the utilitarian creature. Testing commenced immediately, with first Christ driving it up a steep grade, impressing Major Lawes, the head of vehicle testing. Satisfied at this initial accomplishment, Lawes took a short turn driving the vehicle. Lawes, who had driven and tested all the different vehicles at the test facility, returned shortly thereafter, declaring the vehicle would make history.

Despite Bantam's unexpected triumph the company would lose out on the ¼ ton jeep military contract to Willys-Overland. The Army, not altogether heartless, threw the company some bones in the form of a contract to build military trailers. I guess the company built those trailers pretty well, because Bantam Trailers still appear for sale on Craigslist.

These are only snippets of the jeep story as the vehicle evolved over successive decades, both on the production side and on the consumer side. On the production side, Willys-Overland offered extensive customization options. Dual rear wheels, farm implements of all kinds, utility products, and power take-off options were available.

On the consumer side, people bought their jeeps and modified them to meet their needs, sometimes in beautiful and sometimes in ugly ways. Jeeps also were often given names. I too have named my jeeps, the first one being the 'Great Escape' and my latest 'Lost Biscuit'.

These are the stories I post at eWillys. They reveal the scope of jeep use and modification, including the good, the bad and the ugly. In fact, I strongly believe the jeep was the most modified vehicle in history and the more than thirty thousand pictures on eWillys are a testament to that, as it is difficult to find an original jeep that *has not* been modified.

So, for a few hours every day, many times more, I work to build the website and answer email. Over the span of three and a half years, with help from thousands of readers, my dedication to eWillys has led to a complex, rich site. Yet, it continues to need work and can be even better. Most importantly, eWillys, along with my dream of a museum, have given me important goals, points to reach, which I hope leads out of the economic chaos I see around me, while benefiting others along the way.

3. MAY 16TH, 2011

On the 16th of May, four days after writing Virginia, I spot an email from her in my inbox. I discovered it right after waking, because my daily routine generally goes like this, 1) I wake up and 2) pickup my computer from the side of the bed and check my email:

May 16th, 2011 – 7:58 AM

Wow, David, Yes.

You have reached me. Did I ever wear my hair that way? I joke because I am blown away. I do not recall taking that picture. I would have totally forgotten that walk we took, but it came whooshing back. It is amazing how much information we store. You were the first person to explain the Mason's to me. If I remember correctly, you told me you wanted to date someone whom you were dating when you met me. I thought it best to respond ASAP. I am very busy and did not check email for a few days. So now you can avoid harassing the entire public of Virginia Andersons. Take care and I wish you well.

Virginia

The email leaves me scratching my head. "Blown away" sounds good, while "wish you well" sounds like goodbye. Assuming her response was a positive step, I reply right away, attaching a scanned copy of her note card from 1986 so she could read it for herself:

May 16th, 2011 – 2:55 PM

Virginia,

Hopefully, you are blown away in a good way :-) I don't want you to think I'm stalking you or anything like that! I am relieved that I do not have to harass any other Virginias, though I wasn't opposed to doing it, politely of course, but rest assured you are the first I contacted. One of my skills seems to be internet research and I managed to track you down via a blog entry you made that steered me to your website. On your website I saw your picture and felt confident that it was you. The internet is an amazing (and scary) tool.

Regarding your hair, yes you did wear it that way, but I also probably played a role in messing it up more than normal. I took the picture with your camera and then you sent me copies of that photo along with several other photos with sweet messages on the back. Yes, when we met I had dated someone else a couple of times but it was never serious (and we never went out again).

The summer of 1986 was the beginning of my travels far and wide and you helped make it one of the most interesting summers of my life. Because I've moved around so much, I have a small box of my must keep-items, with a small folder of personal items within it. Your letter is one of three letters I have kept all this time (the two others are from Cullen, my friend from Roche you met, but might not remember). I've kept the letter (which I thought you might enjoy seeing) because you were so warm and kind and honest during our time together. And in return, your letter felt like you were acknowledging that I had shared those same feelings with you and helped you through a tough time. (Lord knows we all need help in tough times). I guess I've met so many people and seen so much, that I really do treasure your friendship, however brief, and the time with you the older I get.

To catch you up, I spent the next 2 summers at Roche (where I moved onto the dinner line) then left to get my Bachelor's Degree and eventually a graduate degree. I am divorced and have 3 great kids who are busy growing up quickly. I live in Idaho, for the time being, but am moving (again) this summer to an as-yet-undecided location. I bounce between here, Salt Lake (where my kids live) and Renton (where Mom and Dad, who need my help, still live). I put a lot of miles on my car!

My hope is that sharing with you how much I still enjoy your letter and the thoughts of you enriches your life a little more and puts a smile on your face, however brief. Too often we are too busy to take the time to share such things.

If you ever need anything, drop me an email. I wish you well, too,

- Dave

I impatiently await a response, but none arrives until the next day:

May 17^h, 2011 – 3:17 AM

David,

I am blown away in a good way and am actually relieved with your detailed explanation as to the history that brought you to write to me so many years later.

I assume you noticed the time stamp on my replies. You wrote just as I had been up nights wondering about my life. I guess we do that as we mature. Examining one's life is crucial. I am relieved you are not a stalker and that our time and my words meant so much to you. I cannot believe that while I was wishing for some answers about how my life has affected others, you wrote.

My story could make an epic movie. The only way to tell you about my life would be over a long conversation or a longer book.

You were blessed to have three children. What happened to your marriage?

This is just too hard to say, so I avoided any mention before. I had a child, but she died with my ex-husband driving in a car accident. Obviously, it was a horrible, emotional time for me. It tore us apart.

So you saw my stiff picture. I am a professional set designer for a company in Seattle and get to travel to locations all over.

So I am that open, honest sensitive young woman you met. This is hard so I am going to stop for now and thank you for your candor.

Virginia

Two hours later, still early in the morning, I receive a second response:

May 17th, 2011 – 5:46 AM

Hi David,

Ok I am back. No, I am not crazy either. I just had to tend to my emails when I realized I had not read the note you had attached. You realize, I was completely free in actuality when you and I met. I was raised Catholic and divorce is complicated for me. I do not think it is always a bad thing. I never even think about the guy I married out of high school and college days.

HOWEVER, I do now recall almost all the time I spent with you. Remember the Hotel at Roche? Somehow my family had something to do with building the fireplace mantel. My Grandfather was best friends with Reuben Tarte, the Tarte son's father.

Back to the note. So you and I never did see each other again. Wow, I cannot believe you still have that note. My penmanship is still no better; however, I love writing.

The key is not to over-write, so . . .

PS There is a full moon, so perhaps there is a measure of lunacy here. (kidding!)

Virginia

After just those two emails, a couple things were clear. First, she was in a relationship. Second, she was unhappy in that relationship. If there is one thing I have learned about women — and after several serious relationships I don't know all that much — is that women tend to be upfront about the relationship status when they are either 'very single' or 'happily in a serious relationship'. Everything between those poles is gray.

I also felt her curiosity about me. There was deep emotion in her, very deep, unexpected by me. She also was cautious, not only with whatever concerns she had about her situation, but also about her feelings regarding me. A certain amount of caution made sense. After all, I could just be some loon (heck, maybe I am a little loony). She couldn't see me; she could only trust my words and the picture. In spite of her raised guard, I feel my emails have pricked something tender. I want to know what and why.

I don't want to push for a meeting. I want to let her feel comfortable with our communication so if we meet, it will be in a situation of trust and friendship. I meant what I wrote. I want to know how she is and who she has become. Yet, meeting her in person interests me, because we had been close, which leaves me wondering if that closeness still exists.

Achieving some understanding about why I continue to keep the letter is important too. Are my memories of Virginia simply a golden haze with the problems dusted away and only the good memories remaining? Did I like her a lot or did I love her? Why didn't I pursue her? The more I think about her, the more the number of questions increase. But, so does my optimism, along with my spirit. After some tough times over the past few years, life seems to be turning a corner and in a little way I feel Virginia adding to the growing light.

Around noon, while working on my website, she responds with a third note:

> May 17th, 2011 – 12:29 PM
>
> David,
>
> *I re-read your notes and realized I had not read carefully; middle of the night reading. So I did not mean to exclude your mother. You are lucky to have both of your folks. My mother and father have both passed away. Tomorrow would have been my mother's birthday. My parents were married for 52 years. According to your life now, you would be closest to me, to arrange a visit, when you are in Renton. Your notes hold so much thought and information that I find myself writing w/o awaiting a response. I think I am taking it in piece by piece and then feel a need to respond. So, sorry to fill your email w/multi-responses. I also have traveled to many countries and cities making movies, have met so many people and CHERISH this connection you have made w/me. I am glad you have caught my humor as well. As you said the internet is amazing and scary.*
>
> *Virginia*

I receive her note while writing this one:

> May 17th, 2011 – 12:52 PM
>
> Virginia,
>
> *Well, a little lunacy is good for the soul every so often :-)*
>
> *I don't remember you telling me that your grandfather was best friends with Rueben Tarte.*
>
> *What I do remember is you in the shopping cart one evening (and us getting busted by Dave, the ops guy at Roche). I remember you walking into the restaurant kitchen in a yellow outfit — a total knockout — and watching Grant's (the cook who owned the trailer I was living in) jaw drop when he realized you were there to see me. I remember that kiss on the dock at the end of our first night of mischief.*

After I received your letter in 1986, I felt very happy for you. I'm not sure I even wrote back (I can't remember), but I had this sense it was time for both of us to move forward, with each of us benefiting from the other's friendship and intimacy, without a shred of bitterness that often accompanies the end of a relationship (whether intimate or not). We learned a little about each other and ourselves and we could move forward enriched.

In 1987 at Roche I met a woman and, three years later, married in Roche's garden. We moved quite a bit due to college and jobs — from Tacoma, to Seattle, to Wisconsin, to Utah — and along the way we had 3 kids and both of us completed graduate degrees. So, why did I ask for the divorce in 1999? That's a long story I will share some day.

During the 00s, I co-launched several companies, the largest of which was ManyOne Networks that had 60+ employees in Scotts Valley, Ca (near Santa Cruz). By 2005 I was making great money, had a net worth of $15 million (all notes receivable backed by stock) and we had a chance to walk our technology into Google. But, unexpected events and funding problems halted our progress and nothing anyone did seemed to help. I lost everything. Again, it's another long story . . .

Because of that experience and others, my trust in people was devastated. So, mostly to heal, I went back to something I knew I could do myself. I built another jeep, similar to the jeep I had when we met. While doing that, I discovered how difficult it was to find parts and I found a number of people who were being dishonest about their jeeps. So, I launched eWillys.com, a site dedicated to helping people in the jeeping community. Through word-of-mouth people started to show up to read it daily.

Children have altered my life in wonderful and difficult ways (no fault of their own, they are great, smart, easy kids). But being a divorced father has brought challenges I both expected and didn't expect. It sounds like you haven't found peace with your decision, but I'm sure you made the best decision given the circumstances.

I just saw a new email from you. Don't worry about filling up my inbox, because I run my own email system. So, write when it feels right.

I'm sorry to hear about your parents. My mom will likely be around another 10 years at least, along with my aunt who is a second mother (she has no kids). However, my father is a different person than he was and can only watch TV and lift weights (which he has done for 40 years). However, due to a back problem he suffered last month trying to push a riding lawn mower, even lifting weights isn't possible.

I'm not surprised at all you are an 'artist'. I know you enjoyed that side of you and am happy you have been successful pursuing what comes naturally to you!!!

Well, time to get some work done. Thanks for your p#. I will be up in Renton sometime in the next three weeks.

- Dave

She responds quickly:

May 17th, 2011 – 1:23 PM

David ... Great Letter!

- Virginia

A short, sweet answer. I want more, but this is fine as my mind is focused on writing content for the website. Also, with a better feel for her writing, my understanding of her style and of the long ago letter she sent increased, too. But, it also leaves me wondering if I had misread it. Maybe she wasn't saying goodbye in her letter, but simply guarded her feelings more than I expected. Had she meant to say that *I am busy restarting my life, I have traveled to see you, now will you come down and see me*? Could I have misunderstood her letter?

4. MAY 1986: MY FIRST VISIT TO ROCHE HARBOR

Concern over my misreading of Virginia's letter haunted me all night. Sorting through my memories of the summer of 1986, my feelings upon receiving her letter and my lack of pursuit once the summer ended, left me puzzled. I couldn't answer one simple question: Why didn't I see her again? I'd had her address and phone number; I could have found a way to contact her.

At the time, as busy as she was remaking her life, I was equally busy living mine. After receiving her letter I spent the next three months traveling, starting with a trip to Expo 86 in Vancouver, followed by a month long jeep trip around the state of Washington, and then ending with a trip to New Hampshire, to visit with my cousins, where I stayed for nearly two months. By the time I returned to the Seattle area in early 1987, my energy was focused on earning money and returning to Roche in April for a second summer at the resort.

Also, by the end of my 1986 summer I was tired from months of long hours running an outdoor barbeque and working inside Roche Harbor's Restaurant. While some events from 1986 remain clear, others are foggy. My memory of cooking on the dinner line for the first time is vivid, as one of the line cooks freaked out during the dinner rush and ran outside, pressing me into service. So too are my thoughts of Virginia, when we met, how I felt, and how she looked. But, I don't remember my reaction to her letter, which arrived in late September. I do know my feelings have always positive about her and the letter, which is one reason why it always remained special to me.

Also very vivid is my memory that I would never have traveled to Roche had it not been for an ankle injury. My entire 1986 experience turned on a freak event: I suffered a terrible ankle sprain playing basketball in April of that year.

Readers of eWillys know I am a basketball gym rat. They usually find out, not because I brag about any particular exploit, nor because I tell some tale about a spectacularly great pass, nor due to some demolishing by a far superior team. No, they learn about my basketball passion because about every six months or so I jam, bruise or damage one of my fingers, making it too painful or awkward to update eWillys that day.

In fact, I am nursing a dislocation-sprain-broken ring finger of some unknown type suffered a few months ago. As mentioned to readers, thankfully, my ring finger took the brunt of the damage. That finger has caused me more problems on and off the court and in and out of court than the other nine fingers combined! Maybe I no longer have a need for that finger?

Despite the occasional website-halting injury, my body has been relatively injury free. At the age of forty, I sprained my left ankle, which kept me out of basketball for a month. At the age of twenty-eight I broke my collar bone in three places following a mountain biking accident in Olympic National Forest (the stump may have only been two inches tall, however its power to upend me was great), but that never seemed all that big of deal, because I wasn't playing much basketball at the time.

Of all those injuries, the worst was my ankle sprain at age twenty. That happened in April of 1986 at a YMCA on top of Queen Anne Hill in Seattle. Late one Tuesday with winter finally gone and spring just arriving, I drove my VW Rabbit, the perfect downtown Seattle car, to the Y to play some evening ball. On this particular night, I played for about two hours. Tired, sweating and breathing hard, I was almost ready to leave when a couple guys entered the gym, asking if they could play.

I agreed to play some more, so they and their fresh legs entered the game. During the course of play, one of the new guys stole the ball from me, so I chased him down. As he drove for a lay up, I jumped and spun around him, attempting to block the ball. Well, my swat missed the ball, causing me to fall awkwardly, landing badly on my right foot as I fell to the floor. The swelling started immediately.

I had to work that night, as made extra money working as the janitor at the BurgerWorks. Moving slowly, unable to put weight on my right leg, I showed up at the closed restaurant at 10pm thinking I could gut through two hours of cleaning, but it took little time to realize this would not work regardless of my best effort. After a call to my bosses explaining the situation, I left for my parents' home.

I spent the next few days in my parents' living room, ankle up and wrapped on their antique love seat, whose high arms elevated my sprained ankle perfectly. With plenty of ice cooling it and the TV numbing my brain, the swelling subsided. A week later, my ankle felt better and I could walk again, though gingerly. About that time one of my bosses suggested I soak my ankle with some Epsom salts. I didn't know anything about Epson salts, so I gave it a try.

Unfortunately, I interpreted my boss's suggestion in the wrong way. I used *warm water* and Epsom salts. Since the swelling had gone down and the ankle was feeling better, I figured a little warm water would make it feel even better. Yeah, I discovered that was a fabulous idea . . . NOT . . . I might as well have injected compressed air into my foot, because after a few minutes of soaking in the warm water, my foot swelled to its post sprain size. And once again it hurt badly. This meant I had to make an embarrassing phone call to my bosses, explaining to them that my return to work would be delayed because I am an idiot.

It's truly amazing how life works, because about that time a guy named Grant, who worked near the BurgerWorks as a boat-builder during the winter and a chef during the summers, gave me a call. He wanted to recruit me to go up to the San Juan Islands to cook for the summer.

This wasn't his first attempt at to recruit me. He approached me a couple times during the previous weeks at the BurgerWorks, suggesting I would have fun and learn a lot at Roche. However, I knew nothing about Roche Harbor, having never been to the San Juan Islands. The only thing I knew about the San Juan Islands was that when I was fourteen a friend of mine was sent by his parents to a Camp Orkila, a YMCA summer camp, for several weeks on Orcas Island. I remember he had a great time and loved the place. Other than that, I knew nothing about the islands. In fact, nothing sounded remotely interesting to me about Grant's offer. Besides, I didn't know Grant well, so he might as well have tried selling me encyclopedias.

For obvious reasons, my bosses weren't thrilled by that idea and downplayed it. In addition, they weren't worried I would accept Grant's offer, because I had already agreed with them to work the summer at the BurgerWorks and planned on racing my jeep during the summer of 1986, as I had the previous summer. Besides, the BurgerWorks team valued me. My bosses worked hard, appreciated my efforts and hoped I could help them grow their company. Therefore, I thought replacing me would be difficult for them.

However, my sprained ankle changed everything. While speaking with Grant on the phone, I realized that my newly swollen ankle wouldn't be good for another couple weeks, which forced my bosses to hire a temporary replacement, so the pressure for me to return to work quickly lessened. I also figured a mostly free trip up to the San Juan Islands, a couple nights on Grant's sailboat, and a sail around the islands, might be worth the trip. As I mulled over the offer, Grant informed me this would be the last time he would ask. So, it was either now or never, did I want an adventure or did I want to remain on the couch for another couple weeks?

The decision was easy at that point. I told him yes. I will make the two hour drive, take the two hour ferry ride, spend a couple nights up there, meet the people and see the area, but I was not yet promising to take the job. He accepted my conditions.

A few days after we talked, I drove to the Anacortes Ferry Terminal, arriving a couple hours early, per Grant's instructions, because, if I missed the ferry, my butt would be stuck in Anacortes until the morning. Grant also told me multiple hour waits for the ferry were common, so he advised me to arrive a couple hours before the evening ferry left.

I paid the ferry toll of $24, holding my money tightly out my car door window so the wind wouldn't blow it away. After paying, I drove forward slowly, staring through my windshield. I saw blacktop and white lanes stretch far in front of me, reaching Canada it seemed. The terminal's ferry lot was a gigantic staging area with white lines separating the different lanes. I couldn't imagine how so many cars could fit onto a single ferry. I proceeded forward in my car until I arrived behind another. I stopped, turned off the car and looked around me.

A few people exited their cars and strolled, their hair and jackets blown around by gusts of wind. Seagulls battled the wind as well. Rolling down my window, a cool gust swiftly entered, followed by smells of salt water from the nearby bay. Though the wind blew and the seagulls squawked, there was a quiet, a peace about the place, drivers and passengers resigned to their wait. I too was resigned, to wait in the car that is, because I wasn't about to go through the gymnastics necessary to leave the car and mount my crutches, my ankle still too sore for walking. Instead, I grabbed a book and relaxed.

• • • •

A couple hours later, the ferry arrived, unloading an endless caravan of cars. But then, it was a Friday evening, so I assumed lots of people were leaving the islands to spend the weekend doing one thing or another.

Once emptied, the ferry began to fill back up, as the lanes of cars waiting to board filed slowly onto it. I carefully followed the car in front of me, listening to the ka-chunk of the tires as I drove over the ramp and onto the ferry deck. A ferry worker waved her hands, directing the car in front of me, and then me, to a specific place on the ferry. Another ferry worker waved me forward until I was sure my bumper would tap the car in front of me, directing me to halt a few inches away. Once stopped, I wondered whether to exit the car or not, as the ride was expected to take two hours. I soon learned it was okay to leave the car, as people, whom I took for more experienced travelers, were hopping out of their cars and heading toward similar points on the ferry deck, stairs probably.

Out of the car I hobbled, carefully navigating through the parked cars until I reached the stairs. While excited about seeing the upper decks, navigating the tight stairway did not look like fun; but, staying in my car seemed less fun, so I worked my crutches and me between the cars until reaching the stairs. As I began climbing the stairs I focused on one step at a time, moving my crutches to the step above my foot and then pushing upward. Move, push, step. Move, push, step. Move, push, step. It was slow and tedious.

Eventually, I made it to the lower passenger deck, where I saw a second set of steps and signs indicating there was food on the level above me. The stairs seemed more formidable than the food seemed appetizing, so I crutched my way over to a soft bench seat next to a window. I looked out the window.

Seated, I saw rows of light beige seats stretching in front of me. In fact, most everything seemed beige or white, interrupted by the occasional forest green accents. People milled about the area, though not many. Everyone seemed to have a different direction to go, some went up the stairs to the second deck, some sat on benches, some walked to the other side of the deck, and still others went out the stern doors to a rear viewing deck. Curious to see more, I pushed myself up and crutched my way to the stern and stepped outside.

It was late in the evening and the sun was on the western horizon, which was the direction the ferry was going. At the trailing end of the ferry, I was looking east, watching the remaining rays of sun cause the ripples on the water to shimmer. I could smell salt water and feel a soothing rumble as the ferry made way to Lopez Island, our first destination. The wind blew my hair about and cooled the air, but my jacket kept me warm. The whole scene lit my imagination.

Here I am in 2011 on a ferry that has left the Anacortes Ferry Terminal and is bound for San Juan Island, 25 years after my first trip in 1986. In the background is another ferry with Cypress Island behind it.

The soothing vibrations created by the propellers left little wake as the ferry slid quietly through the water. Leaning on my crutches against the railing, I gazed at the islands, then to the water, then back. It's not that much was happening on the water or on the islands, which were mostly masses of deep green trees. But, there was something mesmerizing about staring at them, similar to hearing ocean waves crash or watching firelight dance.

After enough time at the back of the ferry my jacket no longer kept me warm, so I sought shelter inside. Going back into the ferry and crutching my way over to a bench to sit, I watched through the windows as we passed scenic spot after scenic spot, marveling at the water, the rocks, and the trees. I felt peaceful as the world passed by me as if the landscape was moving rather than me and the ferry.

From that moment, from that single ferry ride, I loved the San Juan Islands. My passion for the place only continued once I reached the island.

Eventually the ferry docked at Friday Harbor, the largest town in the San Juans, where Grant moored his boat. Driving off the ferry, I quickly entered the center of town. The clean streets were filled with just enough people to look busy, but not too busy. Friday Harbor was a throwback to a time when small towns thrived. There were no empty storefronts, the buildings looked well maintained, there were no stoplights, and people appeared in no particular hurry. Following Grant's directions, I drove through town and arrived at the marina.

• • • •

I spent Friday night on his boat. Saturday morning I explored Friday Harbor. In the afternoon I made the half hour drive to Roche Harbor for my meeting with Reaf, the head chef of Roche Harbor Restaurant.

Grant told me I would have no problem finding the restaurant at Roche. He said it was the old McMillin house perched on the side of the harbor. Sure enough, after parking behind the hotel, I quickly saw where to go. As I hobbled to the restaurant on my crutches, the harbor opened in front of me. To my left I spotted the general store. I passed by a wide path paved with yellow bricks — a real life yellow brick road — then entered the front door of the restaurant. The hostess greeted me and, after explaining to her my meeting with Reaf, she directed me back to the kitchen. Walking to the swinging kitchen doors, I noticed only a few people eating in the restaurant. The dining room was dark despite light spilling through several large-paned windows that faced the busy harbor, a stage for diners to enjoy.

And what a beautiful stage! A boat dock angled across the harbor a stone's throw from the restaurant with a few boats moored in the slips.

Beyond the dock, small floating tires dotted the harbor. I would later learn these were buoys used by boaters for mooring. Beyond the floating tires were more islands full of trees, encircling the harbor and providing it protection.

I walked into the kitchen, not expecting much bustle. Grant told me the resort season didn't launch until Queen Victoria Day, the three-day Canadian weekend preceding our Memorial Day weekend (It turns out Canadians have a three day holiday every month, reason enough to be Canadian).

The white brightness of the kitchen forced me to squint until my eyes adjusted. Once I could see better, the kitchen looked huge, overwhelming. At least, it was huge to me. After all, the only restaurant kitchen I had known was the BurgerWorks' kitchen, which wasn't much larger than the average food wagon. Well, maybe it was slightly bigger than that. For me, Roche's kitchen was amazing, full of equipment I hadn't seen, with a walk-in refrigerator and freezer, an actual cooking line with burners, a griddle, a charbroiler, and ovens on one side and serving and prep space just a one hundred and eighty degree spin away. It had an entire kitchen wing devoted to washing dishes. In the middle of the area was a large salad serving and prep area. It all looked to be a great challenge to me.

While waiting for Reaf to arrive, I watched the waitstaff, two women, produce tickets and deliver food. In between, they introduced themselves and seemed generally interested to learn more about me. Both women were in their thirties and had worked summers at Roche for years. They asked if I planned to work there; I responded that we would know about that very soon. As they left the kitchen to deliver orders, they assured me it was fun.

The kitchen was quiet, except for the lone cook preparing food. A warm breeze, welcome in May, blew through a small open window in the kitchen, the only one I could see. Sunlight filtered through the window as well, reflecting off the recently painted white walls. The floor tiles were an earthy red, a few chipped in their corners. The equipment was all stainless steel, some pieces brightly polished, appearing lightly used, while other equipment, like the sauté station, had burners stained black in spots from heavy use. The counters were a light brown, most pocked with knife slices, suggesting food was prepped everywhere

A thin man about my height sporting a bushy mustache appeared from a stairway. He looked to be in his forties and seemed very official in his head chef attire, wearing a white cooking jacket and white and black checkered cooking pants, a name tag, and a thermometer sticking out of the long pocket on his jacket. He shook my hand, introducing himself as Reaf. He suggested we go upstairs to his office for the interview.

Now, do not imagine the staircase to his office was some kind of large sweeping set of stairs. Instead, the stairs, thin, narrow, vanishing into a dark attic (a really dark attic), were a relic of the old house. Approaching the stairs I realized these stairs were much worse than the lighted stairs of the ferry. The stairway had slasher movie scene written all over it. I was playing the guy with the crutches who couldn't possibly get away from the knife-wielding killer. So, I did my best to focus on the stairs and begin my climb. Once again, I repeated the dance I learned on the ferry, move, push, and step. Move, push, step. Move, push, step. It was slow and tedious. If Reaf was a serial killer, he had enduring patience, for he followed me quietly.

Finally, I reached the second to the last step, with only one more to go. Though my eyes adjusted slightly, the attic was still dark, lit only by light trickling through a window on a far wall. I moved my crutches to the last step and did my push. Only this time it worked out differently. It turned out the ceiling, being an attic, was low and angled downward. This meant that when I pushed upward, my head hit the ceiling, throwing me off balance, causing me to fall.

"Is this really happening?" I thought as I began to fall backward in slow motion unable to stop myself. I know I put my arms straight out to my sides, spreading wide as if doing a reverse swan dive, teetering backward helplessly.

Suddenly, gratefully, I felt a set of arms catch and stop me. It was Reaf, who, thankfully, had been paying enough attention that he caught me to a stop, saving us both. The horror movie, turned disaster movie, turned out to be a feel good movie. He proved to be a savior rather than a serial killer, lucky for me. Between my outstretched arms and him bracing me, we managed to halt a very painful trip back down the stairs to the kitchen. What a great first impression that was!

While I was embarrassed, Reaf took the whole episode in stride as if every person he interviewed nearly fell down backward. We made our way to a table at the attic's far end, where we sat and talked. Regardless of my awkwardness, after speaking with me a while, Reaf offered me a job as a breakfast cook and Sunday cook. I was shocked!

My answer came immediately. YES. Everything felt right about the place. It was one of the easiest decisions I ever made. I was pretty excited about the whole deal. Besides, it was a better wage than the BurgerWorks and a whole new experience. He told me to return June 10th and be ready for work. He also reminded me to be careful going down the stairs. I needed no reminder about that!

With much less drama, I made my down the stairs and back into the kitchen. That's when I met a guy we sometimes called Rocky, though Reaf introduced him to me as David. Yep, it took only two minutes into my work career at Roche to meet another David. Because he was another David, he was given a nickname to differentiate him from me and the other Davids, so someone started calling him Rocky, due to his dark hair, eyes, and facial structure that made him look similar to Sylvester Stallone.

However, I always called him David. Never Dave or Davey, but David, as it was his preferred name. Personally, I never cared whether I was called Dave or David, but he did care, so David it was. David's job at the resort was to manage restaurant inventory. He dealt with food deliveries, making sure delivery orders the restaurant received were properly filled and accepting supplies into the restaurant by sliding boxes of vegetables, fruit, napkins and anything else down a steep box chute paralleling the stairs that staff used to enter the back of the restaurant. As a part of his job he also managed ingredients and food supplies at a remote freezer and refrigerator located behind the general store, because the walk-in freezer and refrigerator in the restaurant weren't big enough to handle all the food the restaurant needed. This meant David had to make daily runs to bring supplies from the remote walk-in freezer and refrigerator to refill the freezer and refrigerator in the restaurant.

After introducing us, Reaf mentioned to David that he needed a variety of items from the remote freezer. He also suggested he take me down and show me around, since I would start work soon. David agreed and told me to follow him, which I did. He led me out the back door and up the stairs to the service road where an electric utility cart awaited us. The cart, a deep green golf-cart like vehicle that needed new paint, actually belonged to the hotel, according to David, which begrudgingly allowed him to use it to ferry supplies. I flopped into the cart holding my crutches. A ride in the cart seemed a welcome relief from crutching.

David was never one to say a whole lot. He was quiet, worked hard, and had little patience for fools. That was my first impression of him and, I learned, what you saw was what you got. However, though he had only been working a few weeks, he did know quite a bit of trivia about the resort and was proud to share it once I got him talking.

From the stairs, we drove past the restaurant along the service road before turning onto the yellow brick road, a road paved with yellow limestone chimney bricks left from Roche Harbor's early life as a lime producer according to David. Down the center of the brick road were benches and flowerpots, giving the road the feel of a pedestrian walking area, which it was. As we slowly bumped along the uneven bricks, to my right were two large flower gardens, described by David as English gardens, separated by a second, but narrower brick path, and topped by an arbor. The gardens burst with flowers, plants and colors, filling the air with wonderful smells adding to the resort's atmosphere.

The yellow brick road at Roche Harbor in 2011 looks as it did in 1986. At that time ivy covered part of the hotel's façade. By 2011 it had been removed.

On our left we passed a large building, the Hotel De Haro, a three story wooden structure with verandas on each level of the building. The building looks settled with the railings no longer straight and level.

Painted mostly white, with some green trim, the hotel contrasted nicely against the deep green of the pine and cedar trees behind it and the gardens in front of it. Thick ivy wound up the columns, obscuring part of the hotel. David said that John Wayne was such a frequent visitor he had his own custom-sized bathtub installed.

Driving slowly so I could look at everything, he mentioned that this year was the 100th anniversary of the founding of Roche, first opened in 1886 as the Roche Harbor Lime and Cement Company by John McMillin. In the 1950s, the Tarte family bought all the property and buildings, turning it into a resort. He said the family still owned and managed the resort. He said that besides the restaurant, hotel, and general store, Roche Harbor also had its own church, cabins, swimming pool, cemetery and mausoleum. Then he gave me a sly look and said there was even a ghost named Ada Beane, the McMillin family's former secretary, who haunted the restaurant. I took it all in.

The yellow brick road ended at the edge of the hotel, leaving the scented gardens behind us and depositing us back onto blacktop, which smoothed the ride. The electric motor whined and the wind blew my curly hair as David sped up. We quickly crossed the store's parking lot. As we angled to the right toward the south side of the General Store, I spotted some pay phones, which later became my link to the outside world. The front of the General Store, painted the same white and green colors as the hotel, stood tall in front of me. Panes of glass formed the front of the store, while offices occupied the second story. According to David, the building had been there since 1886.

As we rounded the side of the store, the blacktop yielded to dirt and rocks. The green accents on the front of the store disappeared into a canvas of plain white. Clearly, this wasn't the finer side of the resort. David stopped the cart in front of a white door. He grabbed a metal loop with an attached key, walked to the door, and opened a heavy-duty lock. He slid the lock out of the door handle, opened the door and disappeared through some plastic sheets. Clouds of white mist rolled out from the freezer, chilling me slightly despite the sunny blue day.

As I waited, I looked across the water at some newer buildings that appeared to be condominiums. They looked nothing like the motif established by the resort. I later learned this was a real estate development whose results had not been as successful as hoped.

David began loading a few boxes into the back of the cart. I turned to see frozen boxes of ribs, some frozen shrimp, and a few frozen pastries. Checking his list to make sure he got everything, he hopped back into the driver's seat, turned the cart around, and began the drive back to the restaurant. Now, I had a clear view of the site where the former lime works buildings had been, the original purpose for Roche Harbor's existence. Gone were the buildings themselves, but remnants of the kilns remained, half-buried in the hillside.

Instead of angling back to the yellow brick road, David turned sharply left, taking me to another part of the yellow brick road that ran along the harbor. He suggested I check out the view from the deck near the bar, one story below the restaurant. Driving me up to the steps of the bar deck, he came to a stop and waited for me to get off, telling me he looked forward to seeing me in a few weeks. I jumped out, crutched up the six stairs, and hobbled to a table that overlooked Roche Harbor.

Roche Harbor's Restaurant with the bar deck in front where I sat during my first visit in 1986. The steeple of the church is just visible behind it.

From my vantage point on the deck, I could see the north side of the store, the post office, and the laundromat. To the right of all that were some flags flying on a land mounted ship's mast. Before me in the water was the same dock I had seen from the restaurant dining area. However, with temperatures around seventy-five degrees and the sky a deep blue, the view and the experience of this day were best enjoyed outside rather than inside the restaurant. There was no question in my mind. I wanted to spend the summer of 1986 right here.

5. MAY 18TH, 2011

Waking up, I open my laptop computer, hoping to find another email from Virginia. Yes, she wrote again:

May 18th, 2011 – 10:34 AM

Good Morning Dave.

It occurred to me that you spent time on your last note and I gave a two-word response. You said you needed to work and I thought it best to keep it brief. So this is the lengthy response. First, I am not technological at all. I only use email and do a little research via internet. I cannot imagine I was on any blog. I never do that.

Much of my work over the years has been people seeing me work and then asking me to do more. I have had a long run at film work behind the camera and live shows. I love what I do, but the economy has really made life tough. Of course the economy has wrung everybody out.

On the side I do interior design, which is a natural sideline. I love working with colors and teaching people how to use furniture, fabrics and features to make their house reflect their personalities. However, the movie work pays much better so I have stuck with that for the most part.

I had not seen your personal website during our first few notes, however, I did go on yesterday and read what I could. I am so happy that you have followed your passions and have discovered your talents and have goals. I understand this is a transitional time for you and are actually moving on to a new place and new project. NEVER GIVE UP!

I felt so bad about the undercurrent of pain you felt in your marriage but the bright side are those beautiful children. You have been triple blessed!!! They look VERY happy and confident. I am sure it is a struggle for you to be away from them.

After the day I wrote that note which you let me see again, I did not marry again for five years. Then, I married and we had Sara. Oh Dave, she was so beautiful. Five years later she was gone, a victim of a freak car accident, of circumstance really. Our marriage melted quickly for truly no reason at all other than our hearts were broken. It took much counseling and do not think of those years because they are so painful.

I feel I have not been able to tell you too much for fear of judgment. I am a loyal, honest and giving person and that has caused me much pain. I realized I was risking my deep feelings the moment I wrote a second time. I cannot see myself starting over and trusting again.

I want to tell you about my life now but prefer not to put it on the internet. Maybe the following will help you see how I think.

> *So I am not sure what Dave and Virginia are to each other:*
>
> *- Like the movie Dirty Dancing-young summer love in a legacy old money resort,*
>
> *- Like the movie When Harry Met Sally-an epic tale of friends meant to be together forever who came in and out of each other's lives*
>
> *- Like the story Bridges of Madison County-two soul-mates who have a deeper connection w/ each other than they ever hoped for but obligation wins out and they go separate ways.*

Silly, I know, to use movies to make a point, but movies are my life and that is what was running through my mind.

Good luck with your transition!! Take care, Virginia

That note thrills me. I can see her opening herself, taking a chance. It is clear to me she needs someone to trust, someone who she knows won't hurt her. She has been hurt and dealing with it has worn her down. I can relate.

As much as I want to use a few movie references over the course of our emails, I also want to avoid them, because Hollywood rarely has unhappy endings. In our case, if she is feeling what I feel, if those memories from so long ago are real, if the feelings are real, then we need to act with maturity and tact; if we don't have some sense about us, we can hurt others around us. I am certain we both want to know more about the other, yet we want to maintain our convictions. We both understand without saying as much to the other that meeting in person has to be handled maturely and in a positive way.

For me, the timing for all this is better than it had been in years, because I really am readying a transition. With the house far along in the HAFA process, I feel strongly I should move to Seattle. I have too many contacts and too much family there not return this time, after living away from the area for twenty years. My very independent parents need my help and, God bless them, they have been there when I have needed them (though for an entire year my mother and I didn't talk, which is part of the reason I was living in my law school office in 2000). So, this seems the right time to move to Seattle.

Having thought about all those issues, I drop her another note:

May 18th, 2011 – 1:37 PM

Virginia,

Since it is already afternoon here, I shall send you a good afternoon. I am writing you from Rembrandts, a wonderful locally run coffee shop operated out of an old church. It seems to be the center of town today, bustling and buzzing with moms, kids, computers and conversation. There is artwork everywhere, interspersed with wood beams and earthy colored walls, a splash of muted mustard on one wall and an orangish-red Mexican tile color on others (sorry, I've never been very good with colors). This is the place I go to write, because, for whatever reason, lately I've been able to write efficiently. And, since I have a company paying me to do contract work, but they have no work to give me at the moment (now there's another story), I've decided that if I can't expand my website now, it will never get done.

But, before I get to work, I want to respond to your email because I am thoroughly enjoying this correspondence with you.

Let me start at the end. I understand the use of movies as an attempt to describe what this connection between us is, especially since you are in the industry! I submit that our movie remains unwritten and we are the authors of its ending. Any movie that is co-written, and has a good ending, requires trust and agreement between the authors. I confess, my part of the script has only a few pages at this point, mostly containing some conversation, a hug, some laughing, and a nice walk.

I should also say that I'm probably as non-judgmental a person as you'll find. Love, sex, life, right, wrong, nothing seems black and white any more. We all seem to face moral dilemmas, situations where each decision path feels both right and wrong simultaneously. It's hard. I've tried to live a good life and try to be honest, but I'm hardly perfect.

I too have endured pain. Honesty and trying to lead a good life doesn't spare one from pain. And, unfortunately, I too have hurt others. I also had a short second marriage that lasted a couple years and that cost me more money to end than the first one did, which occurred at the same time the company was dying.

I don't find your work history boring at all! I think your story sounds great. I want to learn more, as I was always more entrepreneurially-minded than I was academically minded, which is why I didn't go on to get my PhD in finance (it just sounded boring to me). Don't feel intimidated by my ex(s) at all. You have accomplished a great deal professionally; after all, how many people get to design sets for movies?

I have attached a link to the blog I mentioned where I saw your comment.

Technology has been my route to success and survival (sometimes one and sometimes the other). I've built and managed websites for 15 years, along with some other programming...I wouldn't describe myself as a techie nerd, as I am not an accomplished programmer any more than I am an amazing mechanic. I'm still learning both.

I am definitely a better cook than I am either a technologist or a mechanic. One of my favorite things to do is cook for my children. Whenever we are together I make sure they are well fed, with everything as homemade as possible. My oldest is becoming pretty good in the kitchen, too (last year he wanted a food processor for xmas). I'll make pho soup from scratch, thai food, mexican moles, and, one of their favorites, my famous mashed potatoes like my grandmother Eilers used to make. It took me years to figure out how she made lightly whipped mashed potatoes. The secret is to mix together the potatoes, cream, salt and butter and then whip back in some of the potato water. I think about my kitchen as my indoor garage.

Well, that was an entirely rambling letter. I hope you don't mind.

- Dave

Though my letter is long, I feel like writing more, but don't want to overwhelm her, though possibly the horse has already left the barn. Writing these emails is triggering something inside me. There are things I want to say, need to say, not just about her and me, but about my general frustrations with life. I need to express the feelings bubbling inside. Sharing the cliff notes of my life is not enough anymore.

Yet, our relationship is not to that level yet. We need time to reconnect. So, I attempt to be patient and wait for a response before launching another email. I don't have to wait long, because a few hours after I send my email, she replies:

May 18th, 2011 – 5:06 PM

David,

I followed the link you sent and visited the website where I left my comment. Amazing! It was the one time in my life I posted my opinion about ANYTHING. I was so passionate about the marriage of culture and mediums in Sex and the City. I could not sit still and watch the genius take all negative press. At the time, I thought, "No one will ever read this but I feel better". Actually you read it and it made a difference in my life. I think the unbelievable factor lives!!

So you read what I said. I wanted to tell you in person about my life today. I just cannot do it this way.

BTW ; Very special how you cook for your kids and love your indoor garage. I am sure you are talented in both cooking and mechanics of all kinds of things.

You will and can be a writer and seems you are on the right track using down time to advantage, especially if it is flowing. The coffee church sounds great. No day starts for me w/o coffee.

You are such a sweet, interesting man. You cannot blame me for actually engaging in correspondence with you and remembering the youthful passion. Although truthfully I still feel the same in many ways.

I will probably write later ... Virginia

She still feels the same way in many ways? In all the ways? With each passing email I begin to feel we are each tugging at the other, gently pulling one another down a rabbit hole. The hole is dark, the way unclear. We have to step carefully, because the holes and stones of the path aren't obvious. This doesn't feel like infatuation or a youthful passion. As short as it was, could this have been one of the most fulfilling relationships either of us had enjoyed? Do we appreciate it even more now?

Email is no longer enough. I want to see her. I need to hear her voice, watch her reactions, and see how she holds herself as we talk. More than ever, I have to know more about her. So, I write another note:

May 18^h, 2011 – 6:33 PM

Virginia,

Wow, that's cool! I find the only blog post you have made and it was my sole clue to finding you :-)

I spoke with my mother tonight and found out their mower is still down. I figured I had better get up there and fix their mower, so I told her I'm going to drive up tomorrow (Thursday) and see if I can't get that thing going again. I shall be around for about a week if you have some down time to meet and would enjoy some conversation.

- David

She quickly accepts my invitation:

May 18th, 2011 – 6:43 PM

David,

You are coming up? Well, Friday 10a.m.-1:30p.m. or Tuesday. I have some time on every day at different times.

Virginia

I respond, asking her to meet Friday. It has to be Friday.

On Thursday, I jump in my car and begin the eight-hour drive from Boise to Seattle.

David Eilers

6. MAY 19™, 2011

> *"Where'm I going I don't know,*
> *when will I get there,*
> *I ain't certain,*
> *Alls I know is I am on my way . . ."*
>
> Main title song of the musical "Paint your Wagon"

Merging onto westbound I-84 in Caldwell, Idaho, I begin my journey north to Seattle with the main title song to "Paint Your Wagon" playing over my sound system. The beginning lines define my life. I should have them carved into my tombstone, partly because I feel they describe my approach to life and also because I am part of a quiet minority that can sing all the songs to the sound track of "Paint Your Wagon" (few brag about this ability). The words and music are entrenched in my head, the removal of which just might require the extraction of my very soul.

I blame my father for this, because it was he who installed the eight-track tape player in our motorhome when I was just a boy and it was he who only had four eight-track cartridges: the sound track from Fiddler on the Roof (which I didn't like), two John Denver Tapes (which I did like), and "Paint Your Wagon" (which I also liked). Whenever we were on long drives in the motorhome — a mid 1960s GMC that was a truck in the front and a motorhome in the rear, a gawky hybrid vehicle with a non functioning shower, a dead generator, and other features that didn't work — those were my choices for music. Like Dad, I became a John Denver fan as well.

These days I have all my John Denver songs and the entire "Paint Your Wagon" soundtrack on my phone, which at the moment is plugged into my car's cassette player, streaming the overture as I speed along Interstate I-84 to the Oregon-Idaho border.

Daydreaming while driving this route is easy, because I have driven it at least thirty times. The five hundred miles of hills, valleys, canyons, cities, rest stops, and even places with old jeeps are as familiar as my drive from my house to the local grocery store.

> *"Got a dream boys,*
> *Got a song.*
> *Paint Your Wagon,*
> *And come along . . ."*

The rolling grassy landscape of western Idaho, green from all the recent rain, flies by as Pardner's brother dies, his body and spirit eulogized, and then his body flung into the air as the wagon train of farmers turned miners transforms a wilderness into a boom town (don't understand what I have said, watch the beginning of the movie).

As one song gives way to another, I pass my first point of interest, the Idaho Motor Pool, a place that sells military vehicles to the public, including the occasional jeep. Located in Fruitland, Idaho, along I-84, the place always has at least one jeep pointed directly at the highway. It is hard to get a good look at a jeep while driving 80mph, but that doesn't stop me from spinning my head to see what they have in stock. This time I only spot a M-38A1, the military version of the more famous civilian cousin, the CJ-5, or what I call the round fendered jeep due to the front fenders that have a rounded front tip. The CJ-5 was made from 1954 through 1983. Over thirty years, more than 610,000 were produced, the reason why so many CJ-5s can still be found for sale on Craigslist.

Now, that might sound like a lot of jeeps, but consider this fact: more flatfender jeeps (MBs and GPWs were the models) were produced (640,000) during the three and a half years of WWII (1942 to 1945) than all the CJ-5s. With that many WWII jeeps made in such a short time it is no wonder the image of the jeep became universally known quickly. Their bigger-than-life beginning is an important reason they became such a cultural icon. However, at the end of the war, a large percentage were destroyed by the military, in part for their scrap value and also to reduce the impact of returning war jeeps on Willys Overland's sales of civilian jeeps.

As the Idaho Motor Pool disappears into my rear view mirror, so does the state of Idaho, because I am crossing into Oregon. Chances are I will not see another classic jeep until my approach to Baker City, where a poor old flatfender circa 1947 sits among other abandoned vehicles. If it is like other CJ-2As (the model name for the first civilian jeeps produced), it was probably running-when-parked and couldn't be re-started when the owner hopped back into it. Apparently, the fuel pumps on these jeeps equipped with "Go Devil" four cylinder engines were poorly designed and broke often. More often than not, replacing the fuel pump, cleaning out the carburetor, and giving an engine fresh gas will allow jeeps to start that have been sitting in fields, barns and garages for up to thirty years. I have heard that story over and over from experienced jeep hunters.

• • • •

I approach Baker City in Eastern Oregon as the preacher on the sound track sings about the vices of No Name City, the name of the boomtown that booms and busts over the life of the movie. It is particularly appropriate I'm listening to "Paint Your Wagon" because it just so happens the movie was filmed just east of Baker City in the mountains. Baker City's downtown Oregon Trail Museum has a scale model of No-Name City, the artificial town created for the movie, along with some memorabilia and pictures highlighting the ripples the filming made in the region. In fact, the museum is the largest seller of the "Paint Your Wagon" soundtracks in the world, or so said the nice woman working the counter of the museum on the day my kids and I visited it (of course, I *had* to stop there once).

I like to believe that if the pre-stroke version of Dad were going through Baker City, he would make the one-hour drive eastward from Baker City to see the spot marking the filming location where the No-Name City set came to life. But these days, he would rather stay at home, waiting for the movie to make its rare appearance on TV. I have yet to make the drive to the filming location, as I'm usually in too much of a hurry going one direction or the other. Someday, I promise myself, I will camp there.

"Paint Your Wagon" started out as a Broadway musical in 1951 and was successful enough to convince Paramount to do a movie version in the late 1960s. According to the histories I have read, production was plagued by a variety of issues, including budget and filming delays. When it finally opened in 1969, even stars like Clint Eastwood, Lee Marvin, and Jean Seberg couldn't save it from the negative reviews. Despite what critics said, Dad always liked the film, as did I, as did my mother and sister. It was one of the few movies we all enjoyed. As a boy I thought it was funny and silly. Since I knew the music, singing along was easy and fun, too.

The movie's main storyline follows Ben Rumson (Lee Marvin) and Pardner (Clint Eastwood). The two become mining partners, equal owners of both a mining claim and, later, a woman named Elizabeth (Jean Seberg). They aren't so much owners of her as her husbands, because they are all married under mining law, at least that is the movie's premise. It only seems reasonable to the characters that a woman could have two husbands, since Elizabeth was formerly the wife of a Mormon man who had two wives. But over the course of the movie their happy relationship is challenged as more "civilized people", in the form of God fearing farmers, settle into town. Eventually, the town gets swallowed in a damnation-like event as if the Devil himself is swallowing the Godless miners. Satire, whimsy, and in some cases, hokey production values, make this a movie that simply won't appeal to most folks. But, it sure works for my nutty family.

Over the years, as I watch it from time to time, I have come to view it as an unusual film, a very atypical western. First of all, rather than a standard Western — with 'good' characters and 'bad' characters fighting over girls, territory, cattle, or money, — "Paint Your Wagon" is about the evolution of a community in a mining camp, where mixed motives create imperfect characters of different types. In addition, unlike most westerns, "Paint Your Wagon" challenges the notion that civilization is civil at all, that freedom and civilization aren't always compatible, that as civilization attempts to bring order to a chaotic town named No Name, it also brings an oppressive climate challenging the freedom of the miners, who have their own moral and legal codes (mining law) that bristles against the norms of civilization.

Sylvester, the jeep, is on the left. I am next to the jeep, age 16, with Dad next to me. We are camping in the Cascade Mountains during a 1981 jeep club trip.

Dad liked the movie enough to name his jeep Sylvester. Not until my mid twenties did I figure out it was not from Sylvester and Tweety, the cartoon I watched on Saturday mornings on TV. No, it came from a character named Sylvester Newel. Who is Sylvester Newel? Well, only true devotees of "Paint Your Wagon" know that Clint Eastwood's character, known as Pardner throughout the movie, finally reveals his real name at the very end:

> **Ben Rumson:** *You say something nice to her for me, Par... What the hell is your name anyway?*
>
> **Pardner:** *It's Sylvester Newel. Yeah, just one 'l'.*
>
> **Ben Rumson:** *Sylvester Newel. Well, that's a good name for a farmer.*

And, it was a good name for Dad's jeep.

• • • •

Forty minutes later into my drive No Name City collapses, the miners leave town and the music ends. Switching to new music, my thumb slides through options on my phone. Done with show tunes, I decide on Disturb's Indestructible album, music introduced to me by my oldest son. He knows music far better than me and seems to continuously find new music I like. He even knows the classic rock of the 1980s better than me, which is embarrassing to me because I have always enjoyed 1980s rock and thought I knew it well. Fortunately, the pride I feel about his knowledge outweighs any shame I feel about a lack of my own.

I am now approaching the city of La Grande, Oregon, and the Blue Mountains or "the Blues" beyond. The first time I was here I was eight-years-old, attending one of the most memorable summer jeep conventions of my life.

Summer Convention was an annual event held in August at different locations throughout the Pacific Northwest where everyone who belonged to the Pacific Northwest Four Wheel Drive Association (PNW4WDA) could gather, relax, race, and have fun with their jeeps. There were multiple reasons why I remember this event so strongly. Perhaps the primary reason was that it was the longest road trip I had been on to that point in my life and the longest trip I would ever take in my parents' motorhome. It seemed like the trip took seven or eight years, though it was probably more like seven or eight hours. Today, having driven the route between Boise and Seattle numerous times, I know it only takes me about five hours to go from Seattle to La Grande. But, as a kid trapped in a motorhome, time ticked more slowly.

The convention was held outside of La Grande on a cleared tract of land surrounded by tall spruce and pine trees in the mountains above the town. We arrived on a Friday evening after sundown and darkness filled the sky.

As Dad slowly drove through the grounds, the truck's headlights sliced through clouds of red dust thrown up by the vehicle ahead of us as he navigated the narrow paths between rows of campers, tents and jeeps. Riding in the bed over the truck cab of the motorhome, I stared wide-eyed through the windows hoping to see anything exciting. Light appeared from camper windows and flickers of campfire light emerged from between the campers. There was plenty of bustle, as camper after camper, jeeps in tow, followed one another along the driving paths, attempting to locate other members of their club, some of whom might

have arrived as early as Monday to stake out the best areas to camp. With our truck headlights highlighting club banner after club banner, usually tied to the front of a single camper or between two campers, the motorhome's lights eventually found the familiar Wandering Willys Jeep Club logo.

I didn't sleep too well that night. I was too busy peeking out the windows. In the morning, as soon as possible, I threw on my clothes and bounced down the camper steps, ready to find Tim and Steve, jeep club and family friends who were as close as brothers to me, and explore the campsites and courses.

Surrounding us was a vast sea of motorhomes and jeeps appeared. Islands of smoke from campfires rose near and far. The desert air, dry with a crisp wind, was a big change from the Western Washington weather I best knew. Quickly finding Tim and Steve, we began our exploration, marveling at club names we had never known, pointing out unusual jeeps. Even the tires were amazing, as that was the first time I'd ever seen a pair of Formula Desert Dog X tires (tires with big Xs on them for tread). They were so cool! For kids who loved big toys, this was paradise. As more jeepers awoke, so did their jeeps. Unmuffled motors rumbled awake loudly, some stock from the factory while others had engines that were highly modified, built solely for racing. Throughout the morning, drivers readied their rigs for events or for cruising around the area, while the three of us watched gleefully.

Summer Convention could last three or four days in the 1970s. Compared with the very first annual PNW4WDA convention sponsored by a single club (the Longview Trailbreakers) in 1960 and attended by only forty-three people, this convention was immense, sponsored by multiple clubs and attended by hundreds of families. It would take a full day to do safety checks on all the jeeps, necessary before any jeep would be allowed on the courses. Racing and events were opened around nine o'clock in the morning and closed around four o'clock in the afternoon. On Saturday morning or Sunday morning the bi-annual association meeting was held, where official association business would be handled. On Saturday night there would be the big dance, where kids and adults would start off dancing early, then the kids would be shooed to bed and the adults would finish off the evening, as teens either watched from the side or snuck off with their bootlegged beer to have their own private parties. Events would close Sunday afternoon so trophy presentations could take place.

Socializing was an important part of the convention, but so were the events themselves. Unlike the weekend playdays and summer conventions in the northwest today, where the focus is a little more about competition, with specialty built racing jeeps, times, and head-to-head racing taking center stage, there was a wider mix of fun and racing during the 1970s. Below are some of the events that were or are still held:

Jeep Stuffing: In this oddball contest, as many people as possible jumped aboard a jeep.

Jeep Stuffing : The jeep in front is the Hamilton's CJ-5 "Gypsy B".

Barrels: This is a classic event that still endures. Inspired by the barrel racing events found at horse playdays, barrels were positioned in a triangle. The racer starts at a gate, circles around each barrel as fast as they can, and then heads back to the gate.

Water Course: The object is to get around the course the quickest without spilling water held in a cup by a passenger. It's a slow, but comical race. A derivation of this involves an egg the passenger carries on a spoon. The passenger must balance the egg throughout the course. If the egg falls off, they have to stop and can't start again until the egg is back on the spoon.

The Divorce Course: The driver is blindfolded. The passenger must tell the driver how to drive the course. No lawyer is seated at the finish line, but ought to be.

Balance Event: The object is to balance the platform as quickly as possible. The driver drives onto a platform, underneath which is a log or large piece of wood. It can be very challenging.

My mother and sister on a balance beam in 1974. Dad would roll this jeep down a hill within a year.

Tire Pit: This was one the events held during the very first playday in 1962 hosted by the Tacoma Webfooters. Apparently the club thought it would be fun to get their members together and play with their jeeps. Then a suggestion was made to invite a few other clubs. The event was a hit, so they held more.

The tire-pit event, one of the events at the Tacoma Webfooters first playday.

Potato Stab or Balloon Pop: In the Potato Stab, a racer races around a track and stops at each box of potatoes to allow the passenger to stab a potato, put it in a sack, and race onward. The fastest time won. There were variations of this event. One variation involved popping balloons instead of picking up potatoes.

The potato stab and similar events, like balloon popping, were popular events, because both a driver and a passenger are necessary.

Banana Course: In the banana course a driver drives the course with a passenger. At a particular spot, the driver stops and the passenger hops out and runs through a little obstacle, like a barrel without a top or bottom, consumes part of a banana, hops back in the jeep and then the driver finishes the course. How much of a choking danger could there possibly be? This was a favorite event of mine, probably because I never choked. There were variations of this, too.

Tonka Course: Designed as a kid's course, young people put strings on their Tonka vehicles and pull them as they run through a course. There were other kid-specific courses as well.

Race Backward: The racer drives a course forward to a stopping point, and then has to drive the course in reverse as fast as possible.

Pole Bending: Similar to slalom skiing, racers zigzag their jeeps around poles spaced at intervals.

Cross Country Course: This is still held today. It is a fast, long course designed with long straight sections for fast speeds.

Obstacle Course: Generally, this is a tight course, which might include a big puddle or other obstacles. Driving skillfully and choosing good lines is important in this course.

Sprints: In this race, several racers line up on a single-track and try to out maneuver the others to reach the finish line first. The Yakima Mud Races were a famous version of this type of event.

Hill Climbs: To the best of my knowledge, these are rarely held in the PNW4WDA anymore, but the EC4WDA (East Coast Four Wheel Drive Association) still has them according to my readers.

Team Relay: This is the most complex event and is the only team event. It continues to be a traditional end-of-the-weekend Summer Convention race. Involving four teams of four jeeps and four drivers on one course, the object is to make four full laps around the course. Each team is assigned a colored flag to make it easy to identify the teams while they are racing. The top two teams to finish a round advance to the next round. The team that wins the final round wins the trophy.

When I last raced in 1985, this event would take an entire day. There were many, many teams and people. It's a fun event to participate in and watch.

The first time racing this event (March 1985 on a cold weekend north of Everett), which was also the first weekend I ever raced, I broke the front driveline in my jeep in the first round of racing, I broke the front driveline in Tim Carter's race jeep Priority in the second round, and I thought I broke the front driveline of Jim and Patti Carter's jeep, Otis, while racing their jeep in the 3rd round (we lost, so we didn't advance after that — and I was relieved!). I have never broken a driveline since. Weird!

Based on the number of clubs, the number of events held, and the number of participants throughout Idaho, Oregon, and Washington, I believe the 1970s, during which the La Grande Summer Convention was held, marked the golden years for innovation and participation in northwest jeeping. The reasons for that included a strong economic climate across the class spectrum, an open lands policy that allowed for more exploration by jeep, cheap gas prices, low or no insurance requirements, and a culture that allowed weekends off so people could truly meet and enjoy one another. It surely was a different time.

Even weekend playdays, which were regional jeep play events, were popular at the time. Because they were regional in nature, sometimes there could be two or three playdays on the same weekend at different locations throughout the Washington/Idaho/Oregon area. The club or region hosting the event would create the courses, usually with the help of a bulldozer or other equipment. They would collect a fee for playing hosts and award trophies for various events on Sunday afternoon. There might be twenty or so clubs that would show up for a playday, with some clubs more heavily involved in racing and playdays than others. In the early days some jeepers would arrive with tents packed in their jeeps or small camping trailers in tow. They would compete in the events (hoping not to break any parts on their jeeps) and then pack up on Sunday to drive back home. By the late 1970s and into the 1980s, motorhomes towing jeeps (often on trailers — I guess people learned that jeeps can break pretty easily while racing) were the norm. It wasn't unusual to see caravans traveling along I-5 heading north or south, making their way to playdays on Friday night and then making their way home on Sunday.

Someone driving by one of those caravans in the South Seattle area would have seen clubs with names like the Bellingham Trailblazers Jeep club, the Cascade 4x4s, the Cresthoppers Jeep Club, Edgewood Hill Willys, Grays Harbor Stump Busters, Green River Valley Jeepers, Misfits Four-Wheel-Drive Club, Puyallup Bushpushers, Roam-eos Jeep Club, Shelton Timber Runners Jeep Club, Skookumchuck Mud Daubers Jeep Club, Skyway Cliffhangers Jeep Club, Spanaway Moonshiners Jeep Club, Tacoma Mudders Jeep Club, Tacoma Web Footers Jeep Club, Valley Crater-Raiders Jeep Club, Seattle Rump Bumpers Jeep Club, Washington Bobtails, and many more. According to the directory from 1972, in Region One (there are nine regions in the PNW4WDA) forty-seven clubs existed in just the South Puget Sound area alone. Extrapolating across the entire northwest, the number of clubs must have totaled at least a hundred.

That explains why, just in my own hometown neighborhood on Renton's south hill, I often saw members and jeeps from other clubs. For me that was normal life. Whether their jeep sported a club sticker or not, I learned you wave to other jeepers, as motorcycle riders wave to other motorcycle riders. It's just how it was.

• • • •

One hour after La Grande, and five hours into my trip, I leave I-84, taking I-82 north and passing through the tri-cities area of Richland, Pasco and Kennewick. I soon see the Yakima River as it winds through the valley, along with patches vineyards on both sides.

By the time I reach Yakima, I am only two hours (on a good day) from Renton. For me, Yakima means jeeps. In 1947 a group of jeepers in this town incorporated the Yakima Ridge Runners Jeep Club and, arguably, became the first jeep club to incorporate in the United States. Shortly after the Ridge Runners incorporated, other clubs began forming across the U.S., such as the Hemet Jeep Club from California in 1948.

The Ridge Runners Jeep Club was also one of the six charter members of the Pacific Northwest Jeep Association, launched at a 1959 meeting in Long Beach, Washington (in 1965 the name changed to its current name). Other charter members included the Tacoma Webfooters, the Portland

Brush Busters, the Vancouver Four Wheelers, the Seattle Jeep Club, and the Longview Trailbreakers.

The Ridge Runners were made famous in the 1950s by a Life Magazine article, which labeled them "Ripsnorting jeep drivers [who] burn up the Yakima sagebrush". Two newsreels were also produced about the Club. The Ridge Runners received additional visibility on TV in the 1960s when they appeared on Exploration Northwest, a television show produced in the Seattle area and hosted by Don McCune. In the show's episode, Don provides history and narrates the trip as the Club follows the Naches Trail, of which Yakima is the eastern terminus, over the Cascade Mountains.

The Naches Trail is still famous among jeepers in Washington State. While well known for its offroad challenges, only a few know that the route was intended to be the major East-West route over the Cascade Mountains prior to development of Snoqualmie Pass, which I-90 traverses. Government money funded development in the 1850s. Several wagon trains traveled over the Naches Pass before discovering a big cliff blocking their route, a legacy from the lack of funding to complete the pass.

The first wagon train to pass over the Naches, the Longmire train, had enough rope to overcome the cliff. A second wagon train arrived without as much rope. In his memoirs, Ezra Meeker mentions that the travelers, with winter closing in, were forced to kill an ox and make enough 'rope' from it to lower the wagons. Unfortunately, as happens, the histories of these two trains has been combined into a single incident and carved onto a sign that overlooks this infamous cliff, with the Longmire train erroneously given credited for the ox killing incident. I am happy to report that no jeeps have had to be lowered over the cliff; instead, later travelers pioneered another route around the cliff face.

Leaving Yakima, a half hour later I summit the Manashtash ridge on I-82 before dropping into Ellensburg where I will merge onto I-90 westbound. Crossing the Manashtash Ridge forty miles northwest of me is a jeep trail built by the Wandering Willys during the late 1970s. The WWJC built the trail with hard-to-locate entrances to protect the trail from general use.

The hope was to preserve it as a tight, small-jeep oriented trail. It was a fun trail I only jeeped a couple times. Driving down to Ellensburg I wonder to myself if it still exists and is still legally accessible?

If the trail is gone, it is just one of many changes occurring during the decade and a half since I jeeped. There are others. For example, some trails have closed due to over use or environmental sensitivity. Racing on private property has almost completely shut down due to liability concerns. Costs to operate a jeep have jumped, as gas prices are higher, licensing tab costs more, insurance for a vehicle driven a few times a year is now required, and free jeeping has given way to the purchase of annual passes for accessing state and federal lands. It doesn't take a rocket scientist to see how all these additional costs were hitting the middle class in a way that forced them to sell the family jeep, simply because it no longer made financial sense for many to own one.

Add into that the state of the economy and now it was clear why listings on eWillys had ballooned since 2008. Economics have forced people to change their habits and one of the many victims is the jeep, no longer the practical utility vehicle it once was. Even if there is the money for a jeep, many families no longer have the time to participate in associations like the PNW4WDA. Happily, there are still about 250 clubs from the Pacific Northwest that remain active in it, so it remains strong.

However many other clubs and associations have seen membership declines. The weekends once enjoyed by my family have become disjointed for modern families, with work pursing my friends and me on the weekends like a snake that bites us and won't let go. Emails and cell phones are harnesses, enslaving us. The lack of real vacations (and a week isn't a real vacation) have brainwashed us into thinking work is real life, when real life is at home. It is no wonder every one of my friends and every one of my cousins has been divorced.

Even my own hobby, or maybe it is my job, eWillys, is a constant monitoring of my email and site, simply to keep it topical and interesting. Though I don't feel chained to it because I enjoy it, I certainly can't imagine taking a two-week holiday from it, let alone an entire three-month vacation and head to Europe for the summer like my great-grandparents used to do. Sure, they had money to vacation, but they also recognized an importance in doing that. I wonder what we have lost in our own humanity by losing the time we need to exist within the world, the time to meet and talk with our neighbors across the fence, to spend more time pursuing our hobbies, to have weekends free (or any two days off in a row), to have more than two weeks of vacation a year?

If we are just cogs in a wheel, only existing to make enough money to shelter ourselves, feed our family, and pay taxes, then we are truly living in the "Matrix", but instead of sucking electricity, it is our time and energy that we simultaneously burn in hopes of reaching the point where we can live our own versions of the American Dream. That dream, once so close, feels farther than ever to me. Paying child support, managing creditors, dealing with taxes, and handling emergencies comes first. Any dreams beyond that were blown away by the economic hurricane.

Yet, I bristle at the thought of how society leashes me to the "Matrix", which is effectively what third parties credit agencies do, and grimace at the indentured servitude I feel. My salve for this is following what I want to do, so at least my 'job' and interests align to some degree. If there is one advantage about doing eWillys, about not having a real job in this new economy, is that I can leave on a moment's notice and drive north to visit my parents or see a woman I hadn't seen in twenty-five years. Maybe just like jeeps, I don't quite fit into this new world? Or, do I just have to relocate my place within it. As I think back to the experiences I had as a child, with jeeps, my parents, and my life, this new world is certainly unfamiliar, but I have to keep trying, because, in reality, I have no other choice.

• • • •

Continuing westward from Ellensburg, I spot a sign for highway 97, which provides access to Wenatchee and Leavenworth. For me, that area remains a bad memory. In 1975, less than a year after the memorable

Summer Convention trip to La Grande, my life of jeeping was altered forever. I was ten when my dad rolled his jeep, an event that drastically changed our involvement in our jeep club.

I suppose it is appropriate that the only images of Dad's wreck in the Wandering Willys Jeep Club scrapbook aren't as clear as I would want, and, as best I know, are the only images that exist, because the memory of it is also fuzzy. I have scanned, color corrected and sharpened the pictures to provide a clearer picture of the crunched jeep, but even the magic of a photo-editing program still can't provide clarity. Besides, even the clearest of pictures can't really tell the story of the impact of his tumble down that hill.

It was a club weekend in 1975 with hot, bright summer days, on the east side of the mountains in Leavenworth, Washington. For Washington State jeepers, the east side of the mountains means anything east of the Cascade Mountain range, a range that emerges on its north side from Canada, splitting the states of Washington and Oregon into two different regions – the wet western side and the dry eastern side — and then fading into the top of California. Trail driving on the western side means muddy trails, with deep, dark greens of cedar, pine and fir, and gray, drizzly, cool weather as the norm. Trails on the eastern side of the Cascades are full of rocky, dry trails, sunshine, sagebrush, large farms and dust (in the summer anyway). Within an hour of Seattle, people can transform their jeeping. hiking, boating, and biking experiences entirely by heading east over Snoqualmie (pronounced Snow•kwal•mee), Chinook (pronounced Shi•nook), or a handful of other mountain passes.

This particular weekend I remember, and say this with uncertainty as these are more like flickers of a ten-year-old's memory, that we were staying at a community-center-like building where all the club members slept on the floor in sleeping bags in one big space. When I asked him recently, Steve Carter told me it was a community center that also had a variety of cabins. It was used by geology students from the University of Washington for several years during the mid 1970s and was operated, through the UW, by Jim Carter; hence, the reason the club had access to the facilities.

Mom, Dad, my sister Kim and I were all there, which was usual in the days prior to my sister's obsession with horses. And, I really don't mean that in a bad way. It is just that when her passion for horses emerged, it came full force. She lived, breathed, and talked horses. On this day, the Saturday of Dad's roll, the only horsing around we were doing involved playing in the river that flowed by the summer camp complex. Kim and I and other club kids were splashing in the water with Mom watching us. It was a normal, hot, dry, day on the east side of the Cascades.

Then came the moment that everyone experiences, where I expected the ordinary and confronted the surreal. My mother, sister and I heard a distant voice through the trees telling us that Dad had an accident, that Mom needed to get to the hospital, but that Dad appeared to be ok. In an instant, Mom was gone, off to the hospital to see Dad.

The next thing I remember was our jeep as it arrived at camp, towed behind a truck. Bent and twisted, the life had been beat out of it. No angles were true nor smooth, no part of the jeep spared. The front fenders were crushed. The rollcage, which Dad had installed the previous year, was cracked in several places. The windshield was off. Various liquids, most likely engine oil, coolant, and power steering fluid, slowly dripped to the ground.

Dad and Mom arrived soon afterward, with my father sporting a few stitches on his forehead from a loose shoulder belt that hit him during the crash.

I was never surprised to see that Dad survived the crash, because he was Dad. He could do anything or so it seemed. It turns out my neighborhood friends felt the same way about him. I learned this early in 2011 when I met with some friends from my childhood whom I hadn't seen in thirty years. As I described Dad's stroke to them, one said that was hard to imagine, because to them Karl was the guy who dug out and then built a basement by himself. He was the guy who could fix anything, whether a jeep, a go-kart, or a bicycle. One claimed he was a hero of theirs. I think Dad would downplay any talk of being a hero. Instead, he would say that it was the way he was brought up. You help people. And he'd probably tell how as a kid and living on Walker Lane in Holladay, Utah, his family had a truck with a plow and it was he and his brothers' job to plow the street for their neighbors, because that was just being a good neighbor.

One of these neighbors from Holladay, Utah, in the 1940s was Jim Carter. A long time family friend who grew up with Dad, it was he who had arranged the trip to Leavenworth and he who had selected the trail to explore. And, based on what I have learned since, it was he who felt a great deal of guilt about the crash. Apparently, it affected him and his wife Patti enough to make trail runs a little less fun, leading them to become more involved in jeep racing.

As the trail leader on that Saturday in July, Jim drove their jeep Otis up a rut-filled hill above Icicle Creek, but not without some difficulty. Otis always had a knack for reaching the top of just about any obstacle, or so it seemed to me. As Otis and Jim crested the top of the hill following a difficult climb, the Ayers started up it. Dad tells me the Ayers made it part way up the hill in their CJ-3B jeep, but the ruts proved too difficult and they were forced to pull off of the hill to the side, coming to a stop and overcoming the angle of the sidehill that could have caused them to roll. To get them up the rest of the way, a winch line was dropped from Otis and they were pulled up.

Now it was Dad's turn.

Dad was driving a CJ-5 that had a Chevrolet 327 V8 motor with 4:11 gears and a posi-traction rear end. It was never anything fancy, just the family jeep that carried Dad to work on the weekdays and the family into adventure on the weekends. The most important feature about this jeep was the rollcage, which he built and installed into the jeep in 1974. With jeep racing getting faster and more people exploring trails, accidents had increased. One of the biggest safety advances was the full rollcage. A rollcage generally consisted of two inch diameter steel tubes cut, bent and welded into a cage that surrounds the driver and passenger. There was never any standard for building cages, other than the minimum standard adopted by the PNW4WDA for racing. By 1975, cages had become popular and, if buying a jeep in the Pacific Northwest these days, it is rare to see a trail jeep without one.

Normally, on a trail ride like the one, the jeeps would be full of family members. However, this time most of the kids stayed back at the camp, hence the reason we were playing at the river. With Mom watching over us on the river, Dad had been doing the trail ride with a club member named Karen Brown. Before going up the hill, Dad suggested to Karen she jump out of the passenger seat. I guess he was a bit worried about it.

After Karen jumped out, Dad began his climb. Everything was fine until he reached the two-thirds mark of the hill. At that point the front end popped up enough to bounce the back up slightly too. When the jeep came back down, all the weight landed on the rear wheels. At that point, forces collided in a perfect storm corkscrewing the rear driveline apart. This created two half drivelines out of a whole one and these two halves would have been slapping against all parts of the jeep's underside, making a racket. This would also render the rear wheels useless, forcing Dad to rely on the power to the front wheels alone to crest the hill, which wasn't going to work.

As Dad tells it, he knew immediately that he had an issue, so he pulled onto the side of the hill like the Ayers had done. The problem was the jeep didn't want to stay there.

As Dad explains:

> *"I felt the jeep lurch and I could tell it was going to roll. So, I held onto the steering wheel and muttered, 'here we go'. I don't remember much about the roll other than I grabbed a hold of the steering wheel with all my might. I could hear the sounds of stuff falling out, metal crunching and felt the pain from getting hit by something."*

The back of the jeep following Dad's roll at Icicle Creek.

The front of the jeep following Dad's roll at Icicle Creek.

The other club members watched helplessly as Dad started his roll. Beginning slowly, but rapidly gaining speed, in little time the jeep would execute three barrel rolls and two end-over-end cartwheels, reaching ten feet into the air. The windshield would get thrown one hundred feet and land without a scratch or crack (and would be reused on the rebuilt jeep). The fenders, hood, grille and rear corners were crushed.

The rollcage welds cracked during the roll, leading Dad to build a stronger rollcage in the next jeep. The impact on the rear rollcage loop collapsed the rear quarter panels. So, in the next rebuild, Dad built a sub-loop that went underneath the rear quarter panels and connected to the frame.

At the end of the roll club members ran over to the jeep, stunned by what they witnessed and afraid of what they would find. To their anxious relief, Dad's only external injury was a small cut on his forehead. However, mentally, he never really recovered. Understandably, after that he was always uncomfortable with trail rides, causing our participation in them to drop dramatically (especially since we had no jeep for a year).

The main reason for our drop in participation was due to Dad's effort to rebuild the jeep, because very quickly after the crash Dad was removing the parts he could salvage, including all the running gear and the wheels. Over the course of the ensuing fall, winter and spring, I watched as most nights he would trudge out to the garage after work in boots and heavy work clothes. He would light his wood stove and begin welding some part or assembling something else.

From the living room I could watch the flashes caused by the arc welder as he welded piece after piece together. It was a white light, like fireworks going off in the garage, the light flickering as the garage window darkened and lightened, darkened and lightened, in non-random pulses that were almost soothing.

If I went out to the garage to view the progress, he ordered me to crouch behind the car or turn my head when he was welding, so I wouldn't be tempted to look at the light, as it could damage my eyes.

As spring turned to summer, before my very eyes a new jeep arose as Dad completed the welding, grinding, and patching it needed. That has always been a powerful memory. I learned a person could actually build a vehicle. Sure, it would take a few more years to put a paint job on it and add details – Dad was never a big detail's fan – but it ran and could be used. However, for reasons that I don't understand, Dad's roll broke the family jeeping dynamic and we rarely jeeped together as a family again.

• • • •

Continuing west on I-90, I approach Cle Elum. When jeeping, the club almost always dropped into Cle Elum from the mountains above it after leaving Kaner Flats and traveling over the Manashtash Ridge. So, I am very familiar with the town.

Beyond Cle Elum, the memories of jeeps and jeeping become more frequent, as each city or place contained a jeep memory. For example, the Alpental Ski Area at Snoqualmie Pass was a place the entire jeep club went skiing one year, many years ago. Outside of the town of North Bend the club once used jeep winches to ferry equipment for the University of Washington across a stream at Goldmire Hotsprings.

Farther along I-90, I pull into Issaquah to pick up some raw milk — unpasteurized, non-homogenized milk from grass fed cows — and the Red Apple Market in Issaquah is one of the few places I can get it. Issaquah sits at the southern end of Lake Sammamish and is home to Lake Sammamish State Park, where the Wandering Willys used to meet during the summer months for our once-a-month Tuesday evening jeep club meetings.

I had never realized it before, but it seems all over Washington I have some memory relating to jeeps. I really did grow up jeep.

With milk in hand, I jump back in my car and drive the final stretch along back roads to my parents' house anxious to see my father's condition for myself. A light drizzle begins to settle on the windshield as if to say, "welcome home".

7. EVENING OF MAY 19TH, 2011

At 9pm I pull into the gravel driveway of my parents' house. Opening the car door, the strong scent of the evergreen trees surrounds me, reinforcing that I am home. I walk along the path next to the living room windows, the eves protecting me from the drizzle, and step on gravel and pine needles. On my way to the back door I walk past the living room windows to see Dad staring blankly at the television. I am directly in his line of sight had he bothered to look upward.

Entering the back door into the kitchen, I give Mom a hug and receive the latest news on Dad. She says he is still in pain and has little desire to leave his chair in the living room.

I put my suitcase in the bedroom and head to the living room to say hello to Dad. Mom follows. The familiar creaks of the floor in the foyer — unchanged since my youth, with its dark, vinyl asbestos floor tiles, white coat closet, cedar paneling, and a black light switch that needed replacing because it took five or six tries to get the overhead light to turn on — announces my arrival before stepping into the living room.

If any room was Dad's room, this was it. The living room was the first room he remodeled following the purchase of the house in 1964. The house sits on an acre of land and began life as a one-room cabin. Later, some bedrooms were added to the north, followed by a kitchen to the east, and then a living room to the south. By the time my parents bought the house — one that included numerous rodents — it needed work, including a foundation. Dad decided the best way to do the repairs on the living room floor was to remove the floor, dig out a deeper crawl space, and put in a new floor. So, shortly after watching them move into the house, the neighbors were a little startled to see dirt flying out of the living room window. After replacing the floor he rewired the room, installed cedar paneling and added a cedar book case along one entire wall.

Now, instead of actively remodeling it, he passively sits in there, the living room becoming his TV room where he watches sports and westerns. Entering, I announce my arrival, "Hey papa, how are ya feeling?"

His eyes shift toward me and then his head follows, "Oh, hi son," he says, happily acknowledging me, yet seeming surprised I am there despite my mother telling him about my visit. "When are you heading back to Boise?"

One of the stark differences between pre-stroke Dad and post-stroke Dad, or 'old' Dad and 'new' Dad, is that he often organizes his brain around concrete dates and events. Even though I like to tease him about it, I know he isn't trying to get rid of me; instead, he just needs to know what everyone's agenda is.

"Dad, I just got here, do you want me to leave already?"

"No no," he says shaking his head slightly. "I just want to know when . . . when you were headed back to . . . umm . . . to . . .," the place name for my home escapes him. He often struggles like this when speaking.

"To Boise you mean?"

"Yes. No. To Eagle I mean." He still needs precision and knows I don't actually live in Boise, but in a suburb called Eagle. At times he appears clueless about what he wants to say when, in actuality, it is simply an inability to express exactly what he knows.

"Part of that depends on you, but I will be leaving next week," I respond.

"Ok, good. Great," He says, settling into his chair and looking back to his TV. This was unusual as even he, for as little as we talk, usually has more to say upon my arrivals, asking about the weather, or the length of my trip, what gas cost, or some other detail.

Trying to re-engage him I ask him about his leg. "Does your leg still bother you? Or is it your back?"

A few days ago Mom told me that after his back injury in April, Dad spent most of his time sitting in a recliner in the living room. He had no interest in moving and no interest in limping outside to cut wood, which was unusual, as normally he liked to be doing something. Now, any movement seems to cause pain, but his stroke makes explaining what parts hurt difficult for him.

Now that I have brought it up, in halting English he tries to tell me what is wrong.

"Well, it's my leg."

Mom asks, "Karl, what part hurts?"

Dad responds, "It's my . . . ummm . . . my . . . the southern part. South. Dammit, my words, umm . . . it is . . ."

The failure at summoning words causes a grimace to appear. His struggles for vocabulary often turn directional. A compass seems hardwired into his brain and he uses coordinates to explain much about life. Listening to him describe a situation can be as painful for the listener as it is for him. However, patience is often rewarded with him accurately explaining a situation, regardless of his circuitous explanation.

So, with Dad unable to voice exactly what hurt on his leg, other than it is south of some point, Mom asks questions, pointing to his left leg. "Is it your leg?"

"Yeah," Dad auto-answers. The stroke in 2002 created an auto-yes response to most questions. He would immediately answer yes, but then he would often add, "No." He would then look up, his big blue eyes searching the questioner for any recognition of understanding.

Even the doctor they visited could not deduce the source of the pain, as Dad couldn't give him a straight answer. So, the doctor had prescribed pain medication to tackle the general pain, hoping Dad would then be able to pinpoint the source of the problem.

Mom and I continue our cat and mouse game of isolating the pain. We ask questions from multiple directions in an attempt to corner the real answer.

"Is it your thigh?" Mom asks him.

"Yes. No," he pauses. "My back . . . in the rear."

Puzzled, I ask, "So, your leg doesn't hurt?"

"No. My leg . . . my . . ." He stops, focusing, searching for the right thing to say, "My left leg . . . dammit . . . down there to the south."

We know he hurts. We actually believe both his back and his calf are causing him discomfort, but we need him to help analyze it. After a few minutes of detective work, Mom and I give up, unsure our questions are getting us anywhere. Mom suggests to Dad he go to bed, which he grudgingly agrees to do.

If the days are bad, I quickly learn the nights are worse. This is the part of Dad's declining health that is wearing my mother down the most. As Mom readies Dad for bed and gets him into it, I pour myself a glass of milk and wait for Mom's return. She reappears, explaining that in fifteen or twenty minutes, Dad will likely need something.

Sure enough, Dad starts yelling, though it is only the ten-minute mark. It begins with Dad yelling "Maaarrrgggeee", though the verb yell is not quite the right description, as his cry for his longtime wife is more mournful than just a yell. There is a helplessness and an emergency about it. Once Mom realizes Dad needs something, she walks back to the bedroom, the tired floors of the house creaking with each step, until she reaches the bedroom and asks about the problem. I have never heard Dad behave like this.

In fact, the scene is comically tragic. My parents' bedroom is at one end of the house and the kitchen — my mother's command station where she watches TV, operates her computer, listens to her radio, and cooks — is halls and rooms away. So, for Mom to hear him, he has to yell her name loudly. To compound the comic/tragic nature of the interaction, Mom's hearing has gotten worse, so she turns up the television in the kitchen. Dad shouts, shouts again, and then makes successively louder shouts until my mother finally hears him. To relieve Mom this evening, and because I can hear him more easily, I attend to his needs.

The emergencies vary widely in nature. At times he panics because he can't shift his body in bed or he is uncomfortable. Other times, he simply wants to know what time it is and, for reasons Mom and I don't understand, won't look down on his glow-in-the-dark watch he wears on his arm. A few times he even calls my mother, "Mommy", which is strange to hear.

We try to be patient, but the every-fifteen-minutes nature of this evening dynamic wears on us both. As Mom and I talk between his cries, we both console each other, knowing this is not the father I knew, old or new, nor was this the husband she knew. The man crying out in the evenings isn't fighting for life, trying to get better in an obsessively independent manner. He is giving in, the adventure for life and the drive to do things replaced by complacence, by resignation, by following Mom's requests with a submissiveness I have never seen. Since the back injury with the tractor in April, this is the evening norm. I am glad I came, because things aren't very normal.

I have been fortunate to see little family death during my life. My paternal grandfather died when I was six and my maternal grandfather died when I was seven. Both my grandmothers died when I was older, but I wasn't near enough to either to watch their passing. But now, I have a front seat with a clear view of the drama unfolding.

8. MAY 20TH, 2011

Virginia and I plan to meet at ten o'clock this morning. Our rendezvous point is Gene Coulon Park, located at southern end of Lake Washington. The time together will be a welcome relief from last night's time with Mom and Dad. It is no wonder my mother is exhausted!

While driving to the park, I follow streets my eyes have rarely seen since leaving the Pacific Northwest with my ex-wife for the cheese and farms, Packers and Badgers of Wisconsin in 1992. Both of us had newly minted college degrees from the University of Puget Sound. She chose to pursue her Master's Degree in rhetoric at the University of Wisconsin, while I was happy to support her and try living in the Midwest, a place neither of us had been. The solidarity of my support was evident by the sale of my jeep to fund our move, the jeep I custom built in 1985. Selling it felt right, because we would likely rent a place without a garage and a classic jeep, being an imperfect vehicle, needs a garage. So, it made little sense to bring the jeep along. Besides, I could always build another. Little did I know it would take another sixteen years to do it.

Heading north on Benson Road off of Renton's south hill, I drop into town under blue sky, a welcome relief from the past few rainy months. Most of this looks the same — the size of the buildings, the grass and bushes along Benson — though names of businesses have changed. I suppose sometimes a person can go home again, for the area appears little changed.

On Bronson Way, about to turn onto Park Avenue North, I pass over the Cedar River, which splits Renton into two halves, bisecting the city as it flows north into Lake Washington. Glancing to my right I spot the Renton City Library, built over the river. Frank Lloyd Wright-like in its design, the one story, flat roofed-library sits atop a flat slab of concrete spanning the river. As a kid I thought it was cool. My old self still thinks it is cool.

Still on Park Avenue, nearing Gene Coulon Park, I find myself surrounded by former Boeing properties that used to contain large buildings where Boeing engineers worked and parked. My mother and her father worked there. Those jobs have gone elsewhere, replaced by buildings housing box stores, restaurants and services bundled into a project called the Renton Landing, with curved streets and pedestrian walkways. It looks quite nice, but, fortunately for the Renton economy, Boeing still has manufacturing plants nearby.

With Lake Washington in sight, I pull into the park, which looks as if it has doubled in size since the days I swam here as a teenager. It has that eerie familiar/unfamiliar feel. Driving through the park, I am no longer sure where to go with the car, as the park boundaries now extend farther north than they did when I was younger.

I pull into a parking space, shut off the motor and check the time: ten minutes before ten. I glance at a car parked to my right, a glossy white Mercedes. Could that be Virginia? It isn't clear to me it is her, but I hop out and appear to look busy doing absolutely nothing while peering at the other car. Nope, the woman seems a little too blond and a little too young.

I move to the rear of the car, leaning against the trunk. It was a rare beautiful May Day, with blue sky and warm temperatures, which explains all the walkers and sightseers enjoying the park today. I eye them, wondering if one was her. No one looks familiar. Searching the area, I am surprised to see a that Kidd Valley, a Seattle area gourmet burger chain, rents space at the park, along with an Ivars Seafood Bar. That's a big change from the greasy burger and fry restaurant that used to be here.

Staring at Kidd Valley, its existence makes me a little sad, because it reminds me of the BurgerWorks' failure. Twenty-five years ago, before heading up to Roche, before meeting Virginia, Kidd Valley and the BurgerWorks were competitors. The owners' mission had been to build a high quality burger chain in the Seattle area to compete directly with Kidd Valley.

As I think about the reasons why the BurgerWorks died while Kidd Valley thrived, which are obvious in hindsight — neither the kitchen nor the parking could accommodate the big rushes —, I turn slightly to look to my right. Someone is walking toward me, hands high, both waving. It isn't just someone, it is her. She is waving her whole body, saying both "hi" and "here I am" simultaneously.

Virginia. From her gait, to her curly brown hair, to her body size, to her hat, to her smile, she doesn't look a bit different. I immediately move toward her. As I approach her, looking into her eyes, hints of age are not apparent. Impossible. Unreal. I have entered a time warp. However she lives, whatever she does, whether hard work or fortunate genes, she has found her own fountain of youth.

After a quick hug, we step back. We look each other over, up and down. Except for my light beard, shorter dirty blonde hair, accompanied by a gray hair or three, and a few circles of stress under my eyes, I look about the same. We both have aged well and exchange approving compliments.

I suggest we return to my car to show her the pictures she had sent so long ago. As we walk, our conversation is awkward, unsure of what to say, so we smile and say little. I retrieve the pictures, which helps break the ice. In one picture, I'm flashing my twenty-one-year-old smile, with blond curly hair expanding every direction from my head. The picture shows me wearing my lightweight, deep green Roche Harbor jacket, which Neil Tarte, son of the resort owner Rueben Tarte, had personally given me. The resort staff didn't usually get green jackets, but he told me I had been doing such a great job running the outdoor barbeque that summer he felt I deserved one. Behind me in the photo are the phone booths, or more accurately, a bank of phones separated by plywood dividers located near the general store, the same ones I saw during my first visit at Roche.

A picture of me taken by Virginia at the Roche Harbor phone booths, which no longer exist. She took this just before I took her for a ride in a grocery cart.

I show Virginia the picture she took of me posing at the back of the restaurant. At the time I spotted her across the water at the dock. I'd yelled to her, jumped up onto the food ramp, and posed for the picture. I watched her turn around and saw her raise the camera. I'm barely visible in the picture, but apparently made quite an impact on her, based on what she wrote on the back on the picture.

After showing her all the images, we decide to walk to the lake and onto a dock, a wooden boardwalk that floats on the lake, parallels the lake's beach, and then heads back to the beach, creating an enclosure that protects swimmers within its borders. As we stroll, our conversation starts with the weather. Last night's rain had given way to sunshine and clear skies, allowing us to see the tall buildings of Seattle far away. It is a perfect day.

Another of Virginia's pictures. On the back she wrote, "If you look real hard you'll see a crazy man about to jump. This is actually when you stole my heart & yelled my name and then jumped up & posed for me."

The first thing I notice as we walk is her energy, her vibrancy. Once she speaks, the tenderness and kindness I knew long ago becomes evident. Also, I could see she wore no makeup, making her blue eyes stand out. Before I can say anything, she says the Dave she remembers didn't care whether she wore makeup or not, so she knew I wouldn't mind. Besides, she said, she owns almost no make up anyway.

She is absolutely right, I don't like heavy makeup. I like seeing the very essence of who she is, as if she had just woken up next to me. After all these years, she still knows exactly who I am, exactly who she is, and how we blend.

How strange it all seems. We might have traded the resort setting of Roche for Gene Coulon Park, but the twenty-five time span seems insignificant.

We walk for about thirty minutes, speaking lightly, painting stories of our pasts with broad strokes. We both told the other we came to this rendezvous with a great deal to say, things to share, too much to fit into a single morning. Yet, there was no rush to our stories, partly because we couldn't seem to remember what we planned to discuss. So, we interrupt our conversations with silence, just walking and basking in the warm May sun, enjoying each other's presence. Without touching, we are connecting. I feel it, but have no words to describe it.

• • • •

The more we talk, the wider our conversations run. Nothing serious, we are still parting the doors of trust, yet we don't need a crow bar to do the work. Between us, those doors seem to open with ease, naturally.

The more we share, the more we slip inside the other's confidence. We aren't holding hands, we aren't stopping to hug, and we aren't bumping along shoulder-to-shoulder, arm-to-arm. We respect the physical boundaries; however, emotional boundaries are another matter.

Eventually, after much walking, we take refuge from the sun, finding a bench and table where we can have some privacy. Once again she shares how much she is "blown away" at my very sweet gesture regarding her letter. She says she didn't keep my letter or anything else about me.

I tell her, "I have always had such fond memories of our time together that I couldn't imagine throwing the letter away. I've thrown many things out and moved all over, but the letter remained special, well you remained special, and I had to keep it."

Inquisitively, she responds, "Are you sure my letter was the only one you've ever kept?"

"Yes, I have a couple letters from Cullen, do you remember Cullen?"

She shakes her head no. Cullen had been my best friend at Roche. Virginia met him multiple times. It is funny how selective our memories are.

"Well, apart from Cullen's two letters, I haven't saved any others. I guess the reason I saved it was because you meant a great deal to me. What we shared was very special and I always treasured it."

Her eyes well up slightly. An "Awww, that's sweet," emerges from her mouth as she smiles, tilting her head. Then she says, "I'm so happy you remember it that way. I remember it slightly different."

Her statement stops my heart. Huh? What does she mean by that? I am unsure what to expect. I hold my breath a bit and wait for more as she looks away from me to explain.

"I was devastated. When I drove away that last time from the island I felt we might not see each other again. I had really fallen for you and it took some time for me to get over that. I knew that we were at different stages of life, but it was so special . . . ," she says, her eyes welling up again. She shifts them to look at me, into me.

I am shocked. My heart drops, settling at the bottom of the lake nearby. My life shifts. I hurt this woman and did not know it. How could I have not known it?

I say precisely what I am thinking, softly, slowly, deliberately. "I did not know." I pause. "I did not know. I thought your letter was a goodbye letter. That's the way I interpreted it."

"Yes," she responds. "When I read the copy of the letter, I could see how it appeared I was getting on with my life."

How could I have misread her, misread the letter? Why hadn't I chased her back then? Here is a smart, beautiful, exceptionally kind and accomplished woman with whom I might have had a great relationship and I screwed it up? Had I been too young? Had I needed to explore life? Perhaps it wouldn't have worked out after all?

While emotions surge inside me, I could see hints of the pain she had felt at losing me. She had been hurt. Deeply hurt.

Looking at her, likely with a blank stare, I wonder to myself if had I been as deeply hurt as her? And if not, why not? Clearly she made an impact on my life, but had I loved her? I find myself back to the questions that began my search for her. Why hadn't I pursued her so long ago? Why hadn't I contacted her after returning to Seattle before going back to Roche for my second summer?

"I didn't know," I say one more time. "I really didn't understand." It is all I can say.

I loved the beautiful, blunt honesty of this conversation. She told me something I needed to hear and she needed to say. It was hard for her to say. It was hard for me to hear. Yet, she knew how to do it in a non-judgmental, gentle, but matter of fact manner. She wasn't pulling any punches, but she wasn't punching me either. There was no blaming, from either of us.

For all her outside beauty, her greatest strength is on the inside. I now had no doubt about why I kept the letter; I had never stopped caring for her either. And, based on our conversation, neither had she. Whatever had happened between us, whatever that spark, that light, the power which ignites a love, our feelings for each other had never died. It had gone dormant, but could not die. For more than two and a half decades it had burned like a pilot light inside of us both.

I also felt this wasn't a simple lust. This felt different. I wanted to know this woman better. Whether it was love or pain, happiness or disappointment, I had to explore my feelings for her. I would not make the same mistake I did last time. I could not give up so easily. But, that might not be up to me, as we still had to come clean with our living situations.

"This is what I couldn't share over the computer," she continues. "It just didn't feel right. I wanted to see your face and see that you weren't judging me. Doing this, meeting like this is highly unusual for me. Yet, I had to see you. Maybe I never did get over you. I just had to know. Besides, it was so thoughtful for you to keep that card. That really, really means a lot to me."

"I can tell it does," I say. "I couldn't throw it away. Yet, I couldn't have told why. However, after today, I know why. You are an amazing person. It is so clear, well you seem so clear to me."

"So, here's the hard part," she starts. "I have been married for ten years, but the emotion is gone. I would have left, but he came with a six-year-old boy. After the death of my daughter Sara, I couldn't bear having kids, especially a daughter. So, when my husband came along, him only having a son felt safe. But, of course, I have become Mom to him and feel a deep attachment that enriches my life in a beautiful way. My husband said he would arrange to have me formally adopt him, but he's never done that. He feels like my own son; no, he *is* my own son, yet sometimes he reminds me that I'm not his real Mom. It happens rarely, but when it does, I admit it hurts."

She paused a moment before continuing. "So, I have stayed in the relationship despite my issues with my husband. I know he doesn't appreciate me and that hurts. So, I'm there for my son, and I suppose, in a way, for my daughter Sara. This is my lot in life."

She hesitated, taking a deep breath. "All that said, something happened three months ago. My son got into a fight with a couple kids at his high school. He tried to defend a friend of his from two bullies known for causing problems. Teachers quickly stopped the fight, but the kids promised they would get back at him. Two months ago we were all home watching a movie. It was just an ordinary weekday night, when we heard loud pops immediately followed by breaking glass. There were twelve shots in all according to the police. It happened so fast. We were stunned as we heard a car race away. I have no proof it was the same boys and there seems little the police can do, but Dave, I am sure it was them! Can you imagine that? In Issaquah? We are afraid they will come back again, but we can't easily sell the house in this market."

She had to stop for a moment and compose herself. "Dave, I'm scared to be there, but we have no other family that lives close, so we are stuck and I am stuck. I lock the doors all the time. I'm afraid they'll come back. It's just such a mess!"

She stops talking. It hurt to feel her pain. Though I'm naturally a fixer, one of the lessons I have learned, the hard way, is that when women discuss their problems, they aren't always looking for someone to fix it. They simply want someone to listen.

"I'm so sorry." I look out across the water and back to her. Filtered sunlight dances across her face as a small gust of wind stirs the trees above us. She has said what she wanted to say. It is my turn.

"Let me share with you my story and why I'm moving back to the Seattle area." With that I explain my situation with my girlfriend, the house in Boise, my father's health, and my feelings of responsibility.

Virginia smiles with a look of understanding. "I really appreciate you explaining things. It means a great deal that you felt you could say all that."

We fall silent, continuing to savor each other's company. It feels right, yet we know we both have responsibilities. How do we handle this? How do we walk the line between exploring our feelings for one another, yet not violating the trust of those we are with? Could we possibly just be friends or would we yearn for more? There's no manual for navigating these situations. Neither of us had any answers. What we did know was that we HAD to see each other again and talk more.

Virginia breaks our silence, "I hate to go, but I have to head to Woodinville to work with a client."

"I understand. I would like to meet again whenever you have time."

We agree to see each other one more time before I return to Idaho. She suggests we eat breakfast together on Tuesday morning at a restaurant she likes: she loves their scrambled eggs and smoked salmon.

We say our goodbyes with smiles and a friendly hug. After twenty-five years, it feels good and right to reconnect and, just maybe, this can be a positive experience for the both of us.

• • • •

That evening I visit my Aunt Marilyn in downtown Seattle. My aunt's house has always been a refuge for me, even with the bustling traffic on nearby Fremont Bridge, the most frequently opened drawbridge in the United States. Her home has always been magical to me because she lives on a house boat. More accurately, she lives on a floating home, though she refers to it as a floating shack, due to its small size. Perhaps it was a shack when she moved into it back in the 1960s when it was extremely cheap housing. These days it is prime real estate and she has remodeled the shack into a friendly oasis.

Just a few docks down from my aunt is the floating home made famous by the movie Sleepless in Seattle. My aunt's dock is often confused by sightseers as the one in the movie, but the Sleepless houseboat floats on cement while my aunt's on logs stacked in an upside down pyramid. Every so often one of the logs needs replacing, which is no easy task.

Enhancing any visit at my aunt's is the time I spend with her. Her demeanor is calm and thoughtful and she is well read and articulate about the world around her. A longtime architect, her virtues, along with her detail-oriented approach to life, suits her work-life well. Though she threatens to retire, she continues to receive work opportunities, staying as busy as she wants to be.

After spending the afternoon talking with my aunt and Phil, I heat up some of the hibiscus molé, chile verde and black beans I made the day before. I had made the food as a special treat for my mother's life-long friend Judy, who had visited Mom for a few days. There was plenty leftover, so I thought my aunt would enjoy it too. Finding a really good molé, one aromatically rich from roasted peppers, crushed nuts, ground seeds, smashed plantains, pureed prunes and raisins, and more, is impossible, so I learned to make it myself. My favorite uses dried hibiscus flowers, which add depth and a slight sweetness. It is nothing like the canned molés found in grocery stores, which are terrible.

We enjoy a wonderful dinner and talk as the sun sets. They retire to the home's only bedroom, while I settle onto the couch which doubles as my bed. I try to relax and think about my day, but am not tired at all.

Instead, I feel inspired. I am inspired by my meeting with Virginia earlier in the day, inspired to help her feel loved and appreciated. But, I also feel some guilt. I feel a loss of twenty-five years with her that should never have happened. At the very least, it is a friendship lost that could have been. I want to make up for that as best I can. I decide cooking her something special is a baby step in that direction, to make her feel special.

For me, cooking is a way to show someone I care about them, which explains why I cooked dinner for my aunt this evening. I do not envision myself as the world's greatest or fanciest chef, but I am a good cook, because I care about the ingredients I use and am thoughtful in my preparation. Cooking is one way I interact with my kids, which has been a wonderful way to blend with them. Having the chance to cook for Virginia would be a special for me. I decide I will offer to make her breakfast. I will develop a special breakfast for her and cook it at the park.

I write the following letter to Virginia to share my breakfast idea:

May 20th, 2011 – 11:50 PM

Hi Virginia.

The sun has dropped here at the houseboat. All around the city lights, looking like little orange candle lights, puncture the darkness, some dotting the house boat next door in the form of a string of Christmas lights, some in the form of street lights across the lake, a few lurking overhead on the Aurora avenue bridge, and some, colored red and green, are floating by, accompanied by the muffled sound of boat motors. One single light, hovering above me, swings gently with the lapping waves as the water bounces against the bundled logs underneath me, gently reminding me that I'm not on solid ground. Staying here is always a unique reminder of how different life can be. It's a perfect ending to a wonderful day, the best part of which was spending time with you.

I don't know how, I can't say why, but for a couple hours today I was at peace, simply enjoying your energy and the conversation. You certainly had some things to discuss and I hope I could reduce, however temporarily, some of the burden weighing heavy on your shoulders. I will listen any time you want to talk.

I've got an idea for something on Tuesday, which I hope is a treat for you. I'll let you know tomorrow night after a little recon work on my part (and a check of the weather for Tuesday).

I am so glad I emailed you. I hope we continue to enrich the other.

I hope the rest of your evening went well.

- Dave

After sending my note, I drop to sleep. Early in the morning, I wake and immediately check my email and find her response:

May 21st, 2011 – 5:25 AM

Dear Dave. I realize you will go in a few days and that will be that. I am so glad that you found me. I am still absorbing what has transpired. I am asking myself if I can see you. I am asking myself many questions.

I told you, and it is true, your holding my notes and pictures so dearly for 25 years, has really had an effect on me. Especially considering your moving about and marriages. I will always feel good about that. Thank you for treasuring my feelings. I cannot help but treasure you!

Also, it sounds like you have a special idea for Tuesday. I am curious. I will be done by around 9:30ish a.m. with some work I need to finish.

I appreciated what you said to me. I feel foolish for my blatant honesty. I do not even know you very well, but you have been on my mind constantly. I am afraid of seeing you again, although I can think of nothing else. I look forward to knowing you better and staying friends.

You are an amazing writer; I love your notes. I do want your emails, but I can only check them at certain times.

Xox . . . I need to sign off, please, do not write for now. I will call you tomorrow.

Virginia

I appreciate her response. I am finding it easier to read the intentions and emotions within her notes. Clearly she is feeling the same way I am. We are both excited, perhaps even relieved, that the feelings we felt twenty-five years ago really were powerful. Yet, we are also a little scared of those feelings too.

I also like that she was willing to trust me. She barely knows me, but has a deep trust in me already, just like I have in her. That is part of the connection. I guess it always had been.

Saturday evening, after testing out a recipe, I send her this note:

May 21st, 2011 – 10:03 PM

Hi Virginia.

Smoked salmon and scrambled eggs. You mentioned that as a favorite dish from Roosters on Mercer Island. Well, I wondered if I could make something similar. So today on my way home from my Aunt's I stopped to shop for a few ingredients. I brought home my ingredients and made a yogurt/garlic/chive sauce to which I added some cream cheese. I then created an omelet, inserted some thinly sliced smoked salmon, and added some of my special sauce. My mother was hovering around, wondering what I was making and asked for a bite too. Two thumbs up!

So, what I really want to do is find a park with an outlet (for an electric griddle) or a gas stove (which I could supply) and enjoy a little breakfast picnic, with a smoked salmon omelet and some fresh hashbrowns (I shredded a large batch for my folks and sister today, too), which are my own special creation. I can easily whip that up in a pan. It would be a real treat for me to share some cooking with you.

The question of 'where' is a bit of a challenge. There are two locations I considered. One was Sammamish State Park and one was Gene Coulon Park (plenty of covered space) I thought Sammamish State Park was closest for you. It's supposed to be a nice day; at least that is what I read yesterday.

- Dave

Virginia responds with a short email, indicating she wants to meet again at Gene Coulon Park. After reading it, I put down my computer. Thoughts of her bring back vivid visions of my first summer at Roche Harbor. Though I can't think of her without thinking of Roche, for most of the summer she wasn't there, especially at the beginning.

David Eilers

9. JUNE 6TH, 1986: I HEAD TO ROCHE

After my initial trip to Roche Harbor in May of 1986 and my acceptance of the job offer, I returned back to my rented house in Seattle with two important issues to solve. First, I had to transfer my house lease to my roommate and, second, tell my bosses at the BurgerWorks I was leaving them.

The first task was easy. I told my roommate Alan my plans to work at Roche for the summer and he was happy to take over the lease on the house. I figured he would be cool about it, because had he not been cool, I would have reminded him that it was his fault I got kicked out of the University of Washington.

Yes, I got kicked out of the UW after only one quarter there. It all started in January of 1986 when I left on a bike trip to New Zealand with eleven other people. My only concern about making the trip was that I couldn't register for winter quarter. The organizers of the trip, a few years older than me, and also students at the UW, said that all I had to do was have someone else register for me. They assured me it would not be a problem.

So, while I was on my trip, I had Alan pretend to be me so the fake me could register the real me for classes. However, the fake me, when confronted by an official of some kind, revealed that he wasn't me, but him. Strangely, the powers that be at the UW weren't thrilled about that.

Apparently, they didn't like a 'pretend me' registering in the place of the 'real me'. So, I got kicked after just one quarter (shouldn't everyone get kicked out of school at least once?). Therefore, I returned to work at the BurgerWorks, resulting in my sprained ankle in April and, thus, my trip to Roche in May. None of this would have happened if Alan had been a better liar. Sometimes life turns on the strangest situations.

Though my conversation with Alan had been easy, I dreaded telling my bosses. On the Monday following my return from the San Juans I drove to the restaurant and told my boss Willie, who was also my Aunt's boyfriend, I was giving notice and would be going to Roche Harbor to work. Now, I figured Willie and Tesh would be a little unhappy about my decision, but I also figured that since they found somebody who could work in my place it would all be good. However, it seems that they were not thrilled with the new guy and were really looking forward to having me back. Neither was happy about my decision.

In fact, my decision pissed off Willie. I remember telling him in the morning and, after he unloaded his feelings on me, any time I saw him he was waving his arms like he was shouting at me in his head , but knew he couldn't engage me without blowing up again. It took until the next day before we could have a real conversation. I felt bad, but I knew it was the right move for me. As much as I hated to disappoint them, I just knew, deep down, that I had to go. And I would be going soon, because my new job started June 10th.

On the Memorial weekend before leaving for the San Juan Islands, I raced my jeep. I did well. I had fun. What I didn't know was it was the last weekend I would ever race. And it's funny when you are young. Sometimes you don't appreciate how easily one path will change the way you live forever. I had spent a year and a half building my jeep, the 'Great Escape', and would race it only one year. I had a clear life path of jeeps and cooking in Seattle, but my sprained ankle dramatically altered my life by creating a window of time for me to visit an island, that led to a job offer, which changed my life indefinitely. Life sure can be unpredictable!

• • • •

June 6th, the day after my twenty-first birthday, I packed my jeep for the San Juans. I didn't pack much in the back of it, partly because I would be staying in a homemade camper without much room that Grant had offered me as part of my deal to work there. Besides, I couldn't carry much because there wasn't that much room in the back of the still topless jeep.

Leaving that afternoon, I will never forget the scene. Mom was crying as I drove away. I think she understood this would change my life more than I realized. As I drove north, my goal, once again, was to get to the ferry line a couple hours early. Because I tend to prefer getting somewhere early rather than late, I am usually a very good time planner. To this day I hate the stress of getting somewhere late and all the other stress that comes with not planning well. However, even though I gave myself plenty of time to reach Anacortes and the ferry line, I became a victim of circumstance.

About five miles south of Mount Vernon, Washington, my engine suddenly shut down, forcing me to pull to the side of the road. I knew the jeep pretty well by this point, having welded, bolted, glued, and fiberglassed every single part of the jeep together during my time building it. Also since I had stalled on mountain trails, push started it on hillsides, run out of gas, drained the battery a few times, rolled it over, and an endless list of other comical or unexpected occurrences, I knew how to fix anything on it.

I wasn't all that worried breaking down. It was part of owning an old jeep. I climbed from the jeep, undid the hood latches, and took stock of my assets: (1) there was plenty of light, (2) I had money, (3) I had tools — I always carried tools —, (4) I had a sleeping bag, and (5) it was warm. Because I had all these assets, there was no need to worry about my situation. Okay, maybe I was a little bit worried, because I really wanted to make that ferry.

I ruled out engine failure, meaning something was broken inside the engine, because it hadn't made any deathly *kachuncking* noises nor had there been any fire or smoke rushing out of the hood (that wouldn't happen until next year). No, the engine simply turned off while I was driving up I-5, as if I had turned the key and shut it down.

It is important to know that I am no amazing mechanic with the ability to create blazing, high power motors. But, I do know a few basics. For example, older non-computerized engines need four things to run. They need gas, they need electricity, they need air, and they need the timing necessary to intake the gas/electricity/air combo, explode them properly, and exhale correctly. (Sigh . . . if only the modern engine in my BMW was so simple).

Starting with the first item, gas, I was certain my gas gauge was working, so the jeep wasn't out of gas. However, fuel filters do get plugged and fuel pumps do die. If either of those things failed, I might be stuck for a while. The good news was testing for this was easy by removing the air cleaner and looking inside the carburetor while pulling on the gas pedal wire. If the fuel pump and filter were both working correctly, there should be some residual gas in the carburetor that will shoot down the intake. Sure enough, the test showed the engine was getting gas.

Testing for air problems was easy too. I removed the air cleaner and tried starting the jeep. If the air cleaner was blocking air, removing it would solved that problem. Since it still didn't start, the air clean was not the source of the problem either.

Testing for electricity was the next issue to tackle. For the gas and air to ignite, they have to mix in each engine cylinder and then be ignited by a spark. If there was no spark, there was no firing of the cylinder. On my engine, I had a distributor that sent the spark to each cylinder. There are several things that can go wrong with a distributor. Leaning over the fender to examine the distributor, it didn't take long to see the coil wire had come loose due to a broken connector. Yes, this would have the effect similar to turning off the engine with the key.

So, I pulled out my tool chest and started the process of rigging up a solution. While I fiddled with the wire, an old man pulled off the highway and checked to make sure I was getting along fine. I always thought that was real thoughtful. But, being the independent cuss I am, it pretty much takes a near-death experience for me to ask for help. I told him thanks for the help, but the situation was under control.

Because the clip for the wire had broken, fixing the problem took more time then simply reconnecting the wire. Unfortunately, as often happens, the fix took much more time than expected, costing me an hour of time. Hoping for a miracle, I got the jeep running and raced to the ferry dock, but it was too late. The ferry had left without me. The islands would wait an extra night for my return.

Wondering what to do next, I drove back into downtown Anacortes, three or four miles from the ferry dock. It was nine o'clock and the sun was low in the sky. I rolled into a Kmart parking lot, stopped, and pulled out my trusty map to look for a place to camp.

I didn't have that much money, nor a credit card, and had never stayed in a motel. Out of nowhere a kid on a bike appeared. Maybe eleven years old, the kid rode right up to the jeep fearlessly and said, "Cool jeep!"

I responded with, "Thanks." Then I asked, "Do you know any place to camp around here? I missed the ferry and am stuck here until morning."

"You should follow me home. I'm sure it would be okay with Mom if you slept in the backyard. Let's go ask her."

I thought the conversation was strange. After all, who invites a stranger to sleep in their backyard? Truly, only a kid would do that, but I figured it was my best option at this point. Besides, I had never slept in some stranger's backyard.

He indicated he lived just a little ways away, whether it was many yards or a few miles was unclear, but he was the one riding a bike, so I said, "Ok, let's go".

Now the scene of me following a kid on a bike seemed a little odd. Don't people get arrested for this type of thing? Despite that, I followed him across the parking lot, across the street, and down a narrow alley. We quickly arrived at the back of his house. The backyard abutted the alley without a fence separating them. So, I pulled onto the grass and waited while the kid ran inside.

Soon, the kid returned and said I could stay the night in the backyard. I never did meet nor see his mom. I thanked him as he ran off, never seeing him again.

By then it was 9:30pm. The emerging twilight made for a beautiful evening. I sat on the hood, no wind blew, no clouds crowded the sky, and the temperature hovered at a warm seventy degrees. The world about me was calm, comfortable and peaceful. The night was perfect for a campout. Closing my eyes, I soaked up the moment. There are times in life when everything feels just right and this was one of them. With nothing else to do, I hopped up on my engine hood, put on my headlamp, and opened up one of the books my aunt Marilyn gave me for my birthday.

With my windshield as a backrest, I started to read the book "Less Than Zero" that made Brent Ellis Easton an author of note. A great read, written in a short, choppy, MTV-like style, a style strange to me in 1986, it described a Los Angeles world of drugs and sex far beyond my innocent upbringing. Certainly none of those characters would be sitting on a jeep behind somebody's house planning to sleep outdoors. I doubt that they would have said to themselves, "There's no place I'd rather be at the moment." Yet, that was me, perfectly happy sitting on my jeep, reading a book in some stranger's yard.

By the time I was finished reading and tired, it was dark. I hopped off the hood and circled around to the back of the jeep to retrieve the big blue plastic tarp (that doubled as my jeep's garage – I had no top for the jeep at that point). Then, pulling out my sleeping bag, I jumped inside it and flopped onto the tarp, rolling myself, the sleeping bag, and the tarp underneath the jeep just in case it rained. I set the alarm on my watch to make the first morning ferry and promptly fell asleep. No rain fell that night and I slept well until the alarm woke me. Quickly packing, I climbed in the jeep and drove to the ferry to make the 6am trip to San Juan Island.

I never did see that kid again. Once he obtained permission for me to stay there he went in the house and disappeared. It's funny how people can bounce into your life, sometimes for moments, and have big effects. Other people stick with you your whole life. Some play intense roles for short periods and then for a variety of reasons you never talk with them again. Or at least that is the way it is for me.

So, to that kid I say thanks, though he is now an adult in his mid 30s. I am appreciative of what he did, not just because he offered me a place to stay, but more importantly, because it was a chance to live differently for one night. My summer was already off to an amazing start.

• • • •

Nothing about Roche was dull that summer. Looking back, starting my summer sleeping under my jeep just made sense. It was the point where I stepped outside the shadow of my parents for an extended period of time. I am sure they would have been mortified to know about my choice to sleep under my jeep. I, on the other hand, felt perfectly fine to replace their shadow with the shadow of my jeep, at least for the evening. I finally felt free to experience the world at my own pace.

In many ways, I am seeing the backend of that period of freedom. When I left the house at age twenty-one my parents were fully capable, physically and financially, of managing their lives. But, now, Dad is wearing down. I can feel the sun setting just a bit on my freedom and the gravity of the situation pulling me back to the Seattle area. Family responsibilities loom. Little did I know that a force I never anticipated would compound the situational gravity: Virginia.

David Eilers

10. MAY 22ND, 2011

It is Sunday morning, two days since I had seen Virginia. This morning I plop myself onto the living room couch, keeping one eye on Dad and the other eye on my computer while I update eWillys. He doesn't say much while staring at his television.

Last night was another night of Mom wearing a path between the kitchen and the bedroom. Regardless of my attempts to help Dad, he wanted her, no matter how mundane the request. It was clear Mom needed a break. So, with encouragement, on Sunday she finally left the house for an extended period of time, heading down to my sister's place south of Tacoma. She welcomed the break, her first long one in three weeks, and remained gone for much of the day. While she was away, I tended to Dad, who spent nearly all his time in his living room recliner, again.

One big difference between this visit and past visits is his state of confusion. For example, for the past few days, every time he sees me he asks when I am heading back to Eagle. I answer it the same way: this time I am heading to Spokane, Washington, first, before going down to Eagle. Yet, he can't seem to retain this information. His mental state is slipping, for reasons unclear. I am unsure if this is a blessing or a curse, as his life has become an endless stream of western movies on TV, with the occasional film like Sleepless in Seattle or Kevin Costner's Dragonfly thrown into the mix. For some reason, just in the past few days, almost every time I visit him in the living room he is watching one of these two movies. They seem awfully romantic for a guy who loves his western movies, though I suppose western movies are romantic in their own way at times. It makes me wonder, does he remember the movies clearly, or are they so hazy they simply feel familiar?

As I continue to update eWillys, I listen to the TV. The symbol of the dragonfly haunts Costner's character, forcing him to follow his gut, choosing his own way despite the pleas of others to be rational. Perhaps that is why I like the movie, too. Sometimes our paths don't make sense, but we must follow them, for we are who we are. I like to believe that by following my own path my actions teach my children to follow theirs. Or, perhaps that is just me rationalizing my own choices. Whether or not that is true, I do get great enjoyment by operating eWillys. I have made connections and friends all over the world, helped people, and learned a great deal. What bothers me is that my efforts don't generate the living I need. Yet, I knew getting into this that my effort probably wouldn't transform into a living. Somehow, that must change.

With Costner chasing the dragonfly symbol to South America, I check my email, discovering one from a reader named Paul. The timing couldn't be more perfect, because Paul has been following his own Alaskan path for over twenty-five years building (only in the winters) a stainless steel M-38, the Korean War era flatfender jeep built by Willys Overland from 1950-1952 for the Army (and a few for the Marines). As far as I know, that's the longest anyone has spent continuously building a jeep. Of course, Willys never built their M-38s using stainless steel, but Paul is such a magician and artist with a welder, stainless steel was an obvious choice for him. Undaunted by time, he continues forward and should finish by 2012.

Early in our friendship, Paul wrote:

> *My father bought an all-original 1952 Willys M-38 in 1964 from a local guy here in Anchorage who purchased three jeeps as military surplus. The M-38 my father bought came with a full aluminum top and doors (commonly but incorrectly called an Arctic Top), a 20,000 btu Southwind heater with all the heating ducts, a built in gas fired engine*

and battery heater, and a 24 volt waterproof electrical system all coated with numerous layers of olive drab paint.

This was my dad's everyday driver for eight years until it was finally replaced by a new pickup truck in 1972 and the Willys passed into my ownership for the sum of ONE dollar. I got screwed on this deal; here it is thirty-seven years later and I'm still dumping money into this never-ending project. Boy, if you want to really mess with a kid give him a jeep and he'll be twisted for the rest of his life!

Never in a hurry, always striving for perfection, even if it means doing it over, his work on his jeep represents dedication and patience (insanity?) beyond anything I had ever imagined anyone would undertake. If he devotes even half of this effort to his job, flying around Alaska fixing airplanes, I have no doubt his work is as fine as you will find anywhere on the planet. And no doubt his long time partner, whom he calls "the Goddess", has no less patience in his nutty, crazy view of the world. Besides, he knows he is number one in her life, because "she often extends one finger in my direction."

Paul's 25 year project, a stainless steel M-38 full of custom stainless work.

People like Paul, who approach the world in their own way, who rebuild their jeeps to suit themselves, are another reason I continue to operate eWillys. And it isn't so much his skill, or his material investment, or his time in his project. Instead, most importantly, the crazy Willys passion his project so clearly reflects also defines and describes many of the people who make up the ten thousand or so readers who read the site daily or from time-to-time.

In today's email, Paul tells me "Summer is here", as his Alaskan thermometer reads a blazing forty-six degrees and it is raining. He then launches into an explanation of his recent wood project, his jeep put to sleep for the summer, which involves applying epoxy to a Kauri root. He includes pictures, which are always wonderful (and help me make sense of what he is doing). Ending the email with his typical humor, he writes, *"The Goddess is still trying to wear the print off her Kindle, she's reading up a storm. Hmmmm, maybe that's why it's raining?"*

• • • •

Since reading Paul's email forty five minutes ago, I posted twelve jeeps for sale, answered seven emails, wrote a short feature about an Area 51 photo with a jeep on it, and watched Costner find the tattoo on his baby's foot, indicating the movie was ending. Dad has said little, and moved even less as he watches the introduction to Sleepless in Seattle. I decide to move from the couch and do something else. I tell Dad it is time to fix the tractor mower, so I will be outside in the garage. He says "OK" shaking his head yes, without making eye contact. His appointment with the doctor this week can't come soon enough for me.

I take the computer to the guest bedroom to charge, find a sweatshirt I can get dirty, and walk out to the barn built during the mid 1970s to house hay and horses. Looking through the split door in the side of the stall, with the top door open and the bottom closed, I see the stall that used to act as shelter for my sister's horse Tug. It is now the tractor's home, the horses and hay long gone. I try to open the door to enter the stall, but I can't remember how. It has been that long. I finally realize that the heavy door is wedged shut, so I put some muscle into it and it creaks open.

I hadn't looked closely at the barn in more than twenty years. I see dirt, dust, cobwebs, chewed wood, and the ghosts of animals rather than the animals themselves, though I'm sure there are some very real mice in and around it. Wood of all types is piled throughout the stalls, on the overhang, and inside the barn's hay and storage area. Firewood is stacked just outside the stalls under the overhang from the roof. What my parents plan to do with all the boards and wood is beyond me. I suspect it will all still be here when they pass away.

My parents' temporary barn made of wood crates from Boeing Surplus.

Looking up I see the green and white corrugated fiberglass sheets that serve as the roof. Amazingly, after thirty five it stills keep out most of the rain. Part of the reason is that so many plants are growing on top that the rain can't get through to the roof itself.

It suddenly occurs to me that the barn would make a perfect storage solution for me when I move to Seattle. My parents were not using it and it could use a good cleaning anyway. It would also be a good project for my kids and me to tackle together. Best of all, it doesn't leak and is still solid, not surprising, because Dad built it that way. What might be surprising is that it was built out of recycled airplane engine crates. I swear only Dad would think of building a barn out of crate wood.

Dad and Mom launched the barn project in 1976 shortly after Dad completed the rebuild of his CJ-5 jeep following his Icicle Creek rollover. With my sister's interest in horses outgrowing the temporary lean-to barn, Mom and Dad decided something bigger was necessary. Dad somehow formulated a plan to recycle Boeing Surplus crates and use the wood to build a two story, two stall barn with a tack room and a hay room.

For those that don't know, Boeing Surplus (which was closed a few years ago) just might have been one of the wonders of the world during the mid 1970s, at least in my eyes. As its name connotes, Boeing Surplus was the place Boeing sent old computers, desks, drill bits, nuts and bolts, bulk steel, aluminum and, yes, parts crates, crates sometimes twenty feet long, built solid enough to safely transport expensive parts. After the parts arrived, these crates would be sent to Boeing Surplus for sale. Many of the sides of the crates were built using 1" thick rough boards, some eight inches wide. The boxes' frames were made of 2x4s, 2x6s, and 4x4s. Best of all, the boxes were really cheap.

And guess what we used to transport all those crates, no matter the length or width, to our house . . . our jeep. Looking back, I wished we had pictures of the crazy loads Dad would pile on top of his rollcage. For a guy scared of tipping on the trail, he seemed fearless on the roads. He tied awkward loads using bundles of rope with all types of clever knots. I learned a great deal about knots and tying down loads from watching him lash those crates to the rollcage.

The loads likely violated one or more municipal codes, but that didn't stop Dad. He would drive, with me riding shotgun, the five mile distance from Boeing Surplus in the Kent Valley up Renton's steep south hill and our house. He rarely topped twenty miles per hour, slowly making turns.

Fortunately, there were just enough back roads that we could make it home without being in anyone's way.

It turns out, when building a barn out of crates, transportation is the easy part. The hard part was taking them apart. Our family's task, along with any neighbor friends I could recruit, was to pull apart the crates, save the wood as best as possible, and save the nails whenever we could. I have never straightened as many nails as I did that summer. I saved many of them, removing nails one at a time from the bent bucket, pounding each straight, and then putting each one into the good bucket.

After pulling apart the crates, it didn't take me long to figure out why Dad wanted to use that wood: it was strong, good quality wood. For weeks that summer, we would travel down, load up the jeep, bring the load home (slowly), unload it, put the crates on saw horses in the front yard, pull out the nails, pile the wood, and straighten the nails. This process repeated itself until we had all the wood we needed. I guess you could say my parents have always been fans of reuse-recycle!

Once everything was ready, Dad explained he wanted to make the barn a 'temporary' structure. In other words, it didn't have a true foundation. Instead, he laid down cement blocks, like the ones used to build decks, in a fashion that would properly support the barn, yet allow for the building to be disassembled and the wood reused for some other project.

As a kid in my early teens, it was exciting to watch the barn go up. For me, this might have been the highlight of having horses on the property. He showed me the importance of tamping down the ground to prevent the blocks from shifting or dropping. As the barn rose, I learned how to create a solid, level, and square platform on top of which would go floor joists, and then the floor, walls, second level, and roof. By the time it was finished, I treated it like my own fort.

Now, thirty-five years later, that 'temporary' barn still stands, as sound as the day it was built. But, there are no longer any horses, so it is used for storing equipment. Or, after cleaning, could be used to store my stuff, which solves one of my moving issues.

Turning my attention to the tractor mower in the stall, I was told by Mom there were two problems. One was that it wouldn't start. The second was that the rubber power-take-off belt, which ran from the motor of the tractor to the mower blades underneath the tractor, had broken. I suppose a third problem was that I had never used the tractor, so I have to first figure out how it is supposed to work.

A problem that should have taken a few minutes to diagnose takes me several hours. After checking the starter, the battery, the gas, and every other possible problem, I discover why the tractor will not start. Because the mower blades had been removed from the tractor, a safety cable that had been connected to the blades is hanging loose. Once I circumvent the safety cable, I can turn the key, and start the tractor. Problem number one solved. There had never been anything wrong with the tractor. It was operator error.

To diagnose the second problem, I need more light, so I drag the mower attachment to the garage. I flip the mower over and try to spin the two mower blades. Neither will spin. I am sure these are supposed to spin freely, so I locate a hammer and a piece of wood. Putting the wood on the back of the blade, I hit the wood until the blade starts to spin. As I suspect, the shafts of the blades are stuck, which explains the broken belt. They need to be taken apart and the grass/dirt/refuse removed from them before I install a new belt. This will take me a couple hours.

With the blade shafts clean, I just need to buy a belt and everything can be reassembled. It seems easy enough. It isn't.

Even though Home Depot is only twenty minutes away from the house it takes me three hours to get the right belt, because it took three separate trips to Home Depot to get it.

The first time an employee recommended the wrong belt. The second time I bought the right package, but it contained the wrong belt. The third time I finally purchased the correct belt in the correct package. In between each trip I checked on Dad to make sure he was ok; truthfully, to make sure he was still alive.

By the early afternoon the tractor runs and the mower blades spin. Normally, I would have a sense of accomplishment at solving the problem. But, the reason I am tackling the tractor is due to Dad's inability to do it, so my success is tempered with that realization. He was the one that almost always fixed things around the house or could do anything. He was the only father I knew who lashed telephone pole spikes to his legs and climbed up trees to saw off branches (and was still doing so until his stroke at age sixty-nine).

From my perspective dads just did those things. I didn't really think much of it. If I wanted a jeep, I was supposed to build one. If I rolled it down a hill, I should rebuild it. If I didn't have a basement, I should dig one, buy cement blocks, create a foundation, and pour a floor. If I wanted a swimming pool, I should buy one, prepare the ground, install the pool, and build a deck around it. If some part of the world wasn't the way I wanted it, I should change it. If something broke, there was usually a way to fix it. That is why a garage and tools were necessary, to fix stuff (rather than housing vehicles).

Of course, Dad made it look easy. It wasn't always so easy for me. As a teen I would try to build a bench or table out of wood, but it never seemed to go together well. At times, I let failure stop me, because nothing I built with Dad's tools seemed to go together like his projects did. Dad was always good about letting me use his tools, so I had plenty of chances to succeed and fail, usually working on my bike or go-kart, even though sometimes I left the tools out to rust.

Because I failed enough times as a teenager fixing and building things, I never imagined I would have the 'knack' to fix anything. It wasn't until I left college, essentially flunking out of it, that I learned how to build something. And I owe it all to the jeep I built when I was nineteen.

11. 1983-1985: I BUILD MY FIRST JEEP

For my birthday and high school graduation, since they happened on the same day, in early June of 1983 I received from my parents my very own vehicle, a 1950 CJ-3A jeep. For two years I had driven my father's jeep, a CJ-5, but my goal had been to own a flatfender jeep. To me they felt like a big boy's go-cart. Finally, at the age of eighteen, I had my very own.

Even back then fifteen hundred dollars didn't buy a beautiful rig. In fact, the same CJ-3A would likely sell for about two thousand dollars today, maybe less. While the jeep had a strong drive train, with a non-smoking Buick V6 225 motor and a T-15 three speed transmission, the body was a patchwork of, well, patches, some flat steel and some diamond plating, held together with welds and blue paint. The axles were stock. The pedals were stock. The rollcage was poorly built, with straight tubes along the front loop, rather than bending with the contour of the windshield and then bending at the dash on its way to the driver and passenger side floors. However, it did have a nice top, a working heater, and was street legal, important attributes for using it as a daily driver.

That summer, I drove it throughout the Seattle area. Aimless, I didn't work, and had no real plans other than I had to attend Green River Community College that fall. And that was only to please my parents. I went along with the idea simply because no alternative occurred to me.

During the summer of 1983 I attended a few races and explored some offroad trails. It took me little time to conclude that my jeep was inadequate for my needs; it needed improvement (I think all jeep owners can relate to this feeling). I wanted better brakes (like Dad's), better handling and styling (like the Carter's jeep, "Otis"), a stronger motor, and a stronger roll cage. I also wanted to race it, which required additional safety improvements like a scattershield (metal bellhousing) and specific rollcage requirements. Therefore, I wanted to take it apart and make it better.

Blocking my rebuild plans were two major hurdles: I had no money and no job. So, rebuilding my jeep seemed an impossibility. Meanwhile, my parents preferred I go to college or "I would be wasting my life" as my mother so eloquently put it.

So, reluctantly, in the fall of 1983, I started college at Green River Community College, a half-hour drive along country roads from my parents' house. I had always been a good student, when necessary, but if apathy arose, I could fail quite spectacularly. For example, I started off the first quarter of my senior year in high school with a 4.0 GPA, while taking Debate, Latin, German, Calculus, and a couple other difficult classes. The last half of the year, senioritis stripped my passion for school. With plenty of credits to graduate, I became a prisoner serving my time and my grades plummeted. I think my last quarter of high school I got a 2.0 average, my lowest high school GPA ever.

I wish now someone had taken me aside and said, "Go travel and explore the world". Instead, I plunged into college half-heartedly and that is a generous exaggeration of my enthusiasm for it at the time. I took three classes (physics, math, literature), none of which inspired me. It felt like a giant waste of my time and it only got worse.

By the end of November, the days were short and cold. The morning drive required gloves and a heavy jacket. The jeep's windshield, which had no defroster, would ice-over and be difficult to see through until about half way to school when the heater would finally overcome its battle with the cold outside. Drafts snuck through the gaps between the top and the body, more apparent as the temperatures dropped (for several reasons a soft top doesn't seal on a flatfender body as well as on a CJ-5 or later body).

Not only did the daily drive increase my apathy for school, so did my growing lack of interest in the classes. By October I'd stopped going to my literature class. I'd had no interest in reading the books that were assigned or sharing my opinion about them with others. High school had managed to beat out of me any interest in reading, which was puzzling to me, as I loved to read in elementary school.

As fall turned to winter, I cared less and less about college. Instead of doing homework, I drew jeeps (I still have some of the drawings). I passionately wanted to tear apart my jeep and rebuild it into the jeep-of-my-dreams. Yet, I still had no money for this. Moreover, the jeep was my primary vehicle; therefore, rebuilding it wasn't practical. So, I kept on dreaming and drawing.

When I completed my prison sentence, with fall quarter finished, I too was done, never to return to Green River Community College. My grades reflected my effort: one D, one E and one incomplete. Frankly, those were generous grades. The D was in physics and the little success I had there was leftover from information I gleaned while taking high school physics. If I thought my worst high school GPA was bad, well, my first attempt at college was a GPA disaster.

At some point during December of 1983, I told my folks I was not going back to college, well not for a while anyway. So, they said get a job. That seemed fair enough, however it turns out that a high school diploma doesn't qualify a person for very many jobs. Mom suggested I apply at a place like McDonalds, because it would look good on my resume. I differed with her on the value of a fast-food job. Instead, I wanted to find a job that provided me with more skills and a different opportunity.

While full-time work eluded me, I did earn some part-time money rebuilding transmissions and transfercases. Dad's friend Al Carroll, who taught him much about jeeps, provided the work. Al Carroll belonged to the Seattle Jeep Club for years and was old enough that he could have been a founding member. Visiting his house in Burien was heaven, because he had multiple garages that were always filled with jeeps of all types. He bought, sold, traded, and repaired jeeps.

I guess both he and Dad thought it would be a good idea for me to learn something about working on vehicles and rebuilding equipment. With Dad watching over my shoulder in the garage, I would disassemble, clean, check the gears and shafts for wear, and then reassemble them with new bearings, gaskets and grease, learning how to set the bearing tolerances in the process. Initially, I was given simple projects, such as rebuilding a T-90 transmission (a widely used transmission in many early jeeps) or a Dana 18 transfercase (pronounced day • na).

The Dana 18 transfercase differentiated the jeep from other vehicles before it. Designed by the Spicer Company specifically for the first Bantam vehicle, the transfercase sits behind the transmission, so the engine powers the transmission, which powers the transfercase, which powers the wheels. What made the design of the transfercase unique, and thus the jeep, was that before the invention of the jeep, there were either two-wheeled drive vehicles or four-wheeled drive vehicles. Uniquely, the jeep was capable of shifting in and out of four-wheel drive. Not only that, the transfercase also allowed jeeps to travel at roads in high range or creep along difficult hills in low range. Thus it was practical for all kinds of terrain.

Over the fall and winter of 1983 I worked on a variety of transmissions and transfercases for Al, appreciating his faith and confidence in me. After finishing a project, Dad and I would drive across the Tukwila Valley to Al's place near SeaTac airport in Burien to drop off my finished product.

One day in late 1983 as Dad and I approached Al's place my heart fluttered. Parked on the side of the road in front of his house was a green fiberglass flatfender racing jeep with a great looking rollcage, mini terra tires, and enough moss on the body to indicate it had been sitting a while. I wanted it. I'm not sure whether Dad stopped the truck before I opened the door and leapt from it, but I quickly ran over to the trailer and climbed onto it to investigate the racer.

Al appeared explaining he had received the jeep for an outstanding debt owed him. My eyes must have been super-sized saucers because Al asked me if I wanted it. I immediately said yes. He told me he would charge me six hundred dollars, but I could work it off by rebuilding transmissions for him. He also said he'd throw in a couple other items as well.

First, he had a Dana 30 front end from a CJ-5, as that would be a stronger setup for jeeping and racing. He also had a mail-jeep (DJ-5) rear end that had a Detroit Locker (and I'm sure he said locker, but I now believe the DJs only came with limited slips) in it. Then he explained, in his tutorial style, that the mail jeeps were about two inches narrower than a stock CJ-5 rear end, so he had his friend machine two spacers that would sit on either end of the axle, which would allow me to use the stronger CJ-5 Dana 44 30-spline axles in it. He clearly felt very clever about this inexpensive axle upgrade and I was very excited he was both sharing the information with me and throwing it in with the deal.

With Dad's help, we picked up the jeep a few days later and, in the daylight, I could see my new jeep more clearly. I regret that I have lost any pictures of it. It had a metal-flake-green fiberglass body with a six point, frame-mounted rollcage, meaning the rollcage attached to the frame in six different places, sandwiching the bottom of the fiberglass body firmly between the frame on the bottom and the rollcage mounts on the top. The body didn't have any major cracks, though it did have plenty of moss. The bucket seats were fiberglass high-back seats designed for a dune buggy (the same seats I would have to drive to Oregon to hunt down twenty years later for Biscuit). The engine was a Pontiac V8 sliced almost in half, which turned it into an inline four-cylinder engine built to Indy specs, according to the builder. It was a really cool engine, with a Frankenstein-like patchwork of welding marks where various gaps and holes were plugged. Its eight-cylinder intake manifold had also been converted into four, like-wise patched. However, the engine was not part of the deal and Al said that we had to return it to the owner.

Once Dad and I pulled the engine, we drove to the owner's house, which wasn't far away. There we learned more about the jeep. According to the original builder, he and a buddy decided to race in one of Eastern Washington's offroad one-hundred-mile races held in the 1970s. He said they only had thirty days to build the rig, so they slapped a fiberglass body onto a M-38A1 frame, built a rollcage, raised the front springs by welding some two inch square tubes between the spring holders and frame, and put in a motor capable of reaching nine thousand RPMS. Based on the number of torch holes (rather than drill holes) the builders used to attach the rollcage to the frame, I really could imagine that two guys built this race jeep in thirty days.

Apart from the fiberglass body, rollcage and engine, everything else was stock. So, the Indy spec motor (according to owner) was pushing power through a T-90 and Dana 18 transfercase, both built for a low-powered four-cylinder engine, into 5:38 gears. Due to rust and abuse, I would eventually junk the entire drive train. Thus, after tearing it apart, I was left with a body, frame, fiberglass seats, and rollcage as the foundation for my jeep rebuild project.

After dismantling the racer, I managed to get our old Ford Pinto running to use as a daily driver. This is the same vehicle that earned a reputation during the 1970s for exploding after getting rear-ended. However, I wasn't nervous about getting rear-ended in it, because my father, two friends and I had already been rear-ended in 1979 in my family's other Ford Pinto and it didn't explode. The reason it didn't explode was because we only had a quarter-tank of gas. After looking at the rear end of the Pinto following the accident, Dad learned that when hit from behind the Pinto's gas inlet hose pops off the tank. If enough gas is in the gas tank, the gas will flow out of the tank and onto the exhaust pipe igniting it, causing the explosion. So, dad fixed the inlet on both of our Pintos so that the hoses couldn't come off of them.

Now that I had fixed the Pinto (and Dad had secured the inlet hose) I could tear apart my blue jeep too. It didn't take me long to dismantle it, leaving me with a garage full of parts. I was ready to build something. Anything.

So, here I was, a college dropout without a job, wanting to launch a jeep build with a budget of about $0. My assets were a garage full of equipment, which Dad allowed me to use, a set of very patient parents, and a bunch of parts. With no particular time frame or plan, except for the basic concept of how the jeep should look, I began building a jeep. Unfortunately, other than taking a grinder to the frame to clean it up in preparation for the modifications, I had no money to proceed.

Besides, it was winter, too cold in the garage to get much done. The garage was a separate building from the house. It was a dark, damp place to work. Though Dad had had a wood stove to heat the garage when he was spending time in it during the 1970s, by the 1980s the stove was gone, which meant I really had to bundle up when working in there. And, even that wasn't always enough.

The light in the garage was a problem too, because there were only two overhead floodlights. There were additional lights over the benches, but any work done in the middle of the garage required me to pull out the extension cord with a shop light (or a couple of them). I broke a lot of light bulbs.

Therefore, while I schemed and planned, not much work was done that winter. By mid-March Mom was again concerned about my future and, not unreasonably so, which wasn't making me feel any better. About that time, my Aunt's boyfriend, Willie, came through with a job offer. He asked me if I would like to learn to cook, as he and his friend Tesh had opened a high quality burger restaurant called the BurgerWorks, a place near Gas Works Park. After weighing all my options — this was a very quick process as I had no other options — I said sure. Besides, I always liked cooking, what little of it I had done. In addition, I would now be working in downtown Seattle area, which sounded fun.

What started as a part-time job quickly became full-time, as Willie and Tesh expanded the restaurant hours by adding a breakfast menu. I was the main breakfast cook, which was good for me, as now I had a full-time job and could pay for my jeep build. However, first I had to figure out how to cook good breakfasts in a kitchen that wasn't designed for breakfasts. For example, there were no kitchen burners. Instead, we put pans on a charbroiler to cook eggs and relied on a griddle to finish off basted eggs, cook fresh hashbrowns, pancakes and everything else.

At first I made lots of mistakes. I burnt toast, broke over-easy eggs, and screwed up orders. However, with time and practice I became a good short-order cook, particularly a good short-order breakfast cook.

I learned there were two important aspects to being a good restaurant cook: 1) cook food correctly and 2) handle large volumes and rushes without panic. Getting #1 right involved practice and understanding of what the customer expected when they ordered, for example, basted eggs (my goal with basted eggs was to keep the egg white cooked evenly, while maintaining a runny yolk, and attain a nice white glaze over the entire top of the yolk). Once I got it right, the next trick was to make it right every time. This meant understanding the equipment and knowing when it was too cold or too hot.

Getting #2 right meant getting the food right en-mass. It required understanding how to handle many orders and knowing how to execute the orders on autopilot, because there was no time to think. Having food prepped is one key to successfully enduring busy periods and making sure the food is still cooked right.

As my confidence improved so did my cooking skills and my enjoyment of the process. The better I got the more experimentation and refinements I made. I figured out that the best hashbrowns required enough butter melted on a griddle to cook them to a golden, crunch brown, but not too much to make them greasy. Then, after laying the browns on the melted butter, adding some melted butter over the top of them improved the crunch on both sides.

Learning to cook hashbrowns, eggs, burgers, fries and all the other menu items was a wonderful experience. Two of my favorite menu items were the hotlink sandwich and the burger dip. The core of the hotlink sandwich was a special sausage link produced by Better Meats, the company that supplied the meat for the BurgerWorks. The sausage link was heated on a griddle with melted hot pepper cheese, placed on the bottom half on a french roll prepared with, in order, mayonnaise, sliced pickles, alfalfa sprouts and tomatoes. Once the sausage and melted cheese was situated on the sandwich, the top half of the french roll capped it. We then sliced it diagonally. I still enjoy eating this sandwich, though finding the right sausage with the right size and slightly spicy flavor is difficult.

My other favorite sandwich from the BurgerWorks, the burger dip, is similar to the traditional french dip. However, in place of sliced beef, two burger patties topped with cheddar or hot pepper cheese are placed between two halves of a french roll. The sandwich is sliced at an angle and then dipped into au jus or barbeque sauce or, my favorite, a mix of both. I still cook this one often as well.

Though sometimes working at the restaurant was hard work, most of the time I had fun cooking. Even better, I was able to save money for the jeep, despite making only $7.50 an hour. And, in the end, that was my principal goal for working: the jeep.

Since this wasn't much money, I had to improvise. A good example of my improvisation occurred when building my suspension. I wanted to change from the standard 1.5" wide springs to the wider 2.5" springs, to both improve the quality of ride and, because I thought the wider springs looked cooler. Also, the springs needed to be longer than stock springs, but I didn't want to make the front and rear of the frame longer, which would throw off the classic look of the jeep. So, in the front of the jeep the springs would have to extend farther behind the axle than in front of the axle if I was going to use longer springs. Locating a cheap source for the right springs became my biggest issue. Also, I wanted springs that didn't require drilling center-pin holes.

One day I was sitting on my jeep's frame with the garage door open looking at one of our Ford Pinto's in the driveway. Staring at the rear, it appeared to me that the rear springs looked longer in the back of the rear axle than in the front of it. I climbed under the car to look closer at the rear springs. Sure enough, that was the case. I got out my measuring tape. Amazingly, the distance from the center-pin to the front of the spring was the exact distance I needed for my front springs! I immediately went down to the local junkyard, found some Ford Pintos, and got four sets of springs, which I cobbled together, to build my fronts springs.

Early 1984. I am puzzling through how to build the suspension.

Even better, while at the junkyard, I discovered the Ford Pinto Wagons had even longer springs in the rear. So, I grabbed a set of those, added a couple leaves, and used them for my rear springs. This was shade-tree (as in working under the shade of a tree) mechanic problem solving at its finest (or scariest). But then, I never let the fact that I didn't know what I was doing, as I had no engineering or suspension design experience, ever stop me. I just moved forward and did the best with what I had.

The jeep frame was not built to handle the width of these springs nor the length. It also wasn't built to have the rear springs mounted to the sides, which would provide more driving stability. So, with some raw steel and advice from my father (who didn't often offer advice, except for the occasional shaking of his head — and not in a good way — at what I was doing) I created, designed, cut, and welded my own spring holders and shackles.

Summer 1984. The suspension is almost complete.

That might sound like a lot of work, but it was actually worse. I had to cut everything with a hacksaw, a hand metal saw that was powered by the arms of yours truly. On some of the thicker stuff, like the half-inch thick plates of steel I used for spring/shock mounts (that were actually old tie-plates which attached railroad rails to ties), it could take a half hour per cut to slice through them.

It is unclear to me if it was a testament to character and desire or simply reflected some insanity on my part, but I spent hours and hours cutting. I would fall into a trance, remove myself from the situation, and free my arms and body to push and pull the small hacksaw back and forth until it slowly made its way down a plate of steel, though I couldn't get too mindless, for the cuts needed to be made straight. There was a subtle balance between remaining conscious and unconscious as I worked.

Twenty-one years later, while building Lost Biscuit, I had a renewed respect for the accomplishment I'd made on my first jeep. While building my second jeep, I marveled at my ability to construct the first jeep without the internet as a reference guide, let alone without a Sawz-All with metal blades (yeah, no more hacksawing). While my first jeep was far from perfect, somehow I managed to put it altogether with few directions, even with a variety of wholesale customizations. I positioned axles, determined driveline lengths, bounded up and down on the frame to ponder suspension issues, mounted the engine, and more. With each challenge, I created a solution, though not always optimal. Somehow the whole project just made sense to me.

While I abandoned college for my dream project, my friends who were all in college filled me in on what they were doing in school. Or, they'd call me because their vehicle had broken and they needed help fixing it. One friend of mine, who was attending the University of Washington, called me one day to say he was stuck in a parking garage, his car wouldn't start and it leaked fuel onto the ground whenever he tried to start it. So, I made the half hour drive to Seattle, climbed under his car, and discovered his flexible fuel line had become disconnected from his solid fuel line. So, every time he turned on the power to start the car, the fuel pump would start and pump fuel through the flexible fuel line onto the ground. As soon as he turned the car off, the leaking stopped. Somehow, it didn't explode. Luckily, in addition to my tools I brought a small clamp, so the fix was easy. I placed the clamp around the flexible tube, slid the tube onto the solid line, and clamped it tight. He was on the road in ten minutes.

Another time, a friend of mine rear-ended a car. He had an older Toyota Corolla and didn't have money to fix it. He was a pretty smart guy, almost acing the SAT test and earning himself a full-ride scholarship to an ivy-league school. But, he didn't know what to do about fixing his car, except to call me. I told him to bring it by and I would do what I could.

When he arrived, I could see the front right side was damaged, the headlight broken, and the hood wouldn't shut right. With a budget of $0 (why do I always have these budgets?), I told him I would do my best to patch it together to make it legal and drivable. I gave him the keys to my car and told him to come back in two days.

I removed and straightened parts, patched others, rewired one headlight, and spray-painted the areas where metal was exposed. It was hardly a polished solution, but when he came back two days later, his hood shut properly, his headlights and running lights worked, and the exposed metal was painted (though with just some primer). He was not only appreciative, but also amazed at what I had done. From my perspective, what I did just seemed to make sense.

And then he said something I will never forget. He said, "I don't understand how you know what to do. How did you know how to fix the car? How do you know how to build your jeep?"

I stared at him, surprised at his question. Then I began wondering the same thing. How did I know how to fix vehicles? I hadn't known much when I started working on the jeep, but now, in my head it just made sense to do what I did. That's when I realized my brain had been rewired. By building my jeep, something had clicked. By disassembling and reassembling parts, I now understood the different mechanical ways metal connected to metal. When I looked at different things that were broken, I could almost always see a rational solution. It all made sense where it hadn't make sense before.

At that point a realization struck me. I had earned, embraced, inherited what I'd always admired my father for doing; I could fix problems. By no stretch could I do everything he could, but I was on the mental trajectory and had the mental tools necessary to troubleshoot problems. And it had all been the result of working and building my jeep. I matured mentally in ways I had not expected. I'm eternally grateful that Mom and Dad had the faith to let me loose in the garage, to succeed or fail on my own.

The inaugural test of my first jeep in late 1984 in the horse pasture. It still needs some lights, a hood, and a bumper among other items.

With this new found sense of self, I continued my work on the jeep from the summer of 1984 into fall and another winter, slowly and cheaply piecing my jeep together from Chevy, Ford, Mail Jeep (DJ-5), CJ-3A, Fiberglass-Racer, Buick, and even jeep parts. When I pulled the wiring out of our wrecked 1972 Chevrolet Vega (my original first car before Mom damaged it a month before I turned sixteen), I went down to the library (remember, this was pre-internet) and copied wiring diagrams that helped me dissect the wiring so I could adapt it for my needs. When I needed to rebuild my Saginaw power steering, I pulled out Dad's manuals until I found something close enough to guide me through the rebuild.

By the time my fiberglass racing/trail/road jeep was finished in late 1984, it was no masterpiece. A low budget meant there were things I couldn't do, like painting it nicely, which reduced the elegance, but not the utility. It was a solid jeep that served me faithfully, most days anyway.

To complete the build in only a year I made personal sacrifices. At age nineteen, I had no social life, partly due to my work on the jeep and partly due to my cooking schedule, which was five o'clock in the morning to two o'clock in the afternoon, after which I would work on the jeep. In between, I started reading again. And, I rode my ten-speed, that was pretty much my life and I was fine with that. I was doing my own thing, having my own life adventure. That set the stage for much of my life.

The obstacle course at the 1985 Summer Convention at the Thurston County/Grays Harbor ORV Park included a water hole that thoroughly muddied the jeep and me. While waiting to spray it off a woman approached me and took this picture. I didn't know her name or ever see her again. A month later she entered it in a photography exhibit at the Snohomish County Fair. Jim and Patti Carter visited the fair and just happened to see the picture, so they made sure I received a copy. It is the only racing-oriented photo I have with me in it.

Building my first jeep was cathartic. It changed my life. I am now a firm believer that everyone should tackle a large project early in life. I tell my own kids to tackle something big or go see the world after high school. Certainly, at some point college used to provide this type of experience, but I find most colleges are simply white collar vocational training grounds, structured less for the experience of learning and growing and more for positioning folks to get a good job so they can pay off their student loans, which seems suspiciously circular. This might be good economics, but doesn't create enlightened citizens in my opinion.

• • • •

With Dad's mower fixed, and the lawn mowed, I return to the house, grab my laptop computer and sit down with Dad in the living room to check email. As I watch him stare at the TV I realize that not only do I have many of his fix-it skills, but I am also becoming him by repairing a host of items Mom had on her sonny-do list. I am replacing my father. And, because of that fact, I see my future more clearly. I can't help but wonder how long it will be before I am where he is.

What will my end be like? And what kind of life do I want before I get there? Will I find myself stuck in a chair? Will I be in my own home? Will I have health insurance remotely as good as his (I have none now)? I have no answers.

Instead, I must focus on the present. Should I move here, to Seattle, settle down and get a real job? Or do I push forward with my website in hopes it will become something more? Should I write a book? What would I regret not doing most?

One thing I know for sure, no matter what complications seeing her might produce, I feel a strong need to spend more time with Virginia. I also know that not seeing her would is a mistake I would regret.

12. MAY 24TH, 2011

Today, Tuesday, Virginia and I are meeting again, though the sunny weather from Friday has been replaced by a cool and windy morning. These are more like the May days of Seattle I remember, gray days I'd escaped for nearly twenty years. Because of my decision to move back to the area, once again I will be enduring them, but they don't seem so formidable anymore. Whether my sense of responsibility for my parents or simply a need to start again, the thought of moving back to the Seattle no longer bothers me as it once did.

I arrive at the park a little before 9:30am wanting to prep my 'kitchen'. I packed a stove, a small cutting board, some towels, a bowl to mix the omelet, plates, and other items. To supply the cooking heat I purchased a new one-burner stove, a small burner that screws directly on top of a propane bottle. It is efficient and compact. I like it.

After unpacking, I check the email on my phone. Virginia dropped me a note saying she will be a little late. With my kitchen prep complete, I retrieve my guitar to pas the time. I like to sing and play the guitar, but am not all that good. I can only play major chords, especially since I broke my ring finger joint while playing basketball earlier this year, because it no longer bends correctly or tightly. I'm never going to be a rock star; I just want to entertain myself. I like the piano too, which I taught myself to play in 2005, but the piano is a hard instrument to pack into the back of a car, so I thought learning to play something I could transport made more sense.

Most of my life I saw myself as musically challenged. I avoided playing music all through my school years, deftly bypassing music classes in favor of anything else. Now, I wonder why that was, because I am sure I would have done just fine.

What is even stranger is that I'm a great-great-grandson of Rudolph Wurlitzer, founder of the Wurlitzer Company, the world's largest music company for decades. I always thought that was a pretty cool fact, but not cool enough to learn how to actually play an instrument.

With my guitar tuned, I strum Bob Dylan's "Like a Rolling Stone", one of the few songs I know by heart, just loud enough to entertain myself, but not so loud as to bother the few people at the park.

• • • •

Virginia arrives at 10:15am, perfectly dressed for Seattle. Dressing in Seattle is all about layers, more so than any other place I have lived, the kind of layers displayed in a REI catalog. She wears a snug turtleneck, a light jacket, and then a fleece vest, all black. Once again, she has no makeup. I love her look.

She seems excited I am cooking for her. We never discussed whether she did all the cooking in her relationships, but I imagined she did from her response. Her reaction suggests this is an extraordinary event for her and she wants to savor it.

From the moment I fire up the burner we are a team. Saying little, she seems to read my mind, recognizing what needs to be done. She lightly bounces around the table, readying it for our food, while laughing at my improvised salt and pepper containers (a piece of foil) and listening as I explain what I am doing. When the wind blows out the burner, she cups her hands as a wind-break to help me re-ignite it. We work well together, no tripping over the other while completing a task. It feels natural.

I have dated enough to know when chemistry exists and when there is none. I use chemistry as a representative word for something I cannot really define. Is it a spiritual bond, psychic attraction, pheromones, magic? I don't know, but I do know that sharing a powerful force with someone, however defined, is rare. Sometimes the chemistry is forced, because you like someone and they like you, but no real chemistry exists. Sometimes there is a physical chemistry and no mental chemistry. Sometimes the mental is there, but the physical is absent.

Whatever chemistry is, we have it. It is deep and neither of us seem to question it. The air around us is charged. *It feels so good to be with her,* I think to myself, trying to focus on the breakfast instead of her. It's hard.

I hover my hand over the pan to feel if it is warm. Satisfied by the temperature, I place the butter in the pan, explaining to her my process of making fresh hashbrowns. I tell her that my obsession with fresh hashbrowns started at the BurgerWorks. Since all I could find in stores were the frozen browns, I experimented with potatoes until I figured out how to make fresh ones.

The secret, I explained to her, is simple: set the oven to 350 degrees, put some potatoes in the oven, and then cook them thirty minutes. Thirty minutes is long enough to turn the starches to sugars, yet not long enough to soften the potato very much. Once the potatoes are baked, pull them out quickly and let them cool overnight. Finally, peel and shred them the following day. This process creates stronger strands of browns with a satisfyingly firm texture that is better than using baked potatoes, yet the browns don't taste undercooked like the way they taste when fresh potatoes are shredded and cooked.

Grabbing some fresh browns from my ziplock bag, I tell her how to cook them, "With the butter melted in the pan, I try not to get the butter too hot or the whey and other non-oil elements will burn. That is why restaurants often clarify the butter, or melt it, which separates out the different parts of the butter, so that only the oil remains. Removing the whey and other particulates improves the butter's ability to handle higher temperatures. But, clarification also removes some of the flavor out of the butter, so I prefer using all the butter."

"Properly heating butter is key not just to cooking hashbrowns, but also to cooking omelets and sautéed items, especially when avoiding non-stick pans, which is my preference. I like to use carbon steel pans, which are cheap and can be beat up, or cast iron pans for most of my stove cooking. I also like stainless steel electric fry pans."

"If that is the case, why are you using a non stick pan now?" She asks.

"Good point," I say guiltily. "Because the only pan I could find was one of my mother's non stick pans."

With the butter melted and hot, I place a one inch layer of the fresh hashbrowns in the pan, tap them down gently with the side of a metal spatula, square up the edges, and then put a few dabs of butter on top of them. The butter will slowly melt down to help the center area turn golden, yet won't make the browns greasy.

While they cook, I break the eggs, duck eggs with thick eggshells, spilling their contents into a bowl. I like using duck eggs because they have beautiful orange yolks, clearer whites, and better taste than the chicken egg. I add a little salt, pepper, and ground mustard seed. With one eye still on the browns, because I didn't want them to burn, I whip the eggs. Virginia watches me with great interest, telling me how amazed she is at how I have just enough equipment to bring this all together.

With eggs mixed and ready, I watch the potatoes, waiting for the edges to brown. When I think they are ready, I flip them with my spatula. Whew! They look great. Usually about this time I will lay on some cheese, but I kept this menu simple today, so I packed no cheese. Besides, cheddar contrasts poorly with the omelet ingredients.

When the browns are done, I serve them on plates I picked out especially for our meal. I knew to choose the plate color wisely, as Virginia loves color. So, I picked some square black paper plates, which I thought would contrast nicely with the yellow/gold of the omelet, the white of the sauce and red of the thinly sliced, smoked sockeye salmon.

I wipe the pan, put more butter into it and reheat it. Once the butter is hot, I pour the eggs into the pan to make the omelet, occasionally lifting the edges of the omelet to slide the uncooked egg underneath. When the omelet is ready, I flip it into the air, simultaneously showing off and praying the egg mixture will land in the pan, which it does, making her smile. I breathe a sigh of relief, mentioning to her that I am glad that worked because we don't have any back up eggs (and truth be told, sometimes flipping an omelet doesn't always go that smoothly)!

I lay down some smoked salmon on the cooking eggs, spooning some of the cream cheese-yogurt-chive-garlic-cucumber sauce over the salmon. I want the coolness of the sauce to contrast with the warmth of the omelet. The saltiness of the salmon will also blend nicely with the mixture, forming three layers of flavors. With the omelet cooked, I fold the egg over and then slide the omelet onto the plate. For style, I drizzle the sauce over the top. Somehow, it all works like I planned and looks even better than my test version.

Virginia seems thrilled. We sit down to eat. She smiles at the care I have taken, happy that someone wanted to treat her with such a special meal, even if the cold winds and gray clouds are threatening drizzle.

Between bites, our conversation turns more personal. "I wanted to say one more time how badly I felt about hurting you, " I said. "I don't know if I was on your shit list or not, just another guy who hurt you, but I really thought you were saying goodbye to me in your note, so I went on my way. I just didn't know."

"I can see that now," she says. "Yes, you were a bit on my shit list. But I want you to know that doing this, buying a brand new stove, taking the time to cook this delicious food makes up for it. This is really, really sweet and special. No one has ever done anything quite like this for me."

"I'm sorry to hear that. You deserve to be treated well."

We fall silent, looking at each other, looking out onto the lake, then back at each other. It isn't that we don't have anything to say or don't know what to say. Our eyes are doing the talking. We just want to be here in the same space with each other.

Virginia breaks the silence, wanting to learn more about my time at Roche. "So you went back to Roche two more summers after our summer?"

"Yes, the second summer, 1987, I returned expecting to operate the barbeque again. Instead, in mid-April our head chef and three other cooks quit to run a restaurant in Friday Harbor. That left a huge employee hole within the kitchen. The resort scrambled to find a new head chef and sous-chef, but didn't have time to find others. So, suddenly I was one of the most experienced chefs they had. Even better for me, I knew more of the resort staff than any other cook. So, my value to the new chef doubled, with a raise in my paycheck too. I joined the dinner line, learning more about the sauté and charbroiling positions, once again in a trial-by-fire situation."

"The new chef and sous-chef had experience in southern California and Hawaii, so their recipes included a variety of non-northwestern dishes. They made buerre blanc sauces an important part of the menu, including a crab-stuffed halibut with a lemon-lime buerre blanc sauce that was our most popular dish."

As I pause, she asks, "I've never heard of a buerre blanc sauce. What is it?"

"It is a butter sauce, a tricky one to make. We started with wine, shallots, and a couple peppercorns in a sauté pan. We reduced that mixture until the wine was almost gone. Then, we carefully stirred cuts of butter into it one piece at a time, slowly melting each piece until the sauce became almost the consistency of a thin hollandaise sauce. We had to be careful, because if we added too much butter and it got too cool, it broke, but if it overheated it also broke. So temperature management of the sauce was key. It took me a while to learn to make it. Once made, we could add orange concentrate to make an orange buerre blanc, blended strawberries to make a strawberry buerre blanc, and more."

"That sounds good," she said. "And, it was during the second summer you met your first wife and married her in the rose garden?"

"Yes. Well, we met the second summer and married a few years later."

"I admit that hurt my feelings when you mentioned that in your email. A few years ago a friend flew me up to Roche for lunch. I walked around the rose garden and remembered the special time we had there. I mean, it's fine that you did, but it sort of burst my bubble for that special place."

"I'm sorry. But since my ex and I met at Roche, the garden was a natural spot to marry. And it was a nice wedding, too."

"Yeah, I understand," she says, trying to be brave, but still slightly dejected.

Lightening the mood, I change subjects, "That second year, in 1987, I traded up from Grant's tiny camper. I bought my own trailer and towed it up to Roche. I arrived in April, so I had the pick of locations on the hill reserved for employees. Naturally, I selected the best spot. I not only had running water and electricity, but I also had a porch! The outdoor space of the porch made it feel like my living space was double the size. It was the perfect pad for late evening parties, card games and relaxing. I never locked the door, allowing friends to come and go as they wanted."

"But, the trailer had a few unexpected issues. The first inkling of trouble occurred when I hooked up the hose from Roche's water supply to the trailer. When I twisted open the water valve, instead of the pipes pressurizing and the sound of the running water subsiding, the water continued running into the trailer. This puzzled me. When I went inside to turn the water on in the sink, it didn't work. So, I thought to myself, *if water is going into the camper, but not coming out the faucet, it must be going somewhere else, but where?*"

My aunt and I at my trailer during my 2nd summer at Roche in 1987. Half the pipes in the bathroom were missing, causing water to leak through the bottom of the trailer floor. I had to tear up the bathroom floor to fix it.

"I decided to step outside and look under the camper. Sure enough, water was draining from the underside of the trailer. I thought to myself, *that is not a good thing*! So, after swearing, I turned off the outside water faucet, went inside, and tore apart the bathroom floor. I discovered the water system was missing half the pipes it needed. As water entered the system it drained out the open pipe into the space between the floor of the camper and the bottom of the trailer, which was now full of wet insulation. It appeared the previous owners cannibalized the pipes in the camper for some other purpose, though it didn't look like the floor had been disassembled. In fact, I had to tear up the whole floor in the bathroom . . ."

Virginia interrupts me, "Didn't you test the camper before bringing it up there?"

"You know me. There was little planning involved. Two days before I left for the island I made the decision to purchase the trailer. I took the seller's word for it. Lesson learned."

I continued on, "The next surprise was the leaky roof. Fortunately, I always carried a cheap blue tarp in the jeep, so that was easily fixed – well covered anyway — until I got some silicon. Eventually, everything in the camper worked and it became a fun place to spend the summer. Often, I would return to the camper after a late night in the kitchen and find some party already going, usually led by Cullen. I really enjoyed that."

"I like hearing your stories. And, I loved the food you cooked for me. This is so much fun!"

"I'm enjoying you, too. And I'm happy that I could cook you breakfast," I say, remembering another story. "Oh yeah, did I tell you the story of my grand sailing adventure aboard the USS Hobie Cat in any emails?"

"Nope. It doesn't sound familiar. Will I be laughing with you or at you?"

"A little of both I think. It all started when I found a deal on a Hobie Cat catamaran sailboat that needed repairs in February of 1987. Naturally, having never fixed a boat, I figured I could fix it. So, I bought it, fixed it, and trailered it up to Roche for the summer of 1987."

"Now, you need to understand that the extent of my Hobie sailing experience was acting as first mate on my Uncle's Hobie Cat for a total of a couple miles from a boat dock to my grandmother's dock at age sixteen with my cousin, also aged sixteen, during which we managed to tip it over. With that grand and extensive experience under my belt, I felt I was ready to command a Hobie Cat into the wild swirling waters of the San Juan Islands. I mean, what could possibly go wrong with that?"

Her eyes got big, "Are you crazy? Didn't you know how dangerous that could be!"

"Well, not really. I was too clueless to realize it. I mean what could go wrong with the ocean tides swooshing gazillions of gallons of cold water in and out of the Strait of Juan De Fuca every day? Actually, I figured with all the islands around, that I couldn't get into too much trouble."

My jeep towing the USS Hobie Cat to Roche during the spring of 1987, which was the start of my second year in the San Juan Islands. I used the catamaran once, but that one trip was a memorable one.

"The one thing I hadn't thought through — like there was *only* one thing I hadn't thought through — was that the wind was the strongest when the weather was cold, cloudy or stormy. Of course, I didn't have wet suits either, which just meant that I'd have to wait for warm weather before attempting to sail, not that the water was much warmer even during the height of summer. I can't even remember if we had life preservers, though I'm pretty sure we didn't. Such was the extent of my planning, or failure-to-plan, for this adventure."

"Don't let me interrupt your story," she tells me, "But let me clean up. By the way, I am amazed you made it out of Roche alive!"

"Yeah, I've done some dumb things, but have survived them all so far! Anyway, in July some nice weather and wind finally arrived. On the fateful day, Cullen had to work, but my friend David and I both had the day off. With the wind and the weather meeting my crude expectations, I went searching for David to ask him if he wanted to go sailing. He said yes, which makes me wonder if he knew how little I knew about sailing. I'm also unsure whether Cullen understood the trouble we could get ourselves into when we told him what we were going to do while grabbing lunch supplies at the store before leaving."

"As usual, the plan was more a shell of an idea. We would sail out of Roche Harbor northward between Pearl and Henry Islands. Then, we could shoot across Spieden Channel, stop, eat some lunch, and return back to Roche. I was hoping it might take a couple hours. It seemed like a fine plan in my head. David didn't seem real concerned about where we were going, but was all up for the adventure of just going, as his sailing experience about equaled mine, maybe less."

"And everything went according to plan, up to a point. The most important thing we discovered, after sliding the catamaran off of its tiny trailer into the water was that my winter repairs to the Hobie Cat's hull worked and it floated without retaining water. That was a moral victory for me right there!"

"Next, we both climbed aboard, bringing a cooler packed with sandwiches and some water bottles. With the catamaran pointed the direction we wanted to travel, I hoisted the main and jib sails. The blowing wind caught the sails, slowly taking us out of the harbor. It was really easy. We even saw a deer swimming off to the side as we exited the harbor."

"We were fairly cautious at first, slowly tightening the sails until we picked up a little speed. Buoyed by our success, we tightened the sails a little more until we were gliding along on one pontoon, with the other pontoon about a foot in the air. It was just like the movies, water raced beneath us, making it appear we actually knew what we were doing."

"I can't say whether the trip across Spieden Channel took twenty-five minutes or forty-five minutes, because we were so thoroughly enjoying our time. Heading due north, we soon found ourselves nearing the southern shore of Spieden Island with Stuart Island about a mile to the northwest of us. Beyond that is Canada. Having made it this far, we both felt it was time to stop and eat, before turning around and sailing back."

"So we dropped the sails and, having no anchor, drifted. Then we opened the cooler, pulled out some sandwiches and chips, and enjoyed this once in a lifetime opportunity to dine on a fifteen foot catamaran with an amazing view in every direction. It seemed like everything was going our way, even the wind stopped blowing so that we could eat without any sandwich wrappers blowing away."

"I wish I could have been there. That must have been beautiful," says Virginia, putting the leftover hashbrowns and butter into the cooler.

"Yes, it was sublime, as we felt very small surrounded by water and islands. Once finished with our lunch, we raised the sails and readied the cat for our return trip."

Pausing, I raise my voice a little. "But, then a funny thing happened."

I pause again for effect, laughing at the memory, "That wind that had stopped blowing so we could eat our lunch, didn't realize it was time to start blowing again. It had died . . . dead . . . dead calm, going nowhere dead calm. Well, that actually wasn't true, we were going somewhere, because the water was going somewhere. The water was going west and taking us with it. But hey, the wind would return right?"

Virginia shrugs her shoulders, "You tell me."

"Well, we thought it would return. For about the first hour we joked, relaxed and enjoyed our time on the water. The sun was high, the sky cloudless, and the temperature was a perfect mid-eighties. For us it was just an unexpected adventure. However, as hour one turned to hour two, a couple important issues became clear. First, the wind was still not cooperating and, second, we were drifting toward Haro Straight and Canada."

"As hour two stretched into hour three, the seriousness of our situation began to dawn on us. It didn't take a sophisticated sailor to see Poseidon's plan. He was pulling us straight west to Canada and the shipping lanes. Now, I wouldn't say we were scared or anything, as we both realized that even if we got sucked into the middle of Haro Straight, some large boat or ship would probably spot us, eventually, and radio for help. After all, we'd look pretty silly — well stupid — drifting about the international border."

"We did have one big concern, though. What would happen to us if we didn't get to Haro straight until dark. With no lights on the Hobie Cat, we wouldn't be seen until the next day."

"Because of that, we decided to start rowing. Without oars, this seemed near impossible. If the water was warmer, we could have jumped into it and swam to our destination, but given the water temperature, that wouldn't work. So, we had to improvise. We took an inventory of our assets. We had a cooler, a camera bag, some sails, some rope, and our crazy selves. None of these items seemed practical for paddling until we remembered that the cooler lid was removable."

"Aha!," I shout with emphasis, aiming my pointer finger to the sky. "With cooler lid in hand, we now had our first tool. Next we had to make a second decision, to which island do we row? Given the direction of the water current coupled with our distance from Roche Harbor, we felt our best hope, our only hope, was to steer the catamaran to Stuart Island."

"Does anyone live there?" Asks Virginia, "I know there is a lighthouse, but I've never been on the island."

"Well, neither David nor I really knew anything about the island. All we knew was that the ferry didn't go there. However, it was a large enough island to offer us hope and was far better than drifting to Canada, though that might have been quite the adventure too . . ."

She interjects, "I think you would have liked drifting all the way to Canada." She is right. That would have been a great story to tell, assuming we survived to tell it.

"True. Besides, I have always enjoyed Canadians. However, in the midst of our situation, Canada wasn't our favored option. Over the next hour, with the boat angled for Stuart and the current guiding us west, David and I traded turns paddling with a cooler lid. After trial and error we discovered we could sit on the edge of the Hobie's canvas platform, with one foot on the pontoon, and get some reasonable power into the paddle. Amazingly, this worked. Very slowly, we seemed to be getting closer to Stuart. This buoyed our spirits a bit, so we kept at it. About an hour into paddling, Poseidon sent a gift our way in the form of a piece of driftwood. It was big enough, but not too big, to work quite well as a paddle. Now, with two the paddles, we began to make more progress."

"Around four o'clock in the afternoon Poseidon sent a second gift our direction. It was about that time that when David and I were startled to hear a strange noise due west of us. We both looked in the direction of the sound. David spotted them first, an entire pod of Orca whales surfacing and diving."

"Oh, I always wanted to see them in person. I never did," says Virginia.

"Really? I know I drove you to Whale Watch Point on the west side of the island in my jeep."

"Well, we never saw them. Besides, I think we spent more time sitting on that rock looking at each other than watching for whales."

"Good point," I say, smiling. "Well, I think I can show you how they sounded. Try this. Breathe in, close your lips, and purse them slightly. Then breathe outward, putting pressure on your lips and blowing them steadily outward, simulating a blowhole. The exhale should create a whoosh. It's the same sound that your husband might make in bed at night, not quite a snore, but certainly an exhale. The whoosh is the sound I heard as the whales surfaced and breathed."

Closing her eyes and lips, she blows slowly, then tries it again. Opening her eyes, she says, "I can imagine the sound, but I would prefer to think of it the way you describe it rather than imagining it as the sound of my husband snoring."

"Point taken. But, yes, it was amazing to hear. David and I stopped paddling, looked at each other, smiled, then listened and watched as the huge creatures swam away. It was a wonderful few minutes."

"So, while I had seen the whales a few times from the island, there was something mystical about being on the water, just them and us, that made it memorable. The sound of their breathing was richer and fuller than any other time I'd experienced it. This adventure was a lifetime highlight. When the whales disappeared, we returned to our paddling."

"At this point we were racing against time and the current, so we paddled as hard as we could. Our arms got sore. By early evening we were tired of paddling and adventure. Though Stuart Island was getting closer, due to the tide pulling us west, we had passed several points we had hoped to reach, so we were concerned we might miss the island altogether."

"Finally, at twilight, we overcame the current and landed on Stuart Island. Dry land felt fantastic. We pulled the boat as far as we could up the beach and tied it to a log, uncertain how far from help we were. We climbed off the beach and up a steep embankment, found level ground and a wide trail. We walked a while until we spotted a cabin that, to our surprise, seemed to be occupied."

"David and I approached the door and knocked, which probably shocked the occupants. Despite how we might have looked after our long day, the couple who answered the door was very nice and immediately offered the use of their cell phone – a device that amazed me at the time, having never seen one – asking us to keep the phone call short, as we actually had to call Canada and then route the call back to the U.S. in order to contact Cullen, our only hope of rescue."

"What we didn't know at the time was that Cullen had ended his shift at work and become concerned by our absence. He concluded, correctly, that we'd probably gotten ourselves into some kind of trouble and, without any way to communicate, needed his help. Though he had lived at Roche a number of years, he'd never owned a boat of his own. So, he had to pull some favors to convince the head of operations to let him use a small runabout boat to search for us. Apparently, he'd cruised all over, but couldn't see us. He had just returned to the harbor to get more fuel when he heard an announcement over the loud speaker, asking him to take a call, our call. The timing couldn't have been more perfect, especially with dusk approaching."

"After some well-deserved sarcasm highlighting our stupidity, Cullen filled the gas tank and raced to the south shore of Stuart Island. We thanked our hospitable saviors, who wouldn't take any money for the phone call, and hiked back to the boat."

"Because it was getting darker, we raised the sail so Cullen could find us, which he soon did. With the adventure over, we made our way back to Roche Harbor, the catamaran in tow. While it took all day for us to reach Stuart Island, it only took about forty minutes to be towed back to Roche. When we arrived at the dock, because we were slightly embarrassed that we had needed saving, we were thankful for the darkness. No one had seen us get towed back. Not surprisingly, that was the first and last time I ever took out the USS Hobie Cat."

Virginia thanks me for my story, noting, "I'm glad I wasn't there to see it in person or wonder where you were. I have never been lost on a sailboat, but I did get lost in Hong Kong once. I think I like getting lost on dry land better," She stops and looks down at her watch. "Unfortunately, I need to get to work soon."

"I understand," I say, wishing we could have more time. Our entire morning together lasted just over an hour at this point.

Helping me carry the cooking supplies back to my car, she has more to say, "I want to tell you, again, how much I appreciate the breakfast you made. It was wonderful."

"You are very welcome." I respond, adding, "By the way, I created that little meal just for you. I won't make that omelet for anyone else. That is something special just for you and me."

We fall silent as we approach her car. It seems she wants to say something. Suddenly, she blurts out, "I'm so attracted to you. I know it's not right, but I can't help it. I should say goodbye and wish you luck, but I don't want to let you go. I can't let you go. My mind is whirling. I'd love to have you in my life as a friend, yet when we are together I want so much more. It feels so good to be around you. I honestly don't know what to do."

"I understand that. I'm not trying to force myself on you and I don't want to make promises I can't keep. I really feel like I am supposed to be in your life in some manner. I'm not asking you to do anything other than be my friend. I would feel wrong to ask much more than that, because we both have life issues to manage."

"Are you really leaving tomorrow for Boise?"

"Yes, but no. I'm leaving for Spokane tomorrow and then will travel to Boise. I need to get back and get ready to move. I have plenty to do."

"Are you sure you won't be around Friday or Saturday night?"

I pause. That is code for *I will be alone those two nights*, but for reasons I didn't know. Frankly, I didn't want to know. I felt that if we spent the evening together, we would probably end up in bed.

What I didn't know, which she would later admit to me, is that she was so scared of being alone in her house that she wanted me to come over to feel safe.

"No, I won't be around. I must get back."

Opening her car door, she turns to face me. "Dave, as much as I enjoy your emails, I'm wondering if we shouldn't stop. They are too hard for me. I am addicted to them. You write so beautifully, but, maybe every so often would be better?"

Was this her way of giving me a chance to back off? I wonder if it is a test to see how serious I am about her. On the other hand, it is easy for me to believe my emails are throwing her life off balance. I think she does want rebalance and to try to understand how I might fit into her life, both in a short-term and long-term manner. The complexities of her reality are all too apparent.

"Virginia, I don't want to be a burden to you. I can ease up on the emailing if it helps you. However, I don't want to lose touch with you. At the very least I can be a good friend."

She smiles, "Ok my friend, we both need to run. Let's stay in touch and let me know when you are back in Seattle."

"That sounds good. Enjoy your day Virginia."

"You too Dave."

I wonder whether this is the last time we will ever see one another. I know neither of us wants to say goodbye. I feel my heart ripping a little as we drive away in different directions.

• • • •

I am barely out of the park before when I realize I want to share more. I drive to the closest coffee shop, the Caffe Felicia at the Renton Landing. I order a black tea, needing some caffeine to focus my thoughts, but before taking a sip I open my computer and write Virginia an email:

May 24th, 2011 – 1:05 PM

Virginia,

I need to send a note. Thanks so much for spending the time with me. I do appreciate the time, along with our renewed friendship.

You are, in such a deep and rich way, the same person I met so long ago. I now understand why I kept the letter and the pictures; it was for the same reason I landed on your S$%t list. Maybe we just didn't know how to convey those feelings so long ago and tripped over ourselves in the process?

> *Even if the thoughts of 'what-could-have-been' inflict a bit of torture on my weary heart (now that I understand how you felt), it feels good just to feel again.*
>
> *If you need anything, just let me know.*
>
> *- Dave*

And perhaps that is the most important thing: I feel again. It feels good to open my heart. I am not afraid of being hurt by Virginia, because hurting me will only happen with the best of intentions (being responsible to others she loves). No, it will not feel good, but to feel the hurt, to feel something I had boxed out long ago, is rejuvenating in its own way.

She soon responds to my email:

May 24th, 2011 – 1:25 PM

> *Dave,*
>
> *Not just your heart. I never told you I would be alone Friday and Saturday nights, for fear we could not resist the chance to spend time together. I wished you could stay with me, even if it was just for time spent, not mischief. I realize that was just wishful thinking and not at all based on reality.*
>
> *I drank you in and savored your creation. I cannot remember ever feeling so deeply warm. I keep replaying our brief encounter. My mind has not been on my tasks at hand. I took mental pictures of you, for me, to hold dear after you held my photos and notes so dear.*
>
> *Switching gears here, the encounter was flawless. However, (if I am your friend) I will tell you to wash that orange shirt, my dear. I hesitate to say. I do not want to hurt your feelings, but I do not want you embarrassed.*
>
> *You are so attractive to me after all these years. I am in a daze. I realize you will be out looking for someone soon and will probably get involved. I must face that and accept my responsibilities. I have no right to feel a loss. Of course I wish you the best of everything.*

I have become addicted to your emails. I must let go. It sounds as though you were saying good-bye, so shall I. You made me feel very special, VERY SPECIAL! For that I will not forget you for even a day. Thank you for letting me know that I could ask you for anything. Thank you for everything!

Love Virginia

I pull my pumpkin colored turtleneck to my nose. She is right, my shirt really did smell a little musky. Again, honesty delivered so directly is refreshing. My ego is not so fragile that I need yes-people around me. I need someone who will tell me if I smell, feel safe to say my singing isn't all that good, and to mention something doesn't match. Virginia's magic is that she can do it with tact.

I dash off another note:

May 24th, 2011 – 2:00 PM

Virginia,

When you mentioned Friday/Saturday night at the park, I immediately knew you had the time alone. I could tell by your voice, your eyes . . . well, somehow I knew. And, I knew it wasn't for mischief, but I believe you feel my energy like I feel yours. I know that warmth you mentioned and feel it too. It's a really safe place, being with you. It always was and, apparently, still is. I don't understand it and can't quantify it, but it's there. And, it is the reason I can be, at the very least, your friend, forever.

And, as much as I would want to be there (or anywhere) with you for a longer period of time in that intimate of a setting, I'd rather wait for a time when we could be alone in a more neutral setting, because I doubt either of us would be completely relaxed there.

I am definitely not looking for someone else. I would rather be single for a while. What I really want to find is some peace, and for our short time together I found it. I've learned that peace is a really rare commodity in my life; but today I got to bask in it, nothing else mattered. That is truly special.

I told my mother today that it was time to move up here, for the reasons I discussed with you today. She seemed to understand that I was serious about it, too.

Regarding the emails, it seems I both hurt you and lost you last time because I didn't write back after your long ago letter. So, I'm having a little problem not writing back when you write (my issue, I know). But, I'll reduce their frequency to help you, as I'm sure these are as gratifying as they are distracting/confusing.

Sorry about the stinky shirt. It was the first time I wore it on the trip, so I'm not sure why it was stinky. Now that you mention it, I have noticed that some shirts do seem to make me more smelly than others. I probably don't notice so much anymore, so I do appreciate your honest feedback :-)

As usual with us, there was plenty more we wanted to say and share and not enough time. I'm confident we'll get to enjoy each other's company and confidence, silliness and frustrations, kindness and thoughtfulness. Until our paths intersect, remember I'm only an email or phone call away.

It seems fitting that when I drive away, I'll do it heading east, into a sunrise, though technically it's almost midday, but that messes up my metaphor.

So, for my purposes, it's a sunrise and a new day, a new week. Once again you've managed to enter my life and make it richer. I may not be the smartest guy in the world, but even I have lived long enough to know that having someone enrich your life twice doesn't happen every day.

So, I'm toasting you with my black tea, to our future, however that may be, for we still have a script to write.

Finally, I can't say goodbye and don't want to, so I won't (it's my script)! :-) Instead, I'd rather think of this visit as a big hello. Besides, I need to spend some time working out my stuff (finances, family health issues, etc), so just to know you are still out there and still care really does mean the world.

Love Dave.

I am not the only one who wants to maintain contact, for she returns a letter a few hours later:

May 24th, 2011 – 6:09 PM

David,

Great , all great. You are right. I wanted something I knew neither of us could handle. I knew it. That is great that you could read my eyes.

I cannot help writing back either. I am glad you spoke to your mom. I think you are doing the right thing. Your script unfolds. I am glad you and I had peace and began friendship. I am glad we talked about the past and our perceptions.

Maybe we could see each other in the morning tomorrow. Bad idea?

Virginia

After an exchange of emails in which we agreed to meet at ten o'clock in the morning at the park one more time on my way out of town, she writes the following mournful note:

May 24th, 2011 – 8:52 PM

David,

Here it is almost 8pm. I am home with my son and no word at all from Larry. No wonder I am starving for the gesture you brought to me. I can see your face telling me, I am the only one whose special mementos were treasured through all kinds of life changes. Dave, I am still-blown away . . .

Virginia

She needs a friend, someone to listen and respond:

May 24th, 2011 – 9:09 PM

Virginia,

Not calling and it's 8pm? Well . . . I'll just stop there. Yeah, you should feel frustrated by that.

There was never any question about keeping the letter. Like I said, I didn't know exactly why I kept it as time passed, I just knew I couldn't get rid of it. I suppose that's why I contacted you, because I just had to know what happened to you. But, now I know why I kept it; you are something special .... and you should hear that more often!

- Dave

Still awaiting her husband, she expresses her disbelief once again.

May 24th, 2011 – 9:38 PM

Dave,

I cannot get enough of you telling me the details of how you treasured my card and photos.

I keep going to my laptop to see if you have responded. BTW I have never had an email relationship. NEVER!

V

That makes me laugh a little. I have been using email for years. Much of my world is virtual, collections of bits and bytes.

May 24th, 2011 – 9:53 PM

Virginia,

I've used email intensively for 12 years, so I've just about got the hang of it. Maybe if I practice more with you I'll really get it down!

Tomorrow afternoon I'm driving over to Deer Park to meet a guy named Dan and then heading down to Spokane to spend the night at my cousin's place. She is an absolute sweetheart — kind and full of love. It will be good to connect with her, as I haven't seen nearly enough of her.

- Dave

• • • •

That night while exchanging emails with Virginia and updating eWillys, I sit in the living room near Dad and talk with him a little. He is mumbling more, retaining little information, repeating questions recently answered. I leave the living room and speak with Mom. We are both worried and both see the same decline. I tell her I can stay if necessary, but she tells me to leave, that she will be fine. If she needs help, she will call my aunt.

Besides, I knew she had already made an appointment with the doctor and is waiting for the scheduled day. Hopefully, we will know more after that visit. Until then, I am resigned to leaving and she is resigned to returning to 24/7 care and another evening of running from the kitchen to the bedroom, as Dad's mournful cries begin anew, every fifteen minutes, once he goes to bed.

• • • •

Virginia and I meet Wednesday, as agreed. The meeting is brief. We promise to keep in touch, we hug, and we say goodbye. Though we never say we love each other, we know it. We have a bond that time hasn't broken, that I believe will remain forever, no matter our future paths. I have renewed confidence that we will see each other again, but I do not know when.

13. JUNE 1986: I START WORK AT ROCHE

Arriving at Roche Harbor on June 7th, 1986, one day later than planned due to my sleepover in Anacortes, I parked my jeep next to a shiny aluminum camper that would be my home for the summer. I describe it as shiny aluminum because Grant used sheets of glossy aluminum on the outside of it. There was no other way to illustrate it!

I arrived a few days early to acclimate and also to explore the island before starting work. Within days, I was being called Jeep Dave, which was better than "the Dave who lives in the aluminum camper".

Growing up in elementary school, I was never just 'Dave' or 'David'. I was 'David E'. The obvious reason for this was the proliferation of kids with the name David. It's a big part of the reason why I was in agreement with my ex-wife to provide unusual names for our children. Neither of us wanted their names to be arbitrary or capricious; they had to be grounded in their family's history or mark a milestone in some way.

So, I was not surprised when, at the start of the summer of 1986, I discovered there were a bunch of Davids working at Roche Harbor. There was the aforementioned David, asking not to be called anything else, who maintained restaurant inventory and with whom I became good friends. There was Dave the operations manager. There was David the restaurant server. There was Dave the bartender, who worked at the bar below the restaurant. There was a Dave who worked the boat docks. And then there was me. Naturally, we all needed ways to keep track of the different Davids, so various nicknames were employed. Given I drove a jeep, and an unusual jeep at that, I became "Jeep Dave".

The person who christened me Jeep Dave was Cullen Finley. I met Cullen on my second day at the resort. At the time, in 1986, about one hundred yards or so behind where the hotel is located (before they built homes there) the resort owners allowed workers to stay onsite in campers for the season. That is Grant kept his camper, so it is where I lived that summer.

It was a custom slide-in camper, shaped like the type normally carried on the back of a pickup truck. The interior was homemade and felt like the inside of a boat, probably because Grant was a boat builder. A queen size bed was located in the cab-over area of the camper. Above the bed was a plexiglass hatch that swung open, so if I wanted some fresh air or to look at the stars, I could open the hinged hatch and lay it on the roof. There was a small sink, stove and refrigerator. It also included a portable toilet that I had to carry to a sewer line to dump; therefore I seldom used it. In other words, there was no standard flush toilet, nor was there a shower. Fortunately, there were toilets and pay showers next to the post office at Roche, normally used by boaters.

After settling into my new home — which really was my home, however temporary it was, because everything I owned was with me — it was time to explore. Since the day was warm, I was dressed in a jeans and a t-shirt, my standard outfit. Without a map, I crossed the road near my new home, the one that wound down to the harbor, and stepped onto a dirt road that led south into a forest. Seeing no "Keep Out" or "No Trespassing" signs, I ventured forth, unsure of what I would find, not knowing if I was still on resort property or on private property.

While exploring, I climbed an upward sloping path that was wide enough for a jeep. As I walked higher, the forest canopy gave way to an opening with a view to the west and north that overlooked Roche Harbor. Beyond the harbor were views of Henry Island and Stuart Island and the tops of the Canadian Gulf Islands on the horizon. It was as beautiful as it was unexpected.

I stood soaking in the view on the warm June day, when unexpected voices behind me interrupted the peace. I turned to discover two guys sitting around a small fire pit with a tent behind them. I hadn't seen them as I walked up the path because they were hidden behind a rock outcropping, obviously trying to hide from the occasional hiker. I walked over and introduced myself, meeting Tim, a resort gardener for the summer, and a read-head named Cullen, who worked at Roche's store.

This is the view from Cullen's former camping spot. Spieden Island is the bare island off to the right. The Canadian Gulf Islands are in the background.

Cullen was a bundle of energy with a hard working and loyal attitude. He was eighteen, just graduated from high school, and the tent was his home. Originally born in Michigan, he spent his teen years in the Roche Harbor area after a traumatic boat trip. It seems his mom and dad decided to move from Michigan to San Diego. In San Diego they bought a boat and cruised up the West Coast to Roche Harbor.

Apparently, it scared the living hell out of them — the ocean can have that effect on people — to the point that they never took the boat anywhere again. They settled into a slip at Roche Harbor where his parents became integrated into the daily life of the tiny community, with

Cullen's mother becoming postmaster. The funny thing about the post office was that it wasn't an office at all — I've seen bigger hot dog stands. Instead, it was a tiny little room with a dutch-door; this allowed only the top part of the door to be opened. The office was located on the dock, integrated into the side of the old General Store. The view of the hotel, restaurant, docks, and rose gardens just might have been the prettiest view from a post office in the whole country!

Growing up on a forty-foot boat and not getting along with his father real well, Cullen couldn't wait to get off the boat. He was a smart guy, even qualifying for West Point, but he didn't go (I don't remember what happened). So, he stayed on the island, lived in his tent and worked in the store until something else came along.

Cullen and I quickly became close friends. During that summer, we found ourselves involved in all kinds of adventures, from late night explorations of the mausoleum to jeeping in places on the island only a local would know. For me, he was my key, my entry card into local life. I became more accepted as an islander rather than simply a seasonal worker. For him, the fact I was reasonably intelligent and had decided to forgo college for a while provided him with a kindred spirit, reassuring him that he wasn't alone in choosing not to go to college. Also, because of our attitudes and the jeep, adventure together appeared around every bend. Mostly though, we meshed well and trusted each other. What was mine was his and his mine. I felt comfortable throwing him my keys to the jeep so he could use it when I was working. Conversely, if I wanted to borrow his scooter I could take that.

We were both competitive and challenged each other in all kinds of games. However, we also had our specialties, his being tennis — he beat me every single time — and mine being basketball, which I won most days. However, that summer we played little of either, instead choosing to play hours and hours of ping-pong, card games (hearts and rummy), and karate video games. The best thing about ping-pong was that the table was under a cover in the pool area, with views of the bikini-clad female tourists, which explains why we played so much ping-pong. Well, that, and the fact that his fine-looking friend, Christy, was the manager of the pool area, so we could wander in at midnight, turn on the lights, and play for as long as we wanted. It turns out Christy and I had a bit of a crush on each other and only Cullen knew that. And Cullen strangely didn't think that was something Christy and I should know about the other.

Though, I quickly developed a social life at Roche, my purpose up there was to cook and that was the part of my life I had to figure out for myself. I had to learn to sauté, to use a six burner stove, a charbroiler, a convection oven, a meat oven, an auto-sham (a refrigerator-sized warming unit), and how to properly use and take care of knives.

Early on, Grant watched over me and offered advice, but he was the dinner sous-chef while I, for the most part, worked during the mornings and lunch. I was starting over, learning how to cook again, expanding my knowledge beyond burgers, fries and short-order breakfasts.

Not long after I started, one of the cooks befriended me, a guy we called Big Ron. Ron worked as a chef at Washington State University on the mainland during most of the year and lived in Friday Harbor at his mom's place over the University's summer break. While staying on the island, he earned extra money at Roche Harbor. He showed me how to function in a big kitchen and shared stories of his time at a culinary school. He treated people fairly, was fun to work with, and taught me a variety of new skills. He also taught me how to catch an octopus, using both legal and illegal methods.

One thing I'd learned while completing my diving certification is that Puget Sound is home to some of the biggest octopus in the world, growing to ten feet in length. Being pretty large, an octopus gets hungry from time-to-time and, during high tides, they will venture very close to the shore, burying themselves under rocks near the shore to eat crab or other delicacies.

According to Ron, sometimes an octopus gets so focused eating that it forgets that the tide recedes. They often get stuck beneath a rock, high and dry, with no water around them. So, they must wait for the tide to rise once again. The strategy of the wily octopus hunter is to investigate large rocks on the beach following an extreme high/low tide to see if there are any pieces of shellfish kicked out from underneath the sides of it; find a rock with pieces and there may be an octopus underneath it.

According to Ron, there were two ways to catch an octopus. The way he did it was to mix some bleach and water together in a spray bottle to temporarily blind the octopus so he could reach under the rock, grab it and pull it out. He felt that was the most humane way to catch it.

But doing that was illegal he said. Instead, again according to Ron, the fish and game folks requested hunters use a hook, similar to a hay bale hook. This time the hunter must reach underneath the rock with the hook and try to swipe the octopus with the hook, pulling it out. To me this hardly seems a pain-free experience for the octopus. In my opinion, the bleach/water mixture seems less invasive than piercing a leg with a sharp hook and wrenching it out.

Now it's one thing to talk about hunting an octopus, it's another thing to watch it happen. One day, Ron invited me to catch an octopus, to which I agreed. The next morning we went looking for them. It was gray and slightly chilly. I thought we would have to search all morning to find an octopus, but instead it took Ron only two minutes to locate a rock with the telltale signs. We dug out the sand around the rock a little bit and, sure enough, we could see something was hiding underneath it. Ron looked around to make sure no one else was watching, then bent down to the rock and squirted a little bleach/water mixture. The octopus immediately rocketed from underneath the rock. Ron grabbed it by the tentacles, pulling it to a bucket of salt water he had ready. The great hunt was over before it had barely begun. Ron said he would take it home, kill it and gently smoke it. One day he shared his finished octopus with me; it was tender and delicious!

Ron became a good friend and ally in the restaurant. About ten years older than me and certainly more experienced, he was gracious enough to teach me a few things about cooking and surviving the politics of the restaurant. It was he who taught us how easily hollandaise sauce could be made.

Though we had served hollandaise at the BurgerWorks, ladling it over eggs benedict and hashbrowns, it was always the Knorr Swiss packaged variety (which works fine for some applications). At Roche, how to make Hollandaise from scratch was one of the first things I learned. It was a moderately difficult and time-consuming sauce to make, or so I was told while watching a couple different chefs whisk eggs, lemon juice, and melted butter for nearly 20 minutes until they created a large bowl of fresh hollandaise. The tricky part is the beginning. We started with some egg yolks, a little water, and some lemon juice. They were combined and slowly heated, while stirring constantly. When the yolk mixture was hot, but not so hot the eggs curdled into scrambled eggs, melted butter was carefully whipped into it. Once enough butter was added and enough sauce was in the bowl, then the process became less difficult, though by that time a cook's arms were very tired of stirring the wire whisk, making the cook wish they were an accountant, bus driver or anything else.

One day Ron asked the morning chef, Joe, if he had ever made hollandaise in a food processor. Now Joe was an odd guy with a few strange behaviors. For example, he would light order tickets on fire if he didn't like the way the server had written them. I saw him do it. He just laughed. I stared, thinking, *did that seriously just happen?* I never liked working with Joe.

With Joe looking at him suspiciously, Ron, who didn't like Joe either, asked Joe why he still used the "old" method. Joe asked what he meant. Ron replied that he could use a food processor to quickly make hollandaise sauce. Joe thought Ron was nuts. So, Ron, Joe and I walked around the corner of the kitchen to a prep area where Ron had warm butter, egg yolks, lemon and a little water staged, ready to make sauce. As we watched, he poured the ingredients into the food processor and, in moments, had hollandaise sauce. Ron smiled, while Joe shook his head, unsure he had seen what he just saw, but to his credit, said it would be worth trying.

That's why I liked Ron. He was a nice, funny guy who always had good ideas and was willing to share them. Yet, I wouldn't work directly with Ron for very long, because management decided they had a higher calling for me.

It turns out, that besides running a restaurant, the folks at Roche liked to have an outdoor barbecue, too. For reasons only known to Reaf, the head chef, I was offered the opportunity to run it. As the barbecue chef, it was my duty, every single night for the summer, weather permitting, to run an outdoor barbecue that might serve up to one hundred people a night. This wasn't some six-dollar buffet barbecue; the owners wanted it one step below the fine dining that was available inside the restaurant. I didn't really understand this or several other important details, but I said yes anyway, because it was something new to try. I remember Ron's reaction when I told him I had been offered and accepted the new position. His worried look said it all, asking me if I was sure this was the right thing to do. Cullen's reaction mirrored Ron's. He warned against it. I wondered if I had made a mistake.

Yet I liked the idea of being on my own, of being in charge of my own destiny. One of my friends, Jack, after working with him at ManyOne Networks a few years ago, told me that he thought I was happiest when I could manage a risky situation. He meant that when I was in control of a difficult project, when there was no preordained success or failure, I was happiest because hard projects and high risk challenge me. Jack nailed me perfectly.

And that explains why I jumped at the chance to operate the barbecue: I was in charge. I did all the cooking, I directed the waitstaff and had the responsibility of satisfying the customers. I believed it could work because I wouldn't give up until it did, but there were some challenges.

I return to the former barbeque area in 2011. Ivy covered some of the area and a large tree grew to the left of the fireplace. Customers ate at tables on the grass. My wide arms attempt to describe the width of the barbeque I used in 1986.

For example, I had never cooked any of the items on the menu. I had never cooked salmon, I had never cooked halibut, I had never cooked a real steak, either ribeye or new york, I had never cooked ribs, and I had never cooked a half of a chicken. Since that represented all the main course items on the menu, my learning curve was one helluva upward slope. And, just to turn up the heat on the challenge, I would be cooking over large pieces of mesquite on a half-barrel grill — no gas — something else new to me.

Also, I did not know that the last two summers of outdoor barbeque had gone poorly, which explained Ron and Cullen's reactions when they learned about my new position. Not only was management concerned about it failing again, but they'd also decided, I learned later, if it didn't work this time, they would no longer offer the barbeque. It's a good thing

I didn't know all that, because the extra pressure wouldn't have helped. Unaware, I jumped fully into the situation assuming the barbeque would succeed.

The first thing Reaf taught me about the barbeque was that I was my own prep cook along with being cook. I also told me I had to carry all the ceramic — no paper or plastic — dishes out to the barbeque. This was a daily workout. Nestled inside plastic milk crates, I carried them two-crates at a time down the back steps of the restaurant, up a full flight of stairs, along the blacktop road, and down and up a few more stairs to the elevated barbeque area. Every night I had to stock my barbeque kitchen with supplies (food, utensils, charcoal and anything else) and, once done cooking, would have to bring them back to the restaurant to be washed.

One thing I didn't have to do was the salad bar, well most nights anyway, because there was somebody assigned to do that. During the summer, I went through a variety of salad bar helpers. One of the more memorable ones I had was a beautiful student on summer break from her biology studies. She had cute cropped blond hair, blue eyes, and a quick wit. She liked to analyze and point out various body parts of shellfish. She was a kick.

Reaf suggested I arrive at 2pm, get everything prepped inside the restaurant before 5pm. This included filleting salmon or halibut, which was one of my favorite parts of the job. I learned that with a salmon one could either remove the fine rib bones and work downward to the spine or fillet down the spine first and then carefully carve out the rib bones. I always preferred the latter method, but a couple chefs I watched were really proficient with the former method.

One of the handiest skills I learned was how to remove fish skin. For example, to remove the skin on salmon, fillet it first. Once filleted into two halves, find a large dull chef's knife (for most people that is likely the only chef's knife they have). Lay a fillet on a large surface skin-side down. Put your left-hand fingers on the tail of the fish. Then cut into the fishtail's meat near your fingers with the blade angled down at a twenty-five degree angle and slide under the meat. A dull knife won't cut through the skin, so the angled blade should separate the skin and the meat. As the knife moves along, shift your left-hand forward so it can grasp more skin, which makes the process easier. When done correctly, no meat remains on the skin; the result will be a perfect fillet ready to portion into smaller sizes.

Once I had all my prep done, I walked to the barbeque, put some blackened pieces of mesquite in the two half-barrels, and lit the mesquite. It took an hour for the mesquite to reach high enough temperatures to cook. While waiting for it to heat, I carried out all the prepped food and readied it for the night. At 6pm, with everyone ready, we opened.

The barbeque area was a grass courtyard north of the hotel with a grand fireplace on a raised concrete platform. I positioned the barbeque in front of the fireplace, whose mantle read "Friendship's Fires Are Always Burning". The cooking area was my stage, three feet above and facing the long grass lawn where people dined. The area had been used for decades as an outdoor party space for banquets and hotel events. Early photographs show large canvas canopies draped above the lawn to keep the rain and sun off guests.

Playing the role of barbeque chef from the stage, I was always on view. Thus, I was careful about what I said and how I did things. When not busy, I smiled, greeted people, and talked with guests. When cooking, I never swore, remained composed, and maintained the flow of food off the grill in a way that best aided the staff. As my experience with the barbeque grew, I enjoyed it more and more. For a shy guy, I'd found a breakthrough role.

Perhaps my biggest failure was not staying clean, because mesquite is black and dirty, the fish marinade I used was buttery, and the barbeque rib sauce was messy. I went through a couple aprons a night, but rarely managed to stay clean.

The barbeque remained open as long as there was daylight. However, at dusk we didn't just hang out a closed sign. Instead, our closing was defined by the announcement of Colors, a nightly tradition at Roche where the flags of Great Britain, Canada, and the United States were lowered at sunset.

As I understand it, resort owner Reuben Tarte started Colors in 1957 after watching a similar ceremony in Canada. Roche's ceremony involves a few employees assuming the role of the Color Guard, marching out to a mast positioned at the end of Roche's pier. On the mast flies the flags. As the Color Guard lowers each flag the national anthem of the country sounds from speakers hidden throughout the resort. Then, a cannon salute marks the end of the evening, often followed by the sounds of boat owners honking their horns.

For the waitstaff, Colors was an opportunity to catch our breath. Because the resort management required us to stop working, we shut down services temporarily. This could be a challenge, because we had to time orders so I didn't finish cooking during Colors, since waitstaff couldn't deliver food or bus tables until the end of the ceremony.

Once Colors finished, the barbeque was closed, except for serving seated customers. We then returned all the equipment, dishes, and left over food back to the restaurant.

Each night, once I was done with my barbeque duties, I checked with the dinner line to see if they needed any help, which they usually did, resulting in plenty of overtime for me. When my evening inside the kitchen ended, so did my night usually, because I was exhausted. As I gained experience, the barbeque became more and more fun for me.

However, before it was fun, it was hell, especially that very first week. We'd opened in late June because the weather was good and we (the waitstaff and I) needed practice before the Fourth of July weekend, the busiest weekend of the season. This was our test week, with our unsuspecting patrons the guinea pigs. Because I had never cooked any of the main dishes, Reaf told me, "Don't worry, I'll be out there to help you. I'll teach you what to do."

That would have been all well and good, except that after cooking only two items, a steak and a piece of fish, an emergency arose in the restaurant and I didn't see him the rest of the night, nor any of the other days that first week. *No wonder the damn barbecue failed year after year; no one ever got properly trained!*

Once he left, I was on my own. Well, I did have the waitstaff. So I muddled through, asking servers, after I cooked each order, if they thought the food appeared cooked correctly. I had zero idea how to tell the difference between a medium-rare and medium-well steak. I didn't know how much to cook a piece of salmon or halibut. It turns out, as I would learn over the ensuing weeks, the waitstaff didn't know much more than I did. To make matters worse, I couldn't start practicing by cooking foods and eating them in front of the guests. So, at the end of each night, I would fix myself something and test the food that way, which helped immensely. I was a nervous wreck during that first week.

We didn't serve many orders that week, maybe thirty or forty total. So, I couldn't have screwed up too badly. But, I did make enough mistakes that the early reviews were mixed. Each day that week I started early, making sure I was prepared. I didn't even charge the restaurant for the first couple hours of my shift. I just wanted to get it right.

About halfway through my second week, I learned Reaf had heard enough about the barbeque — not all good things either — that he was bringing his entire family to test me. It was essentially put up or shut up, pass or fail, sink or swim, choose your favorite. I admit being nervous about it; yet it was also a relief. Maybe I had made a mistake accepting the role. Maybe cooking on a grand stage in front of a big fireplace with a mesquite grill just wasn't my thing. I would soon find out.

On that fateful night, Reaf and a dozen of his family members of all shapes, sizes and ages arrived. Just to complicate things further, it would be the largest single order I had done to date. Even though I knew his family would be there that night, I prepared like every other day. I wanted to treat them like any customer. Okay, truthfully, maybe I did take some special care with them, as my fate was in their hands.

When the server presented the order to me I saw it included everything on the menu in various amounts. I gulped, nervously. I started with the ribs and chicken, which were pre-cooked, and began warming them on the barbeque. Next, I placed the steaks onto the grill near a hotspot to insure the grates charred the meat with marks. When the steaks were halfway done, I placed the salmon and halibut orders over hotspots. One thing I had learned during the past week was that I didn't like overcooked fish, so I wanted to serve the fish barely undercooked.

Though most kitchens have heating lights to keep food warm while it waits to be served, I had no such luxury. Even worse, the outdoor temperatures could cool food quickly. So, I had to complete all the items on an order as closely as possible along with insuring the waitstaff was ready to serve the plates as I finished them. In this particular case, with Reaf's family waiting, I didn't have to cue the waitstaff. They were already queued when I began plating the food, because they understood the significance of the order. The servers looked at the food approvingly as they organized the plates on the trays. They hoisted the trays onto their shoulders, walked down the steps and over to the tables. I always had great respect for the waitstaff's ability to carry multiple plates of food on a tray without dropping it. Personally, I was never comfortable enough carrying a tray to do that.

I held my breath, trying not to stare too intently for reactions. Instead, I stole sideway glances, continuing to cook another order with a faux confidence as I awaited feedback. The first bit of good news was that nothing came back immediately to be re-cooked. Then, about ten minutes into the meal a guy stood up and walked toward me. I smiled, unsure of what to expect, wondering, *Oh God, what now.*

The man stepped to the edge of the lawn where it met my stage. I moved to him, leaned over, and asked, "Is there a problem?"

He responded, "Nope. I just wanted to tell you that was one of the best steaks I've ever had. Great Job!"

Stunned, I thanked him graciously. Then a sense of relief flooded over me; at the same time, I wondered how that possibly could have happened. How could I have cooked such a good steak, because I still felt clueless. What had I done right? All I had done was take a new york cut of steak, put it on the grill, cook it a little, shift it ninety degrees to insure it had intersecting grate marks, cook it some more, flip it one time, make grate marks on the other side, cook it even more, and pull it off the grill. That was the extent of my skill. There was no special sauce, no spices, no nothing. My only involvement was the timing. And even that was a lucky guess. Maybe, I thought, I could get the hang of this.

After Reaf and his family were done eating, he came to me and said I had done an outstanding job. He told me the man who'd approached me was his brother and that his brother had been thrilled with his meal; I was equally thrilled by Reaf's response. From then on I owned the barbeque. Soon, I acquired a new nickname: Barbeque Dave.

From Reaf's perspective, having me run the barbeque was one less headache for him. So with my evaluation complete, I had free reign to do as I pleased, running the barbeque in my own way, choosing my own hours. I worked every time it was open, during high season working forty days in a row. As seasonal servers and salad bar workers came and went, I was the glue that held everything together. It was mine and I felt a responsibility to make it work, because I felt my reputation was on the line. I was Barbeque Dave after all.

At one point, without asking permission, I recruited a guy to play the mandolin at the barbeque. I met him the night before at an evening bonfire where a bunch of us were hanging out after work. He was visiting the resort for a few days and brought his guitar to the campfire. One thing led to another and Cullen and I started singing a John Denver song. The next thing we knew, he began playing the music by ear, having never played the song. Impressed, I asked him if he would come play at the barbeque for a few nights in exchange for anything he wanted for dinner. He was all for it. As promised, he appeared, but instead of the guitar he brought his mandolin. He was wonderful and we all — customers, waitstaff, and I — enjoyed a unique, private concert. I made sure he ate well, too.

One of my favorite experiences was when a group of four guys, two Canadians, one American, and one Brit were visiting for a week late in July. Their first night at Roche they came to the barbeque and ate. They didn't say much, but seemed to enjoy themselves. After eating in the restaurant the next evening, I noticed they were back at the barbeque. The following night they were back again. On the next night, their last one, I learned more about them. They got together annually and, after trying the barbeque and the restaurant, found they preferred the quality of food at the barbeque. Then they bought and gave me a bottle of wine to thank me for making their stay enjoyable. It was a thoughtful gesture and I never forgot it.

That very same week I met Virginia.

14. MAY 25 ᵀᴴ, 2011

On Wednesday, after my brief meeting with Virginia at the park, I begin a five-hour drive east on I-90 bound for Spokane to meet with Dan, an eWillys reader. As I pass through Issaquah, I wonder, *can I see Virginia's house from the Interstate?* Then ask, *can we possibly maintain a friendship with desire haunting us?* Time will tell.

Outside of North Bend, the highway curves upward to Snoqualmie Pass. As often happens, the mountain range corrals the clouds, causing it to rain harder as I get closer to Snoqualmie's summit. My wipers pound rhythmically clearing the water off the windshield. I don't want to listen to music; I want to think and plan. I need to resolve the logistics of packing, the timing of my move, and the best way to break the news to my girlfriend of four years. I also wonder if and when the Boise house will sell and what happens if HAFA fails? I have plenty of issues to resolve.

Dad's health situation is the worst of all. I wonder if I must also prepare for his death. What will it mean for my mother?

Amidst this mental chaos, I have another decision to make: where to be with my kids during their four week visit with me this summer? Perhaps I should stay at my parents, where my kids would offer Mom a welcome distraction from Dad's issues.

The questions seem endless. I tick through them one by one. How can I pay my graduate loans, now in default due to the drop in my income? Should I continue to operate the website? Should I continue to apply for work?

Applying for jobs seems futile as my resume is hardly normal, due to my entrepreneurial activity over the past ten years. The lack of available jobs doesn't help either. In response to the meager job market, some of my friends have falsified their resumes, hoping to snag an interview, calculating that getting an interview with a false resume is better than no interview at all. For one friend this method paid off with a six figure salary. However, that's not my style.

In an effort to clear my mind, I roll down the window to inhale some mountain air as I drive along Lake Kachess, named for an Indian term that means "more fish". It is a man-made reservoir, just east of Snoqualmie Pass. Though the rain has turned to drizzle, the air that blows in is still damp. I roll up the window as I look out over the reservoir, which spring rains and melting snow have filled to the rim; there will be plenty of water this summer. The lake is beautiful when full but ugly when low, with knarled stumps creating a ravaged-looking landscape. It makes a good metaphor for life's ups and downs: when life is full, it is beautiful, and when empty, it can look and feel ugly.

I have seen Lake Kachess at all levels, because my trek from Seattle to Spokane is a familiar one, a path worn by three generations of my family. My mother's parents, my mother and her sister Marilyn, and my sister and I have traced this route since 1934, watching it improve over the years from a slow two-lane highway to the four-lane interstate of today.

My maternal grandparents had moved to Seattle from their rural life in Idaho because my grandfather had earned a degree in aeronautical engineering and went to work for Boeing. My paternal grandparents had retired to Idaho to live in a house that clung to the side of a tall hill above Hayden Lake; there was no backyard and the view of the lake was stunning, but getting to the beach required descending a staircase that zig-zagged back and forth against the hill. Twice a year my parents transported my sister and me out of the green and damp Western Washington to the much drier regions of Spokane and Coeur d'Alene to visit with relatives that remained in the area from both sides of the family.

For me, north Idaho remains a collection of wonderful memories. I explored old farm buildings, rode motorcycles, visited my grandfather's mine, water-skied, played golf, and slept on the porch with my cousins at my grandmother Eilers' Hayden Lake house, awakened by the sounds of squirrels chirping to a summer sunrise.

The Hayden Lake house was a direct reflection of Grandma, because following grandpa's death she lived alone there for ten years. I remember old books on shelves in multiple rooms, polished wood floors, and antiques and art thoughtfully arranged throughout the house. Everything was dusted, floors were swept, and the luxurious throw carpets vacuumed. Yet, it also felt comfortable, calm, and peaceful. She kept a closet full of games for my cousins and me to play, bought books for us to read, cooked plenty of great food, and always seemed to have a pint of my favorite Oregon Blackberry ice cream in her freezer. The sounds from the great room's mahogany clock set the tone for our stays there, ticking the seconds away slowly and heralding the hour marks, never in a hurry.

Grandma always dressed tastefully, wearing nothing flashy. She had beautiful silver-white hair, wore chained reading glasses, and had a timeless elegance about her. She was fully capable of getting her hands dirty landscaping the property or refinishing furniture, yet she had never eaten pizza with her hands, until my cousins and me encouraged her to do so. Despite her polish, she never exuded superiority. Her skills as a gracious hostess reflected her east coast finishing school upbringing. How she wound up at a Lake House in north Idaho is a long story.

Grandma Eilers was the product of Virginia Quaker parents whose lineage stretches back to pre-Revolution American. In 1930, she was nineteen and working as a teacher in lower Manhattan when my thirty-one-year-old grandfather Fritz proposed. Fritz's parents hosted an engagement tea, announcing the event in the New York Times so that women could meet this lucky bride-to-be, for she was marrying into a family who had made millions in the smelting and refining industry.

Today, most people know little about the smelting and refining industry, which, at the simplest level, processes raw ore from mines, extracting the valuable minerals, like wheat from the chaff.

What most people *do know* is that smelting and refining sites are often Superfund sites, polluted areas requiring government money to clean them up. That is how I perceived a company called ASARCO, a huge player in the smelting industry. One of their smelters was near the University of Puget Sound in Tacoma, Washington, where I completed my undergraduate degree. At the time I attended the University, many of ASARCO's structures were still standing. Whenever I rode my bike past the fenced and abandoned buildings, I mentally cursed those involved in the business.

A few years later, interested in researching Dad's family, I was in a narrow aisle among the stacks of the Wisconsin State Historical Library holding a book about mining in my hands. I remember the low ceilings feeling claustrophobic and the buzz of the fluorescent lights breaking the silence. I was just beginning to research my great-great-grandfather Anton's company, called the American Smelting Company. As I leafed through the book's pages, I came across a surprising reference: "American Smelting Company (also known as a ASARCO)".

I blinked. I stopped breathing. I was in the middle of a life changing, holy crap moment. The light dawned.

That is when I realized that the full name of the American Smelting Company, was *American Smelting And Refining Company!!* My great-great-grandfather co-founded the same company I cursed when riding my bike past Tacoma's ASARCO smelter. Holy Crap!

Why hadn't I known that earlier? Because, to that point, all the references I had read about Anton referred to the company as the

American Smelting Company, shortening it from its official name of American Smelting and Refining Company for obvious reasons. Then, in 1975 the company changed its name to the acronym ASARCO. Because I had grown up hearing the term ASARCO, I never linked the old name with the current one.

This discovery further fueled my interest in family research. I needed to know more about their involvement with ASARCO and the industry. I eventually learned that my great-grandfather Karl also worked for American Smelting and was head of western real estate for ASARCO in 1905. It was he who'd purchased the Tacoma site for the company.

Anton Eilers sits in the center. His son Karl stands. Karl's son Farny sits next to Anton, while his son Fritz (my grandfather) stands next to him. 1908.

By 1920 Karl was vice-president of ASARCO. After a dispute with the president of the company, he launched a shareholder challenge against the famous Guggenheim family, which had a tight grip on ASARCO. When the dust finally settled in 1924, the Guggenheims lost control of the company. Meanwhile, my family ceased involvement with ASARCO and, as my uncle once told me, Karl declared that the name "Guggenheim" should never again be uttered in the house. He'd discovered, among other things, that the Guggenheims had moved assets from American Smelting into their own Guggenheim Brothers' private partnership.

As a result of the family's success in smelting and refining, my grandfather Fritz was wealthy when he married my grandmother in 1930, and stood to inherit a sizeable fortune. They were financially set, or so they thought. But, over the next few years they learned the same lesson I recently learned: the economic landscape is full pitfalls. In response to the changing financial climate of the Depression, my grandfather took the family west in 1936 and we never moved back.

The Depression hit the family hard financially, just as I have been hit hard. Because of this, I hoped their experience might teach me some lessons, but I have only gleaned one: keep moving forward.

• • • •

I complete the ten-mile descent on I-90 to the town of Vantage on the banks of the Columbia River, where I exit. A gas station and tiny restaurant anchor the area, the rest of the town farther north and out of site. I stop for gas and a bottle of water. As I climb out of the car, a strong gust of wind blows down the river, ruffling my clothes. The high, bare cliffs of the surrounding gorge and the dearth of vegetation encourage the winds, which explains why every time I stop here the wind seems to be bending the dry desert grass and rolling a few tumble weeds across the road.

I remember a particularly windy trip through the gorge when I was twelve. We passed through here in the motorhome, towing the jeep behind us. Our destination was the Beverly Sand Dunes, which is twenty minutes south of Vantage. The winds gusted hard that dark night, rocking the camper as we drove along the river. When we arrived at the dunes, Dad got out to secure the camper for sleeping. He discovered that the coffee mug he had absentmindedly placed on a ledge, that ran across the back of the motorhome, before we left was still there. It had survived both the three hour trip from Seattle and the winds of the gorge. Even more miraculously, it still held coffee, though the coffee had cooled considerably. We were amazed!

• • • •

Back on I-90, I cross the bridge that spans the legendary river and climb ancient red bluffs until the steep terrain of the gorge yields to flat farmlands. Though gray clouds remain in the sky, the rain has finally stopped. I turn off the wipers. The only sound I hear is the hum of the tires on the road.

Farmland fills the horizon as the interstate becomes mind-numbingly straight, their existence in this arid land only made possible by the pumping of irrigation water from reservoirs many miles away. I pass through the small town of George, Washington. The place may be small, but the name is unforgettable. However, these days the town is better known for its concert amphitheater, which grandly overlooks the Columbia River gorge, than it is for being named after our first president.

A half hour later the fields give way to the city of Moses Lake. Hidden just south of the interstate are the Moses Lake Sand Dunes. Though larger, yet not much farther than the Beverly Sand Dunes, we rarely jeeped here. I think our club preferred the quiet of Beverly. My most vivid memory of Moses Lake isn't from jeeping; it was my parents' complaints about the price of gas during 1974: sixty-six cents a gallon!

East of Moses Lake the interstate straightens and the farm fields returned for the remainder of the trip. From here my parents used to drive non-stop to Hayden Lake. Though for years this trip was a bi-annual tradition, that all changed for me in the mid-1980s, with work and college keeping me busy, curtailing my Idaho vacations.

In 1988, Grandma Eilers died and her home was sold. A few years later one of the huge ponderosa pines, whose enormous cones dotted the landscape that surrounded the house, crashed onto her old home, damaging it badly. The new owners cleared away the grand old lake house, along with all the trees, and built a modern house, destroying the intimacy of a place I loved.

The one positive outcome from her death was my exposure to books she and Grandpa had carefully stored for decades. I didn't know of the books nor much about the family history when my grandparents were alive, other than the family had been successful in mining. Then one day in 1991 at the age of twenty-six I discovered an old cardboard box with some books in my parents' basement, books I later learned Dad had inherited from Grandma.

Curious, I removed the box's lid. A slight odor of mothballs, which grandma used throughout the house to keep "critters" at bay, coupled with aged bindings made it obvious these books were old. The first few I examined had copyright dates from the early 1900s; they were handbooks for mining engineers, printed in small type and covering every engineering topic imaginable. As I browsed through more books I stumbled upon one that stood out: a memorial book for Anton Eilers. The book was nicely bound with a gray cover and professionally typeset. I opened it. The first

thing I saw was a picture of a barrel-chested man in his sixties, dressed in a fine suit, his face covered by a bushy, well-groomed, gray beard. He posed on a chair, sitting on it sideways, his right arm reaches over the top of the chair and around the side so one hand can hold the other. The picture suggests power, yet informality. This was the first picture I'd ever seen of my great-great-grandfather. I immediately began reading the book.

The memorial starts with a friend of his, Professor Rossiter Raymond, eulogizing Anton's passing in 1917:

> *He was at first my employee, then my assistant in public service, and then, to the day of his death, my business associate. I have seen him under circumstances of hardship, peril, conflict, doubt, apprehension, discomfort – and discomfort is no mean enemy to the sovereignty of a man over himself and his fate; — but always and everywhere he was the same simply, earnest, upright, thorough, dauntless, generous soul. He could not do a mean or tricky thing. More than once I have heard him say of some plausible business scheme, "That would be convenient and profitable; but we couldn't do it, you know!" What he said, he meant; what he promised, he performed. In business dealings he matched with his transparent honesty, frankness and justice the skillful strategy of other men. Over and over again, disputes have been settled by the final decision, "Let's leave it to Eilers!" Both sides rested content with the verdict that this fair-minded, incorruptible man, who incarnated in these modern days the ancient motto, "Noblesse oblige!" without preaching and without pretense.*

Three pages of remarks by Raymond were followed by glowing tributes from leaders of industry and family friends. Over the course of fifty pages, Anton emerged as a real man who possessed character, celebrated success, and was a dean of an industry until the end of his days, transforming a messy rule-of-thumb smelting industry into a science-based process. I learned how he built his fortune, managed his business affairs, and lived his life. Being his great-great-grandson suddenly filled me with pride.

What I found most powerful about the book was that it reflected a good man, who appeared to live an honest life and was successful doing it. He was a man I could both understand and emulate. I *had* to know more about him, because this man reflected the temperament of life I hoped to live and the kind of success I hoped to achieve. It also made me want to become an entrepreneur and create my own businesses just as he had. His legacy taught me that good men can finish first.

• • • •

The farm fields of eastern Washington are behind me and bull pine trees now dot the landscape as I near the Spokane Valley. In downtown Spokane I exit the interstate, turning north. I arrive at Dan's house an hour later.

Readers of eWillys like Dan are scattered all over the world, from soldiers in Afghanistan, to jeepers in Bali, South Africa, Russia, Europe, Alaska, South America, Tahiti and beyond. This in part explains why I don't meet them too often. Truth be told, usually I'm too busy being virtual to take the time to meet readers in person, something I'm not sure how to fix. So, on this occasion, to accept a long standing beer invitation from Dan is a perfect distraction from the rest of my life.

Dan is a long time reader and contributor. As a tribute to his grandfather and a treat for him and his family, he has been slowly rebuilding his grandfather's 1955 CJ-5, which he drove as a teen. He has plenty of memories of the jeep and his grandfather, one of which he shared with readers:

> "One day my grandfather decided to transport his two horses in a single axle trailer behind his jeep. While going down the road he noticed that something was wrong. The engine rpm was increasing, but he was slowing down.
>
> After pulling onto the side of the road and looking things over, he noticed that the horses had moved as far back in the trailer as possible and that was lifting the rear tires off the ground.
>
> He thought about it a moment and, deciding he was already half way there, he put the jeep in 4wd and finished off the trip.
>
> When he was done he swore he would never do that again."

But, it has been a few years since the jeep has pulled any horse trailers. Neglected by others, Dan inherited a worn down vehicle with little more than habit to keep it together. The jeep needed a full restoration to be operable. But, Dan didn't want to invest a ton of money, so he made hard choices along the way.

Dan meets me at the car as I pull up next to his newly-built shop. After he introduces me to his wife and kids, he and I talk inside the shop while drinking a beer, the jeep awaiting inspection nearby. After finishing our beers and sharing stories, we check out his jeep.

Top: Dan's jeep the way he inherited it. It is a mess.
Bottom: The CJ-5 reborn, nearly ready for driving.

When he first emailed me pictures, I saw a jeep without wheels, the hubs of its axles sitting on concrete blocks. It was missing seats, a windshield, and many other parts. Most people would have sent a jeep like that to the salvage yard, but not Dan. He was confident he could save it.

And save it he did! Looking it over, the jeep shines with new tires, wheels, seats, brakes, diamond plate corners and other parts. Dents are pounded out or filled in, the body smoothed, and the paint color applied. It appears ready to drive, but still needs the engine and transmission installed.

As he shows me different aspects of his jeep, he describes some of his low budget solutions to challenges he faced. For example, he welded diamond plating to the rear bed rather than using a more expensive replacement floor pan. Also, he used spray cans to paint the jeep rather than pay for a more professional, expensive alternative. He sounds slightly apologetic as he explains these and other decisions, because he knows the project isn't as polished as some jeeps I publish on eWillys.

I dismiss any concerns he has; instead, I urge him to complete the jeep so he can use it, because he is on the right path for his needs. Some people, I tell him, get so wrapped up in the building of a vehicle that they forget about actually driving and enjoying it. Many of these projects never get finished and, instead, get listed for sale on eWillys.

I share with Dan that I never launched eWillys to encourage perfect builds. I want to inspire people to get back into their garages and get their jeeps, jeeps of all flavors, running again. That is why I feature projects of all kinds on the website, from flawless stainless beauties to flawed, homely, practical builds.

I tell Dan that I think his grandfather would be proud of his work. Dan has built a jeep that meets his needs. Moreover, I feel Dan's jeep is the perfect type of build; he loves his jeep for all the memories of his grandfather it embodies and wants to create new memories with his own family. If there is a better use for a jeep, I don't know what it is.

I drive away from my meeting happy to call Dan my friend. I feel proud that my website has helped provide him with ideas and inspiration. I look forward to riding in it sometime, once the jeep is ready to go.

• • • •

Following my visit with Dan, I head south to Spokane where I've arranged to spend the night at my cousin Anita's house, before heading to Boise tomorrow. My visit isn't entirely social, because there is something I want: photos of paintings owned by my cousin and painted by our great-great-aunt, Emma Eilers.

Emma Eilers, or Tante Emma as Dad calls her — Tante being German for aunt — was a regionally known artist in New York City in the early 1900s. The family has always been proud of her paintings and my grandmother Eilers had them hanging throughout her house.

Two Girls in the Forest. This painting by Emma combines three of her favorite subjects: Long Island trees, women, and Hempstead Harbor. Circa 1915.

Before my research, no one in my immediate family knew much about Emma. It took me years to learn anything beyond the dates of her birth, in 1870, and death, in 1851. With enough digging I found out she graduated from the Packer Collegiate Institute in Brooklyn in 1889, and, soon after, co-founded the Club of Women of New York (which later became the National Association of Women Artists). Never marrying, painting consumed most of her life. Impressed by his daughter's skill and dedication, Anton had a two-story wood-paneled studio built on the family estate in Sea Cliff, complete with an Inglenook fireplace, a vaulted main room, and many thoughtful architectural details. I recently discovered the studio still stands, with the woodwork and fireplace saved and beautifully integrated into a modern house.

Emma painted in spite of her "palsy", which caused her to shake constantly. It is unclear how long palsy afflicted her, but Dad, his brothers and cousins remember she shook badly at the dinner table, with her silverware clanking against her plate. Looking back, they admit feeling guilty for laughing at her uncontrollable shakes, but they were just kids.

The very same hands and arms she couldn't control at the dinner table transformed in the paint studio. A determined painter, her brush would vibrate up to the point it touched the canvas. Once on the canvas, her hand became steady, allowing her to create beautiful paintings. As the Brooklyn Eagle reported in 1897, "Miss Eilers of St. Mark's Avenue does some of the strongest and best work at the league [Art Students League of NY]. Her painting of the figure is fine, unsurpassed by any other attendant at the famous art school, so current opinion has it."

Dad told me his family traveled to Sea Cliff following her death, where he saw hundreds of paintings piled all over the studio, many unfinished. He said some of these were sold at her estate sale, some were inherited by family members, others were given away, and the unwanted paintings were destroyed.

As a tribute to her, I have assembled a biography and a website, uncovering sixty paintings so far. Adding photos of the Emma paintings owned by Anita to my digital collection is one of the reasons I am visiting with my cousin today. Spending time with Anita is equally important.

Finding Virginia

• • • •

Due to our frequent trips to Idaho, when I was a boy Anita had been more like a sister than a cousin. She is a year younger than me and, belying her pretty looks, grew up a motorcycle riding tomboy.

Over the last couple of decades our visits have been rare, but that has been true of my interactions with much of my family, as I have been on the go, living, moving, working, and parenting. Ironically, because of my research, I know more about my dead family members than the living ones. I'm not sure what that says about me.

As I pull into Anita's driveway, I glance at her two story, split-level subdivision house, probably built in the 1970s. It is my first time here. The grass is cut, the shrubs and flowers are nicely trimmed. As I walk to the door to knock she opens it.

Anita is excited to see me. Like her mother, she's a hugger, putting everyone at ease. I step back from her to get a good look, finding her long curly hair, now with a splash of gray, and beautiful smile familiar and comforting. As soon as she welcomes me, Anita asks how long I can stay, tells me where to place my things, and says to make myself at home. Everything she does reminds me that I am welcome, am family and loved. Her warmth is a salve for my wounds and her interest in me genuine.

She introduces her husband, whom I am meeting for the first time. After the three of us talk for a little while, Anita suggests she and I go upstairs to see the paintings and let her husband watch his baseball game. So, I sling my computer backpack over my shoulder and pick up my suitcase for the walk upstairs.

She shows me to a sizeable guest room. It is clear that when guests are not visiting, the space acts as storage, with several boxes, two dressers, and piles of odds and ends filling the room. While I arrange my things, she opens the curtains to let in the last rays of the evening's sun, sliding open the window so sweet spring evening air can drift inside. We talk the entire time, sharing updates on our personal situations and family gossip. It feels good to reconnect with her.

Caught up on the latest news, she shifts the conversation. She asks if I want to see some of her albums. I tell her that sounds fine to me. I assume the photos are recent, showing her, me and our families. I sit on the bed while she shifts some boxes around. After some effort, she finds the box she seeks and sets it on the bed. Unremarkable and unmarked, I anticipate nothing special from it.

Parting the flaps of the box, she reaches in and pulls out several albums. I immediately realize these are older than I expected. The first album, large and thick, has a leather binding that exudes age and elegance. As she lays the first album between us, she sits on the bed. According to her, she received the albums in 2008, just before her father died in 2009, which was the last time she and I saw each other. Prior to that visit I hadn't seen Anita since the mid 1990s. I guess Virginia isn't the only person that hasn't seen much of me.

Before she opens the album, Anita, her excitement growing, says she rarely has anyone with whom to share these photos. Moreover, she doesn't know who many of the people are or the history behind the photos. But, what she does know is that because I deeply enjoy our family history I will enjoy these albums.

With that she opens the cover, telling me this is a photo album from our grandfather's childhood. I am still processing her statement when I look at the six photos on the first page. I am unprepared for what I see: My family research has suddenly come to life. In front of me are captioned photos of our grandfather Fritz from 1899, only a few months after his birth.

"Unbelievable," I say.

I flip the page and there are twelve more pictures, all black and white, some slightly faded that include Fritz, his older sister Marguerite and his parents Karl and Leonie. I am stunned. After the first few pages I look at

Anita, asking if she knows what she has here. Not really, she says, because she doesn't know who many of the people are.

I flip a few more pages. Soon the pictures include more extended family: all four Tante's, Fritz's paternal grandparents Anton and Elizabeth Eilers, his maternal grandparents Rudolph and Leonie Wurlitzer, and extended family I didn't know he had. Many of the people pictured were only names in my family database, now they were people with faces, posing for photographers at smelters in Colorado, playing during vacations in the mountains above Salt Lake City, Utah, and hosting parties in Sea Cliff and Brooklyn, New York.

I look up at Anita. I am smiling. She is smiling. I ask if is she is ready to jump into this, because it will take a while. I can identify and share stories of all these people, if she wants me to.

"Absolutely!" she replies. But, before we begin, she suggests we have a shot of vodka with a beer chaser (I'm sure our ancestors shifted in their graves at that moment). I agree, so she runs downstairs. Based on our private talk, I learned she needs this time with me as much as I need the time with her.

Upon her return, we enjoy our drinks, relax and travel backward in her bedroom time-machine. We are both more than happy to forget about the rest of the world for a while.

• • • •

Using the photographs as cues, I laid out the family history for Anita, explaining how the people in the pictures connected with others. This album captured Fritz growing up and moving about the country with his family, from Denver, to Pueblo, to Salt Lake City, to Brooklyn and Sea Cliff, as his father, Karl, rose through the ranks of ASARCO.

"Unbelievable!" I uttered again and again as we turned pages. The album contained more than 400 photos, documenting our family's life and travels during the early 1900s. Anita sponged up my endless trivia about family members, thankful that she could share the pictures with someone who cared. I used my digital camera to capture images I liked. After watching me a few times she told me not to bother. She said the albums were mine as much as they were hers. I could take them and digitize them if I wanted. She understood how important the photos were to me and I accepted her offer. That was Anita, always generous and kind.

We finished the first album. I so thoroughly enjoyed the trip through the early 1900s that I had forgotten there was a second album. I didn't know what to expect from it. Once again I was surprised, because it contained photos of a trip Fritz, his siblings, mother, father, and cousins, had taken to Europe in 1924. This in itself was not unusual, as the family had been traveling to Europe regularly for decades. In fact, they got stuck in Munich, Germany, at the outbreak of World War I in 1914.

What made this album unusual was that it recorded Fritz and his brother Farny's three-month automobile trip around Europe and North Africa during the summer of 1924. Based on their itinerary, their trip was meant to be the adventure of a lifetime, yet I'd never heard about this trip. I'd later learned that neither my father nor my uncle had known about it.

At the time, Fritz would have been twenty-six-years-old, his brother twenty-three. This was their interpretation, a rare automobile version, of the European "Grand Tour" that many well-to-do young men and women usually undertook by train or, prior to that, by coach or by foot (which is how family friend Rossiter Raymond toured Europe). The album's several hundred photos weave a story about their travels through post WWI Europe, photographing themselves, their car, and famous examples of architecture from the Eiffel Tower in Paris, to La Pedrera in Barcelona, to pre WWII pictures of Hanover and Dresden, Germany.

Thankfully, many of the photos included notations, allowing Anita and I to track the brothers as they began their trip in France drove south into Spain toward Gibraltar. The car they drove was a convertible four door vehicle with wide fenders that swooped together to become running boards underneath the front and back doors. A soft top shades them from the sun and protected them from rain, but the top had no sides (I later learned the car was a 1920s Fiat 501 series 2 Touring car).

Based on pictures of them bundled tightly in jackets, wearing a hat and gloves, it wasn't always warm either. The photos show that many roads weren't paved, nor were there many indications of signs or directional help. How they navigated from town to town was unclear. The more I looked at the pictures, the more I could relate; this sounded just like a jeep trip to me, as they were open to the elements and driving rough roads without clear directions.

From Gibraltar, the Eilers brothers shipped their car to North Africa and drove from Tunisia to Tripoli, taking more photos of themselves and architectural ruins along the way. In a strange coincidence, I was in the middle of reading a book called "Who Needs a Road?" The book describes a trip taken by Harold Stephens and Albert Podell in 1965. The pair drove a CJ-5 and a Toyota Land Cruiser around the world, at one point following a similar North African path that the Eilers' brothers did. Stephens describes that portion of the trip as punishing; As I read their book, I couldn't imagine my grandfather crossing the same terrain without four wheel drive and the supplies that Stephens and Podell had. Fritz and Farny even took photographs of the same roman ruins that the two authors would take four decades later. I felt a sense of deja-vu as I compared their North African photos.

Returning from the African continent and landing back in southern Europe, Fritz and Farny traveled through Monte Carlo, into Italy, visiting everything from Venice, which they photographed from a hot air balloon, to Pompeii, Rome, and other famous places. After Italy, they drove north into Germany to stay with relatives and then into eastern France to visit more relatives. Finally, the two boys rejoined their parents and sister in Paris and flew to London on what might have been their first airplane trip.

By the time we finished Fritz's journey, Anita and I were tired. She thanked me for sharing the evening with her. I told her that our grandfather, who'd died while we were both young and about whom we'd known little, seemed more real than ever. She nodded in agreement. We exchanged "goodnights" as she left for bed, leaving me alone with my new found treasures.

Tonight validated all the time I had spent hunting down genealogical leads, emailing folks, and searching the internet. All my work had readied me for a moment just like this. I've learned over the years that family research requires walking down an uncertain path; you never know what you'll find or when you'll find it.

I went to sleep thinking about my grandfather's trip. Though I had driven through eastern Europe, I've never been to western Europe. I can imagine re-enacting his journey. It would be a treasure hunt, an adventure where I retrace his drive using the photos as guides. I recognized enough buildings and places that I know many of the exact locations could be found. I could even try to do it in an old Fiat like they used. And, if not that, then maybe an old jeep would be appropriate, for me anyway. Given I have readers in different countries throughout Europe, I even have a basic support system. This is doable, I tell myself, as I drift off to sleep.

15. MAY 26TH, 2011

I leave Spokane and Anita in the morning, with photographs of Emma's paintings stored on my camera and the family albums packed In a box placed on my back seat. Driving east to Coeur d'Alene, I turn south on highway US-95 to head to Boise. I pass through the area just west of Lake Coeur d'Alene. Only a few years ago the road I travel used to be more scenic and slow-paced as it snaked south. These days, thanks to the rebuilt US-95, a four-lane highway slices a much straighter and faster line.

I admit to being a fair-weather, Idaho panhandle lover, preferring the hot, dry summers of northern Idaho to the cold, snowy winters. My favorite part is the area south of Coeur d'Alene along US-95 where I am at now, a strip of land bound by the Bitterroot Mountains to the east and the Washington State border to the west, a scenic mix of undulating terrain, pine trees, farms and Lake Coeur d'Alene.

I have already planned today's first stop: Fighting Creek (which my family pronounces Fighting "Crick"). For most people it is a way-stop on a trip to somewhere else, a place to purchase gas, food or drinks. Today, it is a way-stop for me too, but not so long ago this was the destination for my mother's side of the family. At that time, Fighting Creek was "the farm" and "the store".

Homesteaded in 1910 by my maternal grandparents, who traveled west after tiring of the cold Minnesota winters, Fighting Creek was their rural American Dream. Lucky winners of a homestead lottery, they made Fighting Creek their own by clearing the land of trees so they could farm it. Next, they erected their first building: a one-room cabin constructed from trees they cut down. After that, they built a barn and a house, then outbuildings and finally a general store in 1926. Over the years they logged trees, farmed the land, raised kids, and bred animals. Their store also served as the center of the community for decades.

My grandmother Schmidt grew up at Fighting Creek. She told me about her mother, who sometimes didn't have shoes growing up in Minnesota. When herding cattle during the winter she buried her feet in fresh manure to keep them warm. Stories like these made my grandma value the simple things, like shoes, a great deal. But even having shoes didn't make attending her one-room country school easy, because to get there she had to ride on the back of a horse behind her older sister Myrl. Farm life taught Grandma to be tough and farm finances convinced her to live frugally, lessons she embraced.

My mother and aunt remember Fighting Creek as a working farm, with cows, horses, pigs, chickens and others, but I have only known it as a farm whose time had come and gone. When I saw it during my teen years the giant red barn contained the ghosts of animals rather than the animals themselves. A tractor sat in a garage and hadn't been started in years. The garage and workshop were full of dust, old tools, and piles of equipment, some left over from the electrification of the area.

Inside the two bedroom farmhouse was a den room with old ledgers from the Fighting Creek Store, including an oak desk, which I now own, with a trick drawer that locked all the drawers when positioned just right. The family had run the store since it was built, but family members sold it in 1970 after my great grandmother Claudia died, because family members no longer wanted to operate it. The farm was sold in 1989 when my great-aunt moved away, because no family members remained in the area to own it.

As I approach the old farm in my car, I see the sign for the new Fightin' Creek Smoke Shop mini-mart, built in anticipation of the wider and faster US-95. The original Fighting Creek store building was bulldozed in 2008, to the dismay of some locals. The original store had a pair gas pumps, on for regular and one for ethyl; the new one has many more pumps. The original store was well-aged, eighty years of use reflected by its rough patina, while the new one has vibrant colors, more glass and brighter lights. While these changes made sense to me, one change didn't. Sometime in the 1980s the owners removed a "g" from the end of the store's name, changing "Fighting Creek" to "Fightin' Creek". I wonder if the owners thought dropping the "g" and adding an apostrophe would improve sales? I never learned the reason for the change, but mom and Marilyn find it annoying; I suppose they have a deeper personal investment in the original name. I less so.

My great-grandparents originally named the store for the nearby creek. According to local legend the creek was named for the occasional fight that took place at a dance hall a short distance from the creek. Another resource suggests there was only one fight and it was between two women in 1902. Whatever the true reason, the area was christened Fighting Creek.

I pull into the new Fightin' Creek Smoke Shop mini-mart for gas, the shop sitting where oats were once harvested. Parking at the southern most pump, I hop out and walk into the store to pay in cash and grab a soda: a carb-free Monster®. I rarely drink other sodas, because corn syrup now gives me indigestion.

As I exit the store I look to my right. To the south of me stands the big red barn, built by my great-granddad, less than a stone's throw away from the mini-mart. Still straight and square, the barn will the century mark in 2015. While its duration is a credit to the builders, it looks sorely out of place, an era bygone. I too am out of place here, because the Fighting (with a "g") Creek Store and Farm are long gone. It is time to gas and go.

I climb back into my black 1997 BMW 540i. The rear windows no longer go down, the tires are bald, the power steering mount is jury-rigged together, and the timing chain is nearing the 175,000-mile mark; it is a relic from the fortunes of my ManyOne Networks' experience. Thank goodness I learned to work on vehicles, because I've been able to keep it running. There is no way I could afford to pay someone else to do it.

I buckle my seat belt, feeling out of place in north Idaho, with the Hayden Lake house and Fighting Creek only memories. I wonder whether there is a place where I *do not* feel out of place. Boise no longer feels like home, neither does Salt Lake City, nor Seattle, nor Santa Cruz, California, nor any of the other places I have lived. Since I don't have a place I want to be, are there places I should be? Do I move to Utah to be near my kids? Or do I continue with my plan to head north to Seattle to help my parents? Who needs me more?

I pull out of the parking lot and accelerate to 60mph in a matter of seconds. Yeah, it may be falling apart and a maintenance headache, but it is still a damn fun car to drive. I pass by familiar small family farms, fields, and trees. My view of the rural landscape is abruptly interrupted, jarred by a giant, bright, electronic Coeur d'Alene Resort and Casino sign. To me it is foreign, out of place amongst the scenery I love. A few more miles later I see the casino itself, whose immense size is a shock, more at home in Reno, Nevada, than Worley, Idaho. If building monolithic resorts like this are good for communities, I see no ripple effects in the town of Worley, which looks little changed from years ago. The highway still bisects the town, which clings to US-95 tightly, slowing traffic and hoping travelers will stop.

In 2006, the rural feel of Idaho and towns like Worley attracted me to Boise from California. With my Idaho family roots and memories, I figured the state would be a good fit for me, as I'm an outdoorsy jeans and t-shirts guy.

My close friend invited me to move to Boise in late 2006 so I could work with him and two partners to launch a new company. Making my decision easier was that by 2006 ManyOne was on life support, employees clinging to each miraculous paycheck. Death was inevitable. The only difference between the Titanic and our company was that our captain saw the gashes along the side of the company as mere dents on the path to success. But, the economic gashes sunk that ship, taking me and my credit with it.

Leaving Worley, the four-lane US-95 suddenly downshifts to a two-lane highway, the type that bobs and weaves with the rolling farmlands. There is no time to daydream, as the constantly shifting highway requires my complete attention. Above me gray clouds blown by the wind threaten rain, but none falls. The hills are green, the ponds look high, and the water has puddled in gullies, indicating it has been a wet spring here, too.

I soon roll into the town of Moscow, home to the University of Idaho. I stay on US-95 as it slows through the city, my second stop of the day already planned; I want to shop and eat lunch at the Moscow Food Co-op. The college town's downtown bustles with lunchtime activity.

A few years earlier while driving through Moscow, I stopped at the Co-op, unexpectedly finding a robust, well-stocked and interesting market. For all the "hick" references Idahoans endure, the Co-ops in Boise and Moscow are as sophisticated as any I have seen (and I've seen a lot of them). They carry products like goose eggs, duck eggs, raw milk, raw cream, locally made butters and cheeses, earthy breads, grass-fed beef, locally-raised lamb, regional beer options, organic fruits and vegetables and more. The stores are terrific!

My interest in high quality food stores has grown over the past ten years. It is amazingly difficult to purchase unadulterated food without fillers or superfluous ingredients from the average grocery store. I do not need whipping cream or yogurt to have carrageen, sodium citrate, guar gum, or other products to thicken it, give it taste or provide it longer shelf life. I would rather have my beef grass-fed and frozen than fresh, gassed with carbon dioxide, and wrapped in plastic. I want my grade AA eggs to look like the grade AA eggs, with deep orange yolks and clear whites, like I get with my duck eggs. And if I have to buy chicken eggs, they should be from hens that have eaten bugs, not be one-hundred-percent vegetarian. Quality pork is important, too, so I can use its fat to render rich lard. And breads. It is so difficult to find high quality filler-free breads!

Because I seek out foods like these, some friends calls me a foodie. However, I don't think my tastes are so refined that it is the right term for me. My interest lies more in the nutritional density of food and how my body feels in response to it. Besides, despite my quest for foods like these, I'm hardly a perfect being and I still ingest things that aren't good for me, the drink I bought at Fightin' Creek Store being a perfect example. For me eating well is a goal, not an overbearing obsession.

On this day as I browsed the aisles and read a few labels (I am a label readaholic). I wander to the back of the store where I pick-up a half-gallon of raw milk and a half-dozen goose eggs. Then I walk past the meat and cheese section, heading to the deli counter to purchase a sandwich. As I look over the menu board, the smell of baked bread drifts from the bakery. A noisy lunchtime crowd forces me to speak up as I order. I decide on a Turkey Avocado on freshly-baked peasant bread, a sandwich that includes provolone cheese, tomatoes, mayonnaise, mustard and red onions. My mouth waters in anticipation.

Outside, I slide into the driver's seat with my food. I twist the top off of the milk and take a drink. The milk tastes rich and creamy with a hint of earthy grass flavor. I unwrap the sandwich and take a bite. I expect a good sandwich, but discover it is fantastic. The freshly baked bread is moist and wonderful, the turkey plentiful, the avocado fresh, and the tomato sweet. It all combines together perfectly, the best sandwich I have eaten in some time. The Moscow Co-op will continue to be a must-stop place for me.

• • • •

Two hours pass. During that time I drove down the steep descent into Lewiston, traced a long ascent up to the high plateaus near Grangeville, and passed over the summit at White Bird. From there, I drop into the most scenic part of the trip: the drive along the Salmon River.

US-95 merges with the river just south of White Bird, where canyon walls three-thousand-feet high frame a picturesque river gorge. I am closer to the end of the four-hundred-and-twenty-five-mile river than to its headwaters in the Sawtooth mountains. Much of the river is wild and fast, which explains why its other name is "The River of No Return".

Lewis and Clark found the upper portions of this river too difficult to navigate, so they chose an alternate route. Modern river runners embrace the difficulties of the Salmon; for them the river is a world-class destination, though they must share it with fishermen, who find its fly-fishing world-class too. By the time the river descends through the canyons of the Frank Church-River of No Return Wilderness (a mouthful of a name) and meets US-95 the pace of the river slows, appearing gentle, belying its true force.

Because of the steep canyon walls, US-95 holds fast to the banks of the wide rippling river, following sweeping riverbends carved long ago. It is an easy place to step back in time, the raw power of nature is everywhere. Normally, I feel peaceful as I travel through here. Today, peace alludes me.

Foremost on my mind is my imminent arrival in Boise. I do not want to return there. I need to extricate myself from the situation as gracefully and painlessly, for both of us, as possible. I believe we both know what's coming; if she doesn't, then she's ignoring many signs.

Fortunately, there isn't actual conflict or finger pointing between us. Because of this, I am confident my girlfriend and I can remain friends, which is important to me. That doesn't mean there aren't any problems; it does mean I am beyond the point of wanting to fix them. I am done. Importantly, I've felt that way for months, asking friends and family for advice. While they understand my dilemma, they could offer no better alternative. They said I was doing the right thing.

So, I'd remained in the relationship, making payments for many month on a house that held no value for me so she wouldn't be destroyed financially. Hopefully, soon, she will be approved for the HAFA program so we can both escape the valueless house; I need that critical piece in place to move on with my life.

• • • •

Late in the afternoon I enter the outskirts of Eagle and soon make the right turn into our neighborhood. As I approach the house, I see what I've been waiting months to see: a "For Sale" sign has been planted on the lawn. The HAFA program and short-sale process has been approved.

I have two choices now. I can either tell her I am leaving and start packing. Or, start packing and tell her I will be leaving when I am closer to my moving date. At the end of my second marriage, I did the former, telling my ex-wife I wanted a divorce three months before either of us could move out of the house we were renting. That was hell, living together while avoiding one another.

Because of that experience, I wanted this house in my girlfriend's name, so that if our relationship didn't work out it would be easy for her to ask me to leave or for me to leave. Either way, she would have the security of owning the house. This seemed like a prudent plan, but I never imagined the market would tank as it did.

I exit the car, having already chosen the latter option. I will be friendly and courteous, yet won't make any promises I can't keep. I feel no pride in this decision.

16. END OF MAY 2011

I wake up in the morning; my girlfriend has already gone to work. With the house to myself, I am ready to pack. I decide to tackle the garage first. Before starting, I check my email, but don't see anything from Virginia. I am not too surprised, because between my two long days of driving and Virginia's busy schedule our emails slowed dramatically. In fact, later that evening she writes to apologize for a lack of emails:

>   May 27th, 2011 – 8:50 PM
> David.
>
> *I have been on a dead run and am beat. I have not eaten, have not yet showered after work nor even gone poop! So, I will go do all that and hope I do not fall asleep before I write again or have to get up and do it again!*
>
> *xox Off and running . . .*
>
> *Virginia*

I guess now that we can talk about poop, we really are friends. Besides, that's all we can expect at this time, because neither of us knows when I will return to Seattle. Moreover, she is so busy that it is hard to find time to share time with her. Mostly, it seems to me, we just need to know the other exists and still cares. Perhaps we are timeless friends, one of those friendships that easily resumes no matter how much times passes.

• • • •

Two more days pass. Life is moving forward as my packing continues. During this time Virginia and I exchange two brief emails, our full lives using up our spare time. Then, on May 30th I receive a surprising letter. In it she hints that our email exchanges are taxing her energy and time more than either of us intended. While she describes accessing email as a new daily chore, I suspect she doesn't mean it in a derogatory way. She just means her life is hectic:

May 30th, 2011 – 6:07 AM

David.

I have worked so hard all weekend and have today to do also. I had nothing left to chat via email. I hope I did not write anything to hurt your feelings. I just cannot do it all. Before we connected, I did not check email daily. I would go days between checking. Now, it is another chore for me to get online and check my email. I have not had the energy to do it all, AND I HAVE ABUNDANT ENERGY FOR ANYONE OF ANY AGE!

During the time you were here, I shoved everything aside to spend time with you. I seemed to have been knocked off of my balance beam. I cannot function with confusion w/in myself. I have started to regain my balance.

I appreciated the time you have taken to write and have enjoyed your successes, whether they be Salmon omelets or digging up precious family history.

I am writing now to say I did not have the energy to sit and write over the past several days. I can only do what I can do.

I imagine you are back where you live now. I hope you have arrived safely. Since I have not heard from you, I am a little concerned. Let me know you are well. I realize, that if you plan to move to Renton that this will be a hellish time for you.

Good luck and be well!

Virginia

After reading her email I try to alleviate any concern she might have that I expect quick and timely responses:

May 30, 2011 – 11:20 AM

Hi Virginia,

I did write when I got back, but I might not have actually said I was back in Boise. Yes, thanks for your concern. When I returned, I had a variety of things to catch up on!

I know I've knocked you for a bit of a loop, so don't feel any need to check email more often than is convenient. I can tell you are a busy person and thrive on that busy-ness. You do have abundant energy — I could see that about you :-)

I've realized that I can sell more of my stuff than I thought. So, I'm going to sell some tools this week, making it easier to move. I've told my family about my decision and they are excited to have me back home.

You might laugh, but I was thinking of movies. The movie I keep thinking most about in relation to you is the "Parent Trap". You remind me of Natasha Richardson's character Elizabeth James. Like you, she is beautiful, independent, busy, and brave, but has a warmth, intelligence, and graciousness underneath it all. And, just like Dennis Quaid's character Nick Parker, I keep wanting to say, 'you don't have to be brave all the time'. In other words, around me, I think you relax your guard and, perhaps, feel a little vulnerable, which is part of what throws you off balance.

So, when you have the energy, feel free to write. If you don't have the energy, just read and enjoy.

Happy Memorial Day!!

- D

I guess she felt relief at receiving my email, perhaps afraid I had arrived in Boise and forgotten about her. For all its uses, emails require patience because sometimes intent, feelings, and inflections disappear, confusing the messages.

Virginia responds:

> May 30th, 2011 – 6:55 PM
>
> *David,*
>
> *I love that analogy, her character in that movie was one of my favorite film characters. Isn't that funny?*
>
> *I thought it was hilarious when she got drunk!!!!*
>
> *Dinner is here.*
>
> *Virginia*

I write:

> May 30th, 2011 – 7:07 PM
>
> *Virginia,*
>
> *I too liked the movie and have watched it a number of times. As I understand it, Natasha was as nice as her character, too.*
>
> *I'm spending time scanning the photo albums my cousin loaned me. There are several hundred photos here. I'm having fun!*
>
> *- David*

These and a few other emails reflect a new sense of friendship, a realization we are where we are in our lives. Besides, no matter what happened between Harry and Sally, I believe men and women can be good friends. So, with the idea of friendship and story sharing bumping around my brain, late in the evening on May 30th I write the email below:

> May 30th, 2011 – 9:55 PM
>
> *Virginia,*
>
> *Here are a couple random stories for your amusement in case you wake up late and can't sleep!*

Men's conditioner:

I don't understand it. I went shopping for men's conditioner. I have some American Crew shampoo, so I wanted their conditioner too. So, I figured I'd go buy some. Not only could I not find any conditioner from American Crew, but nearly all the men's conditioner was mixed into the shampoo. Now, I don't know if this is for convenience (as they feel men are simply too lazy to both shampoo and condition) or it actually works better for hair. I suspect it is the former, as all the women's shampoo of any quality seems to be divided into shampoo and conditioner. Personal care is simply too complicated for me sometimes!!

My First Night of Karaoke Story:

About 8 years ago I tried Karaoke for the first time. I really didn't think I had much of a voice, as I have little range, but after experimenting with some songs at home, I figured I could belt out a version Dylan's "Like a Rolling Stone" pretty well. I was pretty nervous about the whole thing, as I had never sung publicly since a Christmas program back in the 6th grade (and I was one of many voices.) So, I decided to memorize the words and practice. On my big night, I had a couple drinks and then walked up to the mic in a local bar in where I lived in Aptos, Ca. The unusual thing about this Karaoke setup was that there was a set of stairs to one side and behind me that led to more of the bar, so the singers couldn't see someone approaching from behind.

Certainly, I was nervous inside, but on the outside I tried to be calm as possible. The music started and the words began flowing. With each line I sang, my confidence grew. As I completed the second of the four stanzas, I was really starting to feel comfortable and having fun. That's when I suddenly felt several hands appear from behind. Four women in their mid 50s had come up the stairs and, I guess jazzed by the music and powered by a few drinks, decided they would have fun, so they made themselves at home around me, putting their hands just about everywhere, grooving to the music, acting as my 'groupies' and causing the audience to explode in laughter. Meanwhile, I just kept singing, focusing on the music and trying not to start laughing myself. My entourage and I managed to bring the song home to a standing ovation. I never again had as much fun singing as I did that first night.

I haven't Karaoke'd in five years, but some day I'll try again.

- D

Expecting to receive a light-hearted response to my email, I am surprised by the email she sends. The message is brief, but earnest:

May 31st, 2011 – 4:50 PM

Dave.

My son tore his ACL playing basketball. I rushed him to the ER. I will be needed much for awhile, more than usual.

Right now I have a broken heart. Everything can change in an instant. I need to get going now. Be well.

Virginia

The swift hands of fate have swept our unfolding script off the table, incomplete, challenging our ability to communicate. I quickly respond to her emergency:

May 31st, 2011 – 5:15 PM

Virginia,

OH NO!! I completely understand. He needs you. I know you'll take care of him well.

- D

Closing my computer, I wonder why my relationship with Virginia has so many obstacles.

Do the Fates dislike us? If so, why bring us together in the first place? Sometimes life is so complicated.

17. AUGUST 1986: MEETING HER

The Fates introduced Virginia and I at Roche Harbor's pool at the end of July, 1986. Cullen and I had gone to the pool to play a few games of ping pong before I went to work. Entering the pool area through the office door, I quickly spotted a beautiful woman with curly hair in a black, one-piece swimming suit.

How I made it across the pool deck to the ping-pong table without hurting anyone was impressive, because my eyes glued to her while my body tried to navigate through people and deck chairs. Unexpectedly, she caught me eyeing her, and eyed me right back, smiling slightly. I looked around, figuring she was smiling at someone else. But, no, she was smiling at me. She was beautiful, a little older than me, very much a woman. Because of that, I wondered what she could possibly find interesting about me.

She was in and out of the pool, part of a group of people . . . friends? Family? Her kids? I saw no ring, but that could mean nothing. We exchanged a few more glances. I was now completely oblivious to ping pong, irritating Cullen as the ball bounced off my face. After exchanging smiles and glances, it was time for me to leave for work. With one more glance, just to make sure she was really looking back at me, I left for work. I felt great.

That afternoon, I filleted my fish, sliced my cuts of new york and ribeye strips, checked my marinating chickens — soaking in half-soy sauce and half-Italian dressing — and slowly steamed the beef ribs. Unlike June, when everything was so new, now I could ready everything on autopilot, the master of my domain. As usual, I prepared everything in the lower kitchen, working near Dutch.

Dutch was a retired gentleman from Michigan who worked as a prep cook for extra money and to keep busy. He was a stocky old guy with white hair, white mustache, big grin, happy attitude, and tired legs, which limited his ability to climb the multiple levels of the restaurant. He told me once that he liked island life, because it was much warmer and more peaceful than his former life in Michigan. Dutch didn't seem to have many different stories, but he liked to tell stories anyway, which meant I heard a lot of the same ones. The one I remember most is his opinion about chefs.

He usually this story because two chefs disagreed about one thing or another. Once the two chefs left the prep room and we were alone, he would flash me with what I can best describe as a Burt Lancaster look, probably because of that bushy mustache of his. He would say, "Dave, if I lined up all the cooks in the world, each one would point a slightly different direction." Then with a smile as wide as Burt's, as if it was the first time he ever shared that bit of wisdom, shaking his head at his own cleverness. What he meant was, he thought every cook had a different opinion.

"Your absolutely right Dutch," I'd respond, each time, with conviction. He might not have been the fastest prep chef, but I sorely missed in 1987 and 1988, after he decided not to work at Roche any longer.

With my prep done that day, the equipment ready, and the mesquite lit, I was ready for another ordinary day as Barbeque Dave. At least it was ordinary until seven o'clock when a large party arrived, sitting themselves at the rear of the dining area where several picnic tables were located for big groups. To my surprise, the party included the same woman I'd seen at the pool. Even better, she'd seated herself at the back of the table, providing her with a good view of me. In no time, we resumed our flirting.

Unlike at the pool, I got it. She was interested in me (yeah, I can be a bit clueless). Though, I'm still not altogether sure what she found so attractive. My blond crazy curly hair was likely wild looking, as it never submitted to control any more than my spirit did. My chef's outfit made few women swoon. I am sure my dirty apron, which had been white a few hours earlier, was hardly an aphrodisiac. But she was looking, I liked it, so I looked back, probably wearing some goofy smile.

Much of that evening is now a blur. I remember her family leaving after finishing their meal, walking toward the store, while she turned the other direction, in no hurry to go anywhere, giving me a glance, and then strolling along the yellow brick road. With no orders in the queue, I took the opportunity to briefly leave my stage, walk over to her, and introduce myself. This bold move might seem simple enough, but it was a new experience for a shy guy like me. But, there was something easy about approaching and talking with her.

As soon as we talked, I felt a connection. I asked her if she wanted a personal tour of the resort after I finished work. She agreed. That night I closed the barbeque as quickly as I could that night, never bothering to ask the line cooks inside the restaurant if they needed help.

At ten o'clock that night we met in front of the barbeque and began to walk. She told me she was visiting with her parents and brother on their boat. She was twenty-six, single, a college graduate, and looking to explore life after ending a long relationship. We walked for a half hour, eventually making our way to my trailer where she pulled out a surprise. She said she rarely smoked pot, but her brother had given her some. Did I want any? Sure, what the hell I thought. Again, with her it was easy. Somehow, I made her feel comfortable enough that she dared ask and, somehow, she knew I would accept.

We each took a couple tokes from the joint. That was all either of us wanted. We never smoked after that. I took her down to the hotel, where I made up a silly tour just for her, mixing fact and fiction in ways that left her giggling and asking more than once, "Is that real or did you make that up?"

Our conversations were silly, fun, and full of "What we liked and didn't like" comments common on first dates. One hour past and then two. Eventually, even the bar closed and we had to say goodnight, so I walked her to the dock. When we neared her destination, she turned and we melted into the other, kissing deeply, surrounded by darkness, the sound of water lapping gently against the boats.

It was a wonderfully memorable kiss and the clearest memory I have of her. All these years later, I can still transport back to that dock. I can feel her lips. I can hear the water.

During the following six days, any time I wasn't working was spent with her. I showed her the San Juan Island I knew. She rode in a jeep for first time. We drove it along gravel roads, into town, and over to whale watch point on the island's west side, where, as she noted, we saw no whales, but saw plenty of each other. I took her to the mausoleum at midnight, which was eerie without flashlights, carefully one step at a time in complete darkness. The more time we spent together, the deeper our connection became. We flirted, kissed, played cards, and talked late into the night.

Too quickly, our week together ended. Her family was leaving and she with them. She said wanted to return, without family, so we could learn more about each other. I told Virginia to come back anytime. Apparently, she took my offer seriously.

18. JUNE 1ST, 2011

Sun. I see rays of sun bouncing off the concrete driveway into the garage as the opener slowly raises the two-car garage door. The light beckons me as I walk out of the garage onto the driveway to bask in it. Finally, the rainy spring has given way to the beginning of summer. It feels cleansing as if a new chapter is opening in my life.

Part of the reason I feel a sense of rebirth is because I have been packing and cleaning the garage for the past few days. I put away all my tools, recycled steel and aluminum at the salvage yard, and listed miscellaneous stuff on Craigslist. I sold my parts cleaner (for cleaning engine and transmission parts), my tube bender (for making my rollcage), my arc welder, my drill press and a few miscellaneous tools. I was pretty certain that I wouldn't need any of those tools in the near term. Besides, if I did, I could use my father's tools, because he certainly wasn't using them.

Amazingly, each tool sale was accompanied by a buyer with an economic tale of woe. As I explained to buyers why I was selling the tools — the house was going through a short-sale and my relationship was ending — the buyers would explain to me how they had already sold their home through a short-sale or they were in a divorce exacerbated by the economy or they had lost their job and couldn't find another. The guy who bought my router lost a job he'd had for twenty-five years and was amazed that, despite a great resume, he couldn't find another one. He felt he was viewed as too old and feared his corporate career in marketing was over, so he decided to earn money doing cabinetry. The frustration with the economy was at the forefront of all these men, whose ages ranged widely. We were all in the same sinking boat with no life preservers in sight. In each case we met as buyer and seller, but left as friends wishing the other luck. We all needed luck.

I head back into the garage and climb onto my workbench. Standing on my workbench, I drop cardboard packing boxes from the high shelf in the garage to the floor. I have stored them since my move to Eagle four years ago. Fruit boxes, thick and sturdy, perfect for storing books, I never disposed of these or other moving supplies, just in case I had to move. My unending sense of being temporary is tiresome. Permanence would be better, but settling for a situation for permanence sake is not an option. Yet, I want to throw away my boxes and find a place to call home. Maybe I will find home again some day, but this is no longer home.

The fruit boxes will store my cookbooks, which I rarely consult any more. They are pre-internet relics from a time I couldn't consult Google for a recipe, but unlike other books I have owned, I can't get rid of them. They feel like luxury items that I don't really need. I also don't want to sell my bookshelves, high quality relics from a 2001 dotcom company implosion I rescued from a storage locker in California. Since, the cookbooks will still have shelves and the shelves cookbooks, I will continue to keep them.

I'd made great progress, filling four boxes of books and carrying them to the garage. I place them next to two suitcases filled with winter clothes and jackets I packed earlier in the day. There is plenty of room to stage my belongings for the move, because of the newly-cleaned garage.

My girlfriend, on the other hand, had not start packing. At one point she asked why I was cleaning the garage and I said that it had to be cleaned because the house was for sale and we would have to move. That was all I volunteered and that was all she asked. Strangely, she didn't see the need to pack or clean.

I decide to break from packing and run to the store in my jeep for some raw milk, bread and duck eggs. I take Hill Road, driving my jeep along the contours of Boise's foothills between the town of Eagle and the city of Boise. Dressed in t-shirt and shorts, the wind blows and the sun warms me as I pass between grassy hills on my left and small homes on the my right. Something inside me relaxes, my cares dissolve away. Once again, my jeep is a source of comfort.

My destination is the Boise Co-op. I pull into the parking lot and find a space. Coming to a stop, I reach down to flick off the ignition and power switches. There are no keys. When I built the jeep, I installed two switches and a push button for starting it. Not only does it make the jeep feel more like a toy, it simplifies my life, because I never have to find a key to start it. As the motor shuts down and I jump out of it, I see a man in his fifties walking in my direction. I can tell from his expression he wants to know about my vehicle.

"Nice jeep. My uncle had one of these. What year is it?"

That's usually the first question I get. I tell him, "According to the title, it is a 1949 CJ-3A. However, the running gear is from a 1973 CJ-5. The suspension is custom, as is most everything else. The body is fiberglass and the hood was handmade by me."

"That's great," he says. Reading the name along the hood, he asks the inevitable, "Why is it called Lost Biscuit?"

"When my oldest son wanted a name for his Xbox Live online account, all the names he wanted were taken. So, he picked two random names, 'Founded' and 'Biscuit', and his username became 'FoundedBiscuit'. Emulating his older brother, my youngest son wanted to be a 'Biscuit,' too, creating the name 'LostBiscuit'. When they told me about the name, I thought it was a great name for the jeep, because I like being lost and I like to cook. So, I asked to use it and they said sure."

"Great story. And what a great day for driving it. Have fun!" he says walking away.

"Enjoy your day," I respond, as my cell phone rings. I recognize the caller ID. It is my mom's cell phone, which she seldom uses. I think to myself, *this can't be good news*. After Mom and I talk, I email the gist of the conversation to Virginia from my phone:

June 1, 2011 – 3:16 PM

Virginia,

My mom called me, from her cell phone no less. This is a rare event. She is worried about Dad. She walked into the living room to talk to him around noon and to ask him what he was doing. He said he was reliving his life. She didn't know what to make of that. Then, she told him she needed to take the wheel chair they had rented back to the rental place, as they had only rented it for the week. A few minutes later she told him she was leaving and he asked where she was going, to which she repeated the rental place.

She is concerned, as am I. I may be up again soon.

- Dave

With the message sent. I digest what my mother told me more completely.

My formerly carefree mood has darkened, piercing my thin emotional shield. I feel tears only a blink away. The possibility of life without my father cannot be denied. The idea overpowers me in a way it hadn't before. Normally I can control my feelings, but now I want to cry.

I turn and walk into the store, determined not to cry. However, they lurk at the surface. I walk past the deli, then past the bread as my eyes moisten. I grab some burger buns, take a breath and keep walking, but I can't shake my emotions.

Memories bubble to the surface. I suddenly remember the time I filled the jeep's gas tank at the age of four with water from the front-yard hose, thinking I was helping. There was the time he showed me how to work an antique whipsaw, an eight-foot-long two-man saw from Fighting Creek, which my friends and I had to use to cut up a fallen tree. And, there was the memorable day in 1985 when he filmed my first jeep test in the horse pasture. As I drove down a hill, I hit a barrel, my tire rolling onto the barrel, which flipped me and the jeep all the way over. (good news, the rollcage worked). I lost the video a few years ago, but it ends with him dropping the camera and yelling my name, "David? David are you OK?". At that point the video turned to checkered fuzz.

As the memories surface, so do the tears. I wander aimlessly, trying to calm them. I take my eggs, milk and buns and leave quickly. Maybe the ride home will calm me.

But, it doesn't. I can't think and can't work. I pace. I always pace when feeling emotional. Sitting still is agony. Because of this, because I couldn't stop thinking about him, his life and him dying, I decide to stop fighting the emotions. Instead, I would harness them. I would write about him. Yes, it feels like a good idea.

I ask myself what would I want to say about him and want others to know about him as part of a eulogy. One thing Dad won't want, is someone telling a gathered church audience about how he is going with as part of God's pre-ordained plan. Nope, that isn't Dad's style. In fact, during a funeral service we attended a few months earlier, he'd rolled his eyes at how much the service was about God and how little it was about the person who'd died.

To understand why the idea of Dad's eulogy entered my head at all requires understanding the research I had done on Rossiter Raymond. It was Raymond's eulogy of Anton Eilers that had launched my family history initially. Raymond wrote and delivered eulogies of famous and not-so-famous people, many of which I have read. For decades he celebrate the life of the departed through them.

Raymond's work impressed me greatly. So, I followed my instincts and wrote about Dad. I spent a couple hours stitching his life together.

• • • •

Karl Emrich Eilers was born Nov 9th, 1933, in New York City at the Lenox Hill Hospital where his grandfather of the same name, Karl Emrich Eilers, was President and Chairman of the Board. Despite arriving in the depths of the Great Depression, Karl was fortunate to be born into a family of substantial wealth, as his grandfather and great-grandfather were world renowned in their knowledge about and the managing of the smelting process, which led to great financial success. However, like many wealthy families in NY, the Depression took a substantial portion of their assets, forever altering the family's finances.

I believe this is why at age three Karl, his sister Anita, and his brother B.B., were taken by their parents to the remote area of Salmon, Idaho, where Fritz bought a gold mine with a partner.

From 1936 to 1941 the family lived in Salmon. Karl's youngest brother Tony was born there. According to Dad, the partners mined gold until they reached a shear wall, at which point they abandoned the mine.

In 1941 the family moved to Salt Lake City where Fritz went to work for Kennecott Copper. After living several places, they eventually bought property along Walker Lane in Holladay, where they built a nice house and a swimming pool. Little Cottonwood Creek bordered part of that property and their father Fritz diverted the water to fill up the pool.

Dad liked to tell a story related to the swimming pool. The family had to dig out their kidney shaped pool by hand and Dad, being the eldest, worked his butt off (or for the purposes of our story, his abs on). Because, he claims, during the process he developed abs that stuck up two inches. I guess he was proud of his abs, because he still tells me that story.

Though life was good to them, their time in Holladay was marred by one significant event, the death of Karl's sister Anita when she was thirteen. That made Karl the oldest sibling. He took on the attributes commonly associated with the eldest sibling, becoming a responsible rule-follower. And that was Karl, the father I knew.

From left to right, my father Karl, and his brothers Tony & BB.

Dad had his first experience with jeeps in Holladay, too. And, as many of you know, throughout my youth and young adulthood, there was always a jeep in the family.

Now, given our history with jeeps you would think that I would have known my father's first vehicle was a jeep — a CJ-2A — which he got when he was sixteen as his first car. But, no, I did not hear this story until 2008. There are several reasons for this, mostly, I suppose, having to do with our father/son dynamic. He and I just didn't talk all that much.

As Dad tells it, the year was 1949, he was sixteen and the family still lived in Holladay. The city sits at the base of nine thousand foot Mt. Olympus. One day, Dad decided to drive his jeep and five youthful passengers up the hill toward Mt. Olympus. Today this area is known as Olympus Cove, but at the time, I'm sure it was the great unknown.

As Dad tells it, he was driving his jeep with his brother BB in the passenger seat and four kids in the back. He says one was his brother Tony and one was longtime friend Jim Carter. Even for kids, four is a tight squeeze in the back of a jeep, so there couldn't have been much room. Dad told me he was crawling very slowly in low range when his left front wheel climbed a bump or rise. Continuing to drive forward, the rise grew, shifting the jeep toward the passenger side until the jeep tipped onto the passenger side, dumping the kids in the back onto the ground.

Miraculously, no one was hurt, at least not severely. The worst damage was to Jim Carter, who suffered a cut on his knee. Apparently, Jim fell the farthest; I guess he must have been on the driver's side back wheel-well. With no one seriously hurt, they tipped it back onto its wheels and drove home.

After graduating from Granite High School, Dad joined the Navy. For a Navy guy, he spent almost no time at seat. He often told me he was third in his class, clearly proud of his accomplishment. Because of this, he had his choice of assignments. At first, he worked in Washington, D.C. Then he wanted to go out west, ending up in Hawaii. While in Hawaii, he managed to hitch rides with some of the naval airmen, traveling to Japan and other places. I really couldn't say much more about his Navy days, because he didn't share them with me.

After the Navy, he moved to the house in Hayden Lake. He first attended junior college in Coeur d'Alene, then attended the University of Idaho in Moscow, before graduating from Gonzaga University with an electrical engineering degree.

Dad's degree landed him a job at Boeing in Seattle. He moved into a house on 52nd south, near Seward Park, in Seattle. Across *the street lived a good-looking woman named Marjorie that caught his eye. Dates and marriage quickly followed.*

Dad would stay with Boeing for thirty-three years, though the last few seemed to be unhappy for him, because he'd been forced to move into management. About that time, my sister purchased five acres with a house, barn and outbuildings that needed lots of work. When Dad retired, he went to work at Kim's, transforming the barn into a horse barn, strengthening buildings, and building fences. He loved doing all that work.

When he was done at Kim's, he had to decide what to do next. He figured he could sit at home and collect social security or go to work and make the same amount. He chose the latter, joining Home Depot. He happily took odd shifts, led education classes, cooked hamburgers for the staff on Wednesdays, and answered customer questions. Dad even got to represent Home Depot on local TV, with callers phoning in to ask questions. Working for Home Depot might have been his favorite job ever.

In the fall of 2002, just a day after his birthday, Mom got up that morning and found him in the kitchen, unable to buckle his belt. She immediately called 911. The ambulance rushed him to the emergency room. By that afternoon, we found out he had suffered a major stroke. For ten days, no one knew for sure if he would recover, remain in a vegetative state, or die. On the eleventh day, he began to show improvements. As he improved, he had to relearn how to speak, read, walk and lift weights, his preferred way of exercising since 1980.

Characteristically, if the doctor told him to walk one mile a day, he'd walk two miles twice a day. He was willing to work as hard as necessary to revitalize his wounded body. While he hoped to recover fully, his right side never recovered nor could he get his brain to coordinate with his mouth.

Over time, we learned there were just some things he could not longer do. Driving was one of those things. This he learned the hard way at the King County waste and landfill transfer station in Renton. Unhappy with the way Mom had backed up the truck, he slid into the driver's seat, his first time in the driver's seat since the stroke, and put it into gear to move it ahead a little.

However, things didn't work out quite like he planned. With Mom screaming at him to stop, his foot got stuck on the accelerator, driving him forward and launching him over a small curb and down a steep one-hundred-foot embankment. Everyone at the facility was shocked as the back of the truck disappeared down the hill. Dad said he knew right away he was going over the edge, so he just held on, as he had 35 years earlier when he'd rolled his jeep at Icicle Creek. Fortunately, he didn't roll the truck and was able to come to a stop far below. It was such a big event that the news copters arrived to capture the scene.

The father I knew was stubborn at times, always kind,, and somewhat stoic. I never saw much anger, or a great deal of emotion, other than a smile. I never saw him smoke and he rarely drank much alcohol. He preferred to wear blue jeans with a shirt or two over which he wore a long-sleeved wool shirt. He was as good a man as anyone could hope to have as a father.

So, Dad's somewhere else now, no doubt looking for new adventures and doing things his own way. Though he is gone, he still remains with us in memories, stories, pictures, and videos.

• • • •

The two hours I'd spent writing helps me feel better. I am more calm and less emotional. Whether any of this gets used is another matter. I can proceed with my day and continue to pack.

The following day, I receive an urgent call from my mother. Dad couldn't get out of bed.

19. JUNE 2ND, 2011

June 2 2011 – 4:54 PM

Virginia,

I'm leaving right now for Seattle. Dad wouldn't get up from bed this morning. Finally, Mom had to call 911 and they all went to the hospital.

- D

The call from Mom came at 10am. Unable to help Dad from the bed, Mom phoned the paramedics. They came and, after evaluating him, took him to the hospital.

I would have left immediately for Seattle, but I had to deal with three issues: renew my driver's license, which would expire June 5th, collect my "stipend" check, and cash the check at the bank, which would pay for my travel expenses. Once those tasks were complete, I could leave for Seattle and be there by late evening.

However, things didn't go as planned. That evening I posted a letter on my website, explaining to my readers why I was in a motel room in Yakima. I titled the post, "And Now For A Special Comment about the Idaho DMV."

• • • •

Dear State of Idaho:

Thank you so much for my new temporary driver's license. Despite the size of the government of Idaho, you've taken the time to use this opportunity to remind me, in a personal way, just how fast and awkward our bureaucracy continues to become and how quickly one's normal function can be curtailed by the state.

And here, I thought you were only asking me to renew my driver's license.

To your credit, the lessons started quickly. For example, I had no idea that my out-of-state check from Washington would be rejected with such zeal when I mailed in my initial driver's license renewal application. You see, my main bank is in Washington State and every other business, utility and government entity in Idaho seems to function perfectly well using my checks.

Naturally, before sending you my check, I looked at the application to see whom I should make the check to and if there were any qualifications. How silly of me to expect that you'd put a "we do not accept out of state checks" notice on the renewal application, or anywhere else for that matter. I guess that qualifier is only for people in the know.

Of course, once I received the declined application in the mail, I headed directly to the DMV, the new one near the Boise Mall. What I learned there is that your ability to manage lines and waiting times is impressive. It really was. I was in and out with my temporary license and my new car tabs in less than twenty minutes.

The downside is, perhaps to make the process faster, you only issued me a temporary permit. Moreover, you took away my actual license, still good and valid up until my birthday. This didn't seem to be a big deal at the time, but that was before I tried to use the temporary permit.

You see, State of Idaho, no one believes the temporary permit is valid. They either chuckle and shake their head at it or look aghast, assuming it is a fake. I find I am no longer a person with the rights the power of a plastic ID bestowed upon me. Instead, I'm a subhuman, I'm a second-class citizen, I'm a paper ID'd pauper. When I attempted to cash a check at a major bank — a bank I had been using for two years — they looked at my paper ID and said it wasn't valid. I responded it was, telling them the State of Idaho issued it and took my expiring ID. They said they really weren't supposed to take it, but they would make an exception in my case. This was fortunate for me, as I had to get some cash to run north to Seattle. However, I left puzzled wondering why something printed on plastic would seem so much more authentic than paper. After all, I can guarantee that I can create a reasonably good fake ID in short order using Photoshop and then transfer it onto either paper or plastic. What's magic about plastic?

As I traveled north, passing through Yakima, my tire blew. After changing my tire and deciding to buy new tires before traveling any farther, I had to get a motel for the evening. Well, it turns out the motel was not going to take my paper ID either. You see, they don't accept a temporary ID as a valid form of ID. After the clerk explained to me that they didn't accept the ID, he mentioned that I essentially didn't exist for the time being. I too was coming to that conclusion.

However, the clerk took pity on me and said, while he wasn't supposed to rent me a room, he didn't want me to have to sleep in my car, so he'd make an exception in this case. Well, gee, thanks Mr. Stereotypical-World-of-WarCraft-playing-kid (yes, as he worked at the desk and, when not helping me, was playing WOW and looked like he had been playing WOW for years).

After putting my stuff in my room, I decided I was not ready to settle down quite yet, so I thought I'd go play some pool. As I walked by the desk, I asked the desk clerk if he knew of any places to play pool in Yakima. He didn't play pool, he said, and didn't really go out to bars, he said — and I'm not surprised by either answer from the WOW playing twenty-one-year-old — but, he did know of at least one place. Then he added the kicker. He reminded me that with my temporary license, I probably couldn't get a drink.

Well State of Idaho, that really was the kicker. My birthday is in two days and it is entirely possible that, as a forty-six-year-old, away from home visiting my sick father, that your stupid temporary ID will make it impossible for me to enjoy a night out with my sister and my cousin playing pool and having a few drinks.

So, until I return to Idaho and get my plastic driver's license, I'm forced to accept my second-class citizenry, paper ID and all. How screwed up is a system that won't let a forty-six-year-old get a drink without ID, won't let him rent a motel room (even bearing plenty of cash), and won't allow him to do just about anything else?

It's always wonderful to have an educational opportunity thrust upon oneself. In this case, I've learned just how fragile my existence as a citizen is.

Yours Truly,

Citizen Eilers

• • • •

Sitting on the bed in my Yakima motel room, I hope the letter will soothe me the way writing about my father did the day before. But it doesn't. My blood still boils. The DMV post reflects a variety of frustrations, some relating to the DMV and some about the world in general. The system, our system — governmental, corporate, and societal — is bent on torturing me.

Of course, it's not just me. I'm not paranoid. But, the realization that it isn't just me provides no comfort. It is many people like me who have fallen into the cracks, who live as "Crackers". Now I know the term Cracker has already been taken and applied in a different way, but for me it is a good description for all the people who are experiencing what I am experiencing. So, I am reappropriating the term for my needs.

You see, we Crackers are the ones that have fallen into the financial cracks created by this recession. We know that cell phone companies like Sprint charge more for paying a bill in cash. We know that Bank of America charges six dollars to cash a check drawn on one of their own accounts, unless the payee has an account, which will cost a fee anyway (in other words, they are no honoring the check at its face value). We know how difficult it is to function in life without a credit card or a bank account. We know we really don't own anything, other than what we can hide from the electronic matrix, for when something exists on the system (car title, house, bank account, paycheck, investments), it can face a lien. Of course, I understand the hows and whys, the history of defaults, cheaters, and mistakes that have resulted in the system we have. But that knowledge does not ease the frustration of being a Cracker trapped in the system.

Cracks in society have always existed and people have always fallen into the and they will continue to fall into them, as no safety net will catch everyone. Self-sufficiency is difficult — try fishing, hunting, growing food or gathering berries in cities or suburbs — due to our reliance on our corporate/governmental system for food, housing and security, we are at greater risk when we fall into the cracks.

Some Crackers excelled for years, even decades, only to be wiped out by the economic collapse. These are accidental Crackers, who get buried by catastrophic or unexpected events. Other Crackers overleveraged and got bit by it when their jobs vanished. Still others got divorced, which can destroy finances and relationships regardless of whatever solid planning the couple might have done. There are many different stories behind the Cracker phenomenon, but the size of the demographic is reflected by the growing number of payday loan places, pawn shops (which have gone from seedy to hip), low cost retail outlets, dollar stores, and other services, which provide support for Crackers. I call them Cracker support stations.

Finally, there are Crackers like me who prefer the irregular-job route, choosing the hard work and risk of a startup. We are heroes when our startups succeed, but, at times, thought as lazy when it doesn't because we have no "real" job.

During my first experience building a cash-strapped startup during the early 2000s, I learned a great deal about life on the financial edge. For all the fantasy of the garage-startup fairy tale, the reality is that businesses that start in garages, or more likely these days in living rooms, do it because they have no money. This forces entrepreneurs to live like Crackers, conserving cash and helping each other. I slept on couches at other peoples' homes for months while launching ManyOne. I drove with no tags on my car and no insurance while living in Utah at a time when both were legally required. Moving to California, a startup mecca, I arrived with tagless out-of-state plates, commuting fifty-five miles each way for six months from Aptos to San Mateo four days a week. I had no desire to break the rules, but I couldn't afford to conform to them. The trick was to watch for police and, if I saw one, turn before reaching them. Also, I obeyed the traffic laws religiously.

With the little money I did make, I faced a moral dilemma. Do I pay child support or pay for insurance and tags and other basic necessities. My kids won out, though it took years to catch up, while my stress levels spiked. I hated having to break the law to survive, but I did it.

Eventually, I thrived, achieving the success I had pursued. The day I could again buy auto insurance and new tags thrilled me. As did the day I could buy new glasses. Luckily, I have never yearned for the latest cars or clothes, but I do yearn for basic necessities, no debt, and a low stress life.

As I have written, my success was short-lived. The economic collapse derailed my plans, making all the risks I'd taken and all the sacrifices I'd made pointless. Now, I am a Cracker again, living on fumes, watching less educated (or more desperate) Crackers live off of payday loans, even though they might have full-time jobs. At least I still have hope for myself, but for many Crackers I think the future is bleak, as they have little education, no pensions, no 401ks, no health insurance and can expect little from social security.

• • • •

My distrust and frustration sour my positive memories about being a part of the system and improving the world I experienced as a child. Back then, the world made sense. I expected to thrive.

How much of my view of the world came through my parents and how much came through our jeep club is unclear, because their values were aligned. One of the strongest values was rule number one: don't litter! This was especially true within the jeep club family, because the penalty was clear: any club member caught littering, whether on purpose or not, had to wear a litterbug cap. I avoided the cap by never littering, because I would have died from embarrassment: "LITTERBUG", the letters boldly spelling out the crime.

It wasn't a one-sided doctrine. We kids were taught both not to litter and to clean up the litter we found. To teach us the importance of cleaning up litter, and to show us how to contribute to the community, the club participated in Operation Shore Patrol, an annual event where jeepers cleaned Washington State's Ocean Beaches. I was one of hundreds of volunteers, each collecting garbage one piece at a time until we'd gathered twenty thousand (yes thousand) pounds in a single weekend. As a child, those huge piles of garbage impacted me.

Through the club I also learned about caring for the planet by planting trees following a forest fire. I can remember climbing hills in national forests carrying little containers full of either cedar or fir seedlings, digging tiny holes, slipping the baby tree into them, and covering over the roots. These events involved multiple clubs and, like the beach cleanup, hundreds of volunteers. Most importantly, these were on the ground, all day, trying-to-make a difference projects. We were the system, working together to make the world better.

Other volunteer projects included trail-work parties, designed to preserve the trails we used, both for our benefit and so that others could use them, including motorcycle riders, hikers, hunters and, even today, mountain bikers and ATVs. I remember the special opportunities for physically challenged kids and adults for whom we organized four-wheel-drive trips. We worked at Seattle's favorite summer party, Seafair, volunteering for the closing event, the hydroplane races, as garbage collectors, bathroom monitors, and staff-support.

Most importantly, from all these activities I learned there was a long list of things we could do to help our communities, both individually and as a group. Since I was never involved in Indian Guides, Cub Scouts, or Boy Scouts, it was through my jeep club and my parents that I formed these views.

That ideal, of helping others and contributing to society, was strongly imprinted on me. I followed rules because of this experience, trying to live up to agreements I made, assuming others would reciprocate. These lessons still act as a guide for how I proceed in life and influence on how I operate eWillys, uncovering misleading ads, helping people who need help, and building a community.

After my financial crash in 2007 and 2008, which sent me back to Crackerville, I lost my bearings. Since I felt so much had been taken from me, I rejected the system, limiting my involvement whenever possible, for reasons my Idaho DMV experience underscores.

To find my bearings, I reached back to a simpler time, to a world that made sense to me. Jeeps. The more I thought about it, the more I wanted to build a jeep like I'd built in 1984. This wasn't just something to keep me busy, a hobby to distract me. Instead, I *needed* the entire process. After the crash of my companies, I *needed* to do something successful. The jeep I built and call Lost Biscuit was my therapy, my Zoloft®, the garage my sanctuary. It kept me sane from 2007 through 2010, as the recession consumed both my assets and income, like the Great Depression had eroded my grandparents' finances so long ago. It was a full circle, so to speak.

I guess I could have given up and turned my back on the world, but that isn't my style. I have to do things. I have to work. So, I began to build Lost Biscuit at the start of 2007. Initially I purchased a modified flatfender for $700. After disassembling it, I realized some of the parts were in bad condition, so I traded the spare parts I didn't need for parts I needed. Next, I bought a 1973 CJ-5 and then a non-running flatfender, taking both apart.

I mixed and matched parts, keeping what worked and shedding what didn't. Despite all the parts I'd gathered, I still had to customize much of the jeep. However, it didn't take me long to discover I'd forgotten many of the practical aspects of building one. I had to re-teach myself how to arc weld. I also had to borrow my father's jeep manuals and tools to rebuild a transfercase. In many cases, I relied heavily on the internet to find information, which left me wondering how I ever built my first jeep without it.

One explicit goal I had was to create the type of modified jeep seen during the late 1970s. So, I turned to the internet and Craigslist to get the styling elements I needed, searching for a Bobcat fiberglass body, dune buggy seats, Desert Dog tires and cast-aluminum hurricane rims. A funny thing happened while searching for parts and information; I discovered it was hard to find the parts I wanted. Older jeeps and jeepers were disappearing, along with the custom old-school parts of the 1970s and 1980s. I also couldn't find a useful resource that highlighted old jeeps for sale across the model spectrum. The most important thing I discovered was, to my surprise, no one had started a museum to preserve jeeps and tell their history.

It occurred to me that if I had these frustrations, others must have had them too. Other jeep lovers must want a museum. Other Willys nuts must want a way to follow the classic jeep market. Other jeepers and former jeepers must be just as crazy about classic jeeps as I am.

Certainly, there are excellent websites out there, but in many cases they are usually focused on one type of jeep. I had a wider vision: a website that was updated daily and shared information about all models. Eventually, I decided to focus on three things: 1) everything having to do with flatfenders, (2) deals on 1960s & 1970s non-flatfenders, such as CJ-5s, M-151s, trucks, jeepsters and wagons, and (3) highlight lesser known jeeps, such as FCs, Jeep Vans, DJ-6s, racers and oddballs. There are no hard and fast rules about what I post, except that I have to find it interesting. Sometimes, my posts don't even include jeeps.

As my vision came into focus, I realized that my website was a chance to pursue a passion and contribute to a community that had been so important to me in my youth. It also gave me the chance to learn what things had changed in the world of jeeps and what were the same. For example, did people in four wheel drive clubs still race jeeps? Had membership in clubs changed significantly? Was there a market for old jeeps? What were people doing with them?

As my interest for launching the website grew during 2007, I realized it could be a useful way to gauge public interest in building a jeep museum. I had two central questions to answer: *if I built it, would enough people visit to make it financially viable?* And *how would I pay for building it?*

I didn't know if the website couldn't provide those answers, but I did know it could answer two other important questions: (1) *what jeeps were still available to put into a museum?* And (2) *what would it cost to purchase different kinds of jeeps?*

I launched eWillys in January of 2008 from my living room couch using Wordpress as the backbone. I sensed this project had legs, the possibility of growing into something amazing if I could realize my dream. Even better, because it cost little to launch eWillys, my risk was low. I told myself that if I just posted ten jeeps per day, everyday, in two years I would have information on about 7000 different jeeps. Feeling like that goal was achievable, I began to post information, using Wordpress' built-in tools — categories and tags — to organize the jeeps into sensible classes. Thus, starting from nothing, eWillys' loosely organized online museum of jeeps has grown a little bit every day.

While I have worked hard to grow the site, devoting roughly 3,500 hours over the last four years to the project, the world-wide community of jeepers has been integral to its growth. Through interest, word of mouth, and comments, we have all built eWillys into an important part of the daily lives of jeep lovers, classic jeep junkies, and those poor folks that suffer from the debilitating Willys Sickness, who understand that owning one jeep just isn't enough.

• • • •

My phone alarm buzzes. Disoriented, I sit up. My computer is on the bed from last night and I am still wearing my clothes. I locate my phone and turn off the buzzing; my sleepy eyes focus on it. 7am. I am still in Yakima. I realize I had fallen asleep working on eWillys. I rub my face and eyes with my hands, trying to wake myself. I need to shower, get an update on Dad, buy tires and get to Seattle.

Before I leave the motel, I check my email. There is no response from Virginia. Given the decrease in our emails over the past few days, I wonder if we will fade apart like friends sometimes do. Or, will she pop back into my life, suddenly, like she did twenty-five years ago when she reappeared at Roche?

David Eilers

20. MID-AUGUST, 1986: A SURPRISE

I will never forget where I was when Virginia returned to Roche Harbor. She arrived around three o'clock in the afternoon in mid-August. I know this because I was in the restaurant doing prep for that evening's barbeque. I was sautéing a pan of Uncle Ben's rice with butter and mixing it with sautéed vegetables for the nightly rice pilaf. Grant came to me and said someone was in the back of the kitchen looking for me. I wondered who that could be, so I turned off the burner and stepped around the corner.

There she stood in a bright yellow dress . . . Virginia. She filled the kitchen with sunlight. Her face beamed, exploding into a huge smile when she saw me. A week earlier the Virginia I'd met dressed in casual clothes, unprepared for romance. The Virginia standing before me now could cause traffic accidents. I walked up to her, mouth agape and started talking, but don't remember a single thing I said. I never thought she'd really come back. But, there she was, all for me.

She understood that I had to work, but wanted me to know she would be around. I probably said something like "mi casa es su casa", telling her to make my trailer hers and to do what she wanted. As she left, I turned to see Grant, who looked at me, then looked at her, and then back at me.

"She's here to see you?" He asked, unbelieving.

"Yep," I proudly replied. I think that day Grant found a whole new respect for me.

The entrance to the mausoleum, "Afterglow Vista", truly a unique place.

Virginia stayed with me for five days. We walked to the mausoleum, peeked in the church, and roamed the docks. We explored new areas of the island by day and slept next to one another at night, sharing stories and dreams. She cut my hair. I fixed her food. The trailer became our fantasy island, our little corner of paradise. In the evenings we walked down to the beach near the swimming pool to relax by the bonfire.

We exchanged more stories. She told me tales of life in Santa Monica, California, where she spent summers during high school with her grandmother, who had been a well-known actress in the 1940s and still made occasional appearances on film into the 1970s. Virginia would accompany her to studios, where she met a variety of stars, including one her all-time favorites, Katherine Hepburn. She'd loved her time with her grandmother.

Me at the mausoleum in 2011, standing just behind the 'broken' column. It looks nearly identical to the way it looked twenty five years ago.

I told her that my parents didn't name me. I lived life as Baby Boy Eilers for two days, because my parents couldn't decide what to call me. I still had no name when family friends and fellow jeepers Jim and Patti Carter visited us. Surprised to learn my parents had yet to name me they suggested one: David Eilers. My parents liked it. I always thought being named by a couple of jeeping friends was appropriate for me. Virginia laughed when she heard the story. Even better, I told her, when my sister was born she spent life as Baby Girl Eilers until Jim and Patti dropped by to suggest a name for her: Kimberly Eilers.

After five days of living in our own world, sharing feelings, kindness, and tenderness, it was time for Virginia and me to part. The one thing we never discussed was the future, our future. Maybe that was because it was still so unclear. We let loose the future to relish the present. But, the present had ended.

With one final kiss, we said goodbye. She teared up, wishing she didn't have to go. I promised to write and she said she would, too. With that, she drove out of Roche Harbor and out of my life. As I know now, she left her heart behind with me.

I did write. I sent her a letter and awaited a reply, a reply that was strangely delayed. It would take more than a month to receive her response. Summer would end and fall begin before her card arrived. Perhaps the fact she waited so long to write back coupled with the content of her letter convinced me she wasn't too serious. Or, maybe it was me, that I wasn't all that serious. Truthfully, from this vantage point, I don't know.

21. JUNE 3RD, 2011

On June 3rd, I roll into Seattle on brand new tires I purchased in Yakima, driving straight to the hospital. I already learned from Mom that doctors diagnosed Dad with a blood infection. The doctors were also worried that his "pig valve", a replacement valve he received several years earlier, might be infected.

Based on their diagnosis, the hospital began administering an antibiotic. They had given him only two rounds of antibiotic by the time I walk into his room, but Dad looks a thousand times better than just a week ago. He is surprisingly alert and chatty, asking when he can leave the hospital.

According to the doctor, Dad could have died, because the infection is quite serious. Despite his already amazing recovery, the antibiotic treatment has only just begun; it will take a total of six weeks to complete. The drug with have to be intravenously administered twice a day, each round requiring one and a half hours to finish dripping into his body. This will be done at home by my mother. Six weeks. Twice a day. Three hours each day. I wonder how my mother can do this and still do all the other things she must do around the house. My list of reasons for moving to Seattle keeps growing.

Dad interrupts me as I ponder what Dad's medicine regime means for my future. He tells me his is ready to go home. I remind him it still isn't time, distracting him with more questions about traveling back to Sea Cliff after his grandfather died. He begins to tell a story that I'd heard before when my sister and her kids walk into the room. Kim wants to show Dad some new tricks Tommy learned on his unicycle, so while she hands Dad the camera, I take some pictures. It's a nice family moment. Given Dad's rapid return to health, I'm beginning to think we might have more happy times ahead.

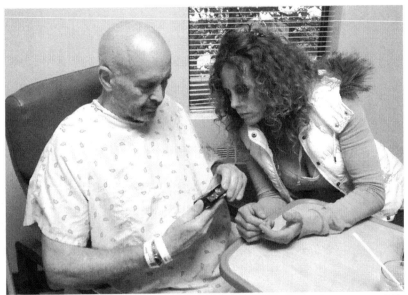

My father and sister. He is watching a video on my sister's camera while he was in the hospital. In just forty-eight hours he improved dramatically.

• • • •

Though I had sent her an email two days ago, I have received no response from Virginia regarding my trip to Seattle. So, having been woken by my father early in the morning and unable to get back to sleep, I try sending out another email. I want to update her:

June 4 2011 – 7:50 AM

Virginia,

I finally made it up to Seattle yesterday, rolling in on new tires. Dad had a miraculous recovery yesterday. By the time I walked into the hospital room just after lunch, he was sitting up, his eyes were clear and his speech lucid. It turns out that he had been suffering from a blood infection, probably for a couple weeks. It only took a couple doses of antibiotic to suppress the infection.

This morning the phone rang at the house at 6:20am. It tugged me from sleep. The phone stopped ringing, so I tried to go back to sleep. A few minutes later it rang again, so I thought I'd better investigate. Sure enough, the caller ID indicated it was Valley Medical Center. I reluctantly answered. I figured it was either the staff asking us to come down right away or it was my father.

It was my father:

> **me (very sleepy):** Hello.
> **Dad (speaking cheerfully):** Hi Son, what are you up to?
> **me:** Sleeping.
> **Dad:** Sleeping? Don't you know what time it is?
> **me:** Yes, 6:20 in the morning.
> **Dad:** Well, I've been up since 5. What's your mother doing?
> **me:** Sleeping
> **Dad:** Oh, ok. Well, I'll let you get back to bed. Talk to you later.
> **me:** Sounds good Dad, talk to you later.

20 minutes later . . .

> **me:** Hello.
> **Dad:** Hi Son. Is your mom up yet?
> **me:** No, it is 6:40 in the morning. She is sleeping.
> **Dad:** Ok. Tell her I called.
> **me:** I will. Goodbye Dad.
> **Dad:** Love ya.
> **me:** Love you too Dad.

15 minutes later . . .

> **me:** Hello.
> **Dad:** Tell your mom I want to leave.
> **me:** She is still sleeping. Are you feeling impatient?
> **Dad:** Yes, when she wakes up, tell her I am ready to go.

me: I will. Goodbye Dad.
Dad: Goodbye.

Yes, my father has recovered some. He almost seems normal. Now, if he would only sleep more, I could too!

- D

Well, normal is a subjective term. He is his normal post-stroke self. He has only been in the hospital for two days, but he already wants to leave. We have to tell him he can't. His release date remains unknown.

While sitting with Dad at the hospital, I use his alert moments to query him about family history and jeeps, testing his knowledge of what I know and hoping to learn something new. Some of his memories are accurate and some are not. Other times he isn't so alert. There are still hints of the confusion I had previously seen, such as him asking questions that I'd answered only to have him ask again.

After a couple days at the hospital, a brain specialist looked at images of Dad's brain, which show a large black hole on the right side. The doctor said he is amazed Dad can do anything at all. Given his history, my father is doing better than he should be, maybe due to luck or, more likely, because he never gives up trying.

22. JUNE 5th, 2011

I turn forty-six today. While Mom is tending Dad at the hospital, I tackle my sonny-do chores around the house, including sweeping the pine needles and moss off the roof (a biannual chore), repairing the door handles in the back bedrooms, pruning some branches from around the TV dish, sawing some firewood, and anything else she can't do.

Late in the afternoon I am standing on the roof almost done sweeping it when my phone rings. It is Mom. She says Dad is especially impatient today, declaring his intent to leave multiple times. His unhappiness turned to belligerence directed at Mom, frustrating her to the point that she left the hospital early and is heading home. The call is less about an update on Dad and more about Mom needing to vent, which is completely understandable. She knows it is his post-stroke persona that is causing his behavior, but that knowledge doesn't always help. This is not the man she married. She confessed a few days ago that she hadn't had a real conversation with him since the stroke, as he doesn't have the ability to carry on an extended discussion. It was a sad admission.

Most of the time, to Dad's credit, he thanks Mom and me for favors big and small. But, the capacity to maintain his cool when frustrated was damaged by the stroke. That is when dealing with him is difficult.

Last summer he and I had a showdown over me driving my kids and their cousins in his truck down to my sister's place. Dad was convinced the six of us were too heavy for the truck, a four door 2001 Dodge, one-ton, four-wheel-drive truck. I told him he was being ridiculous, which he was. He argued it was his truck and his decision. We went back and forth until Mom, disagreeing with Dad in private, yet not wanting to disagree with him in front of me, agreed to follow me down with a couple of the kids in her car. Dad and I remained mad at each other until the next day. Stroke or no stroke, I didn't want to give into the arbitrary nature of his decision, mostly because he wasn't treating me like an adult and that made me angry. It was the first time in twenty years we had argued like that. If I am going to spend time around Dad, I will have to figure out how to deal with situations like this.

Two hours later I am driving my car through downtown Renton, following my mother. We will be celebrating my birthday with a dinner at the Royal Orchid, a thai restaurant on Rainier Avenue. Mom chose this place after asking me what I'd like eat. She said it is very good.

We park and walk toward the front door. The restaurant appears to be a remodeled Skippers Restaurant, though the owners have camouflaged it so well that after opening the front door I begin to doubt my initial impression.

Joining Mom and I are Marilyn and Phil, my sister and her boyfriend Ken, and my sister's kids, Holly and Tommy. As everyone sits down to the table, Mom asks me to order the food, knowing I have specific ideas about what I want. After a quick review of the menu I choose some Tom Ka Gai, the chicken-galangal-coconut soup that caused me to fall in love with Thai food eighteen years ago in Port Townsend. To that I add two orders of salmon curry, which they prepare with thai basil and red pepper just as I like it; two orders of pad thai with shrimp; a massaman curry with beef, which I prefer with sautéed peanuts; and an order of the Royal Orchid Special Noodle, which contains wide noodles seasoned with soy sauce and topped with peanut sauce, a dish I'd never tried.

The order complete, we turn our attention to Mom as she updates us on the latest news from the doctor and explains the events that made her so mad earlier in the day. She is nearly done talking when the food arrives. The noise of serving and passing food is followed by quiet as we consume the delicious dinner. Everyone seems satisfied. All the dishes are very good, but I am particularly fond of the Special Noodles with peanut sauce, making a note to myself to research similar recipes: it is a dish I want to cook.

Stuffed with noodles, curries and rice, we say our goodbyes. Everyone is headed back to their homes, except Mom and me. She is heading to the hospital, while I decide to go shoot some pool and relax.

I play a few rounds of pool and have a beer at the Spot Tavern, but soon grow bored. It is Sunday night and the bar is slow. So, I head home. I arrive at the house and check my email, finding a birthday surprise:

June 5, 2011 – 9:26 PM

I am sorry, Dave,

I read all your mail at once. Between work and my son I am buried alive!!

I am sorry you, your dad and mom went through all that. It seems you are needed now.

You wrote many interesting things and I read it all. It seems the most important news was about your folks and your kids.

HAPPY BIRTHDAY you karaoke stud you!!

I will write at length soon,

love, Virginia

I sigh, happily. Because her emails had grown infrequent, I began to wonder if my contact with her had grown too uncomfortable. However, it appears she has just been busy. Feeling relieved, I share more updates:

June 5, 2011 – 11:40 PM

Virginia,

Thanks for the birthday greeting and the well wishes! I wasn't worried that you hadn't responded. I planned to keep writing :-)

I went out to the Spot Tavern and shot some pool. I beat a guy named Billy two games to one. By the soft shake of Billy's hand and some of his comments, I suspect pool wasn't what he was really interested in . . . but, it was fun to play a few games. I believe he quickly realized that pool was all I was interested in, so he left after three games. After finishing my beer, I drove home.

Dad is really doing much better now. He had a blood infection and some antibiotics really have done the trick. He is back to being a little more boisterous and has more spirit. He's way more lucid. I'll be hanging out through the end of the week. Then, I'll be back in another week with my kids.

My plan is move back permanently after they leave, so mid to late July.

How's the patient doing? And, how are you doing?

- D

I don't hear back from Virginia until the following evening:

June 6, 2011 – 9:47 PM

Hi there Dave,

The patient got bad news today, he will be laid up for a couple months. I am very sad over this but will take it day at a time.

It seems you are helping your folks and it is good you are there for now. I am sure your Dad actually understands when you come and go from visiting, but he is in anguish. We need our loved ones when we are suffering. Men his age do not have honed communication skills, as we discussed.

I hope that your dad can be home and your mom does not get too worn and can enjoy him and her life.

I am glad you averted an illicit gay affair. Although, I was not sure if you were trying to tell me something. I know people do change and I do not want my joke to be in bad taste.

I am off work tomorrow. Maybe we should see each other if possible,

Virginia

I immediately respond with an email, agreeing to her proposal:

June 6, 2011 – 10:15 PM

Virginia,

You are funny :-). No, I wasn't trying to tell you anything other than I thought it was funny. I have had plenty of gay friends (and a couple of gay business partners), but I have never had any interest to 'bat for the other team' as they say.

I think Mom is actually enjoying him in the hospital. She's getting LOTS of work done and doesn't have to worry about him yelling for her. She's 71, but right now she's out there on a ladder scooping pine needles off the roof. She's been up since 6am and won't sleep until midnight.

I did make her dinner tonight as a treat. She's so funny when I make dinner, because she watches me like a hawk; partly she watches me because she wants to know exactly what I am doing when I cook and partly because she can't help but correct me when I'm cooking.

I would LOVE to see you tomorrow. However, I know your schedule is busy, so didn't want to put any pressure on you.

I will be near my computer until around midnight and then will check it around 7am (unless I can't sleep). So, let me know what works for you and I will make it work for me.

- Dave

Comfortable we have a meeting arranged I go to sleep happy. In the morning I find a follow-up email that surprises me. She wonders why it is her who always suggests we meet:

June 7, 2011 – 8:30 AM

Dave-

I am so tired (winded) that I can barely get this email out. When I can let down, my mind and body take over.

The wind has kicked up and it makes me just want to stay in. Last days off were in panic mode. I feel bad because every time we have met it was at my suggestion. I was, of course, so taken by the fact that you had saved pieces of me so dearly. What was I supposed to do?

I am curious, why you never asked to see me any of these times?

Virginia

Her question is fair. I have not pushed meetings because of her situation. She has a tight schedule and a big risk of impropriety, so it makes sense to me that she be the one who suggests meeting times. She needs to know that the passiveness I express is out of courtesy and not due to disinterest. So, I show some aggressiveness to underscore my interest.

June 7, 2011 – 9:00 AM

Virginia –

Why haven't I been the one to suggest the meetings? Well, I will have to look through and see what I wrote in my emails, but I have always wanted to see you.

I know you've been so busy that I didn't want you to feel like you had to carve out another piece of your life to fit me in it (especially given the new patient). So, that's me being a nice guy.

So, let me be a little more forward. Yes, I want to see you. I'd love to kiss you. I would love to run my hand down your body, tracing the outlines of each part of you. I'd like to stay up all night talking. But, I didn't want to come on like a freight train after we re-connected.

So, if you'd like to rest today, do you have time tomorrow?

- Dave

Apparently, that gets her attention:

June 7, 2011 – 9:30 AM

Dave-

Ok, now I am blushing. I cannot handle not knowing the truth. I want to see you but I am exhausted. Maybe you could come up and we can meet at a Starbucks. That way the temptation of the body thing would just have to stay in place.

Either tomorrow at 10 a.m. in Factoria or today around 11 or so, in Factoria.

I know I need to rest, but you may not be up here again for a while. So I am making an effort because you have been a nice guy.

Virginia

I interpret her email as best I can. I think her emotions, her needs, and her obligations are confusing her. She doesn't want to feel like she is chasing me, which is how the meetings have unfolded, due to my effort not to push her too fast. So, I need to lead, give her a chance to respond to me. With that in mind, I decide to stop worrying about her. I decide to focus on what I want. So, I respond with what I want:

June 7, 2011 – 9:45 AM

Virginia,

I want to meet Today at 11am . . . which Starbucks?

- Dave

The answer is more complex than I imagined:

June 7, 2011 – 10:19 AM

Dave-

There are two in Factoria, both in the same complex, on the east side of Factoria Boulevard, just south of I-90.

So the complex has a Bartells set back in the center and a QFC to its left. As you arrive heading north, the Starbucks is on the first right hand space where the L-shape comes out to the road. The complex is directly across from the Factoria Cinemas. The Starbucks is the one more south than the one set back between Bartells and QFC. OK? 11am.

Virginia

I immediately hop into my father's truck, because it is rarely driven and needs to be driven, and drive fifteen minutes north to Factoria.

I arrive early. The weather is cool, so I enter Starbucks, sit down and wait. The clock ticks slowly past 11:00am and then 11:10. I begin to wonder if she has changed her mind or has a problem, but I see no new emails on my phone.

As I look outside, I finally spot her wandering up and down the parking lot. That is when I realize I hadn't told her I would be driving the truck.

I dash outside and yell. She appears relieved, saying she was looking for my car, which prompts an apology on my part as I explain about the truck.

She also says she has a surprise, a special place she wants to share. So, after ordering our drinks from the coffee shop, we climb in our cars and she leads me to a part of Bellevue I'd never seen, a place called Water Tower Park, named for the giant green water tower built on top of the hill. A place I will never forget.

Despite all the time I have spent biking the Renton/Bellevue area, I'd bypassed this hilltop, missing it entirely. We walk side by side up a path as she explains to me how she'd discovered the park while searching for a friend's house. The park is small, maybe just a couple acres.

We sit down on a bench, together, but not touching, not holding hands. We are unsure what to do. We don't say much initially, choosing instead to gaze past the bushes to the beautiful view of Lake Washington in the foreground and the buildings of downtown Seattle in the background. On a clear day, the Olympic Mountains would look beautiful from this spot, but today gray skies and billowy clouds hide them.

Eventually, she says, "I brought you here, because I knew you would love this place."

"You were right. This is beautiful here."

She turns to toward me and struggles with her words. "Dave, this is really hard. I love your emails, but they are ripping me apart. A part of me wants to know more about you and spend time with you. You have been so wonderful, so thoughtful and that feels so good. I have been more lonely than I realized, masking it with work and my son. But, I have responsibilities. I need to be true to who I am. I am unsure I can remain just a friend. There is too much emotion involved. I just don't know if I can handle any more emails."

I thought for a few seconds. "Virginia, I understand. I have no desire to upset you or create any discord within your family. I contacted you because I needed to know why I kept the letter, what your life was like, and whether you were happy. I had to know. Maybe you are right. Maybe this can't work."

She nodded. "Thanks Dave. I am just so appreciative of your keeping my letter all these years. It means the world to me."

I make a suggestion, "What if I email you once a month? I want to maintain some contact, because I don't want to lose you for another twenty-five years. We can let our lives evolve and support each other as friends when necessary. What do you think about that?"

"Once a month would be fine. I think that all sounds good."

The agreement feels artificial, awkward, but we need to try something, because she is unhappy with the current state of our relationship.

We stand up and walk, but I stop her. I want to express to her what I am feeling. But, for all my eloquent emails, words fail me, because I am not sure exactly what I am feeling. As I dig through my emotions I feel elements of caring, love, and respect. Passion lurks as well. I am at a loss to understand exactly what we have and what we mean to the other. But I feel I must say or do something.

So, I turn her and bring her close to me, hugging her as deeply as I can. She hugs me back. We hugged during our last visit, but this time is different. She releases her reservations, melts into me, and then burrows her head into the crook of my neck.

As we hold each other Virginia says something and I ask her what, but she can't speak. She says it again. I think I hear "Oh My God", but I can't be sure. She says it a third time. She is overcome with emotion. Suddenly, she pushes back, separating us. The experience is too powerful, too much. The space between us calms her. Regaining her composure, we walk and talk some more about nothing in particular.

We make our way around the back of the water tower, where she tells me a couple personal stories of adventure with a friend. As she talks, I reach for her hand. It is the first time in twenty-five years I have felt her hand. She doesn't resist, instead holding on to my hand as well. I wish her stories would go on and on, but Virginia's tight schedule forces us to return to our vehicles.

We walk slowly back to the parking lot, our hands no longer together. Before we part, I look into her eyes. It is time to tell her how I feel. She needs to hear it. She is special to me, not as a future lover, not as a potential conquest, but as someone with whom I feel deeply and soulfully intimate. I am sure it was true two and a half decades ago and I know it is true now. I know no other way to express it except to tell her I love her, that I feel love for her.

"I love you." I say it with warmth and certainty. Yet, I do not want to mislead her, to think I am trying to sweep her off her feet with the promise of an intimate relationship. I just feel she needs to hear someone who cares about her share those feelings with her. She deserves that.

A few tears slide down her cheek as she stares back at me. Nothing more needs to be said.

We part. She walks to her car and I walk to Dad's truck. I am about to jump in the front seat when I hear her.

"DAVE!" She yells mournfully. It is a raw, last gasp before her worst fears are realized, that she might never see me again.

I step backward so I can see her behind the truck cab.

"I love you too!" She says tearfully.

"I know," I say, touching my index and middle fingers of my right hand against my lips to blow her a kiss. She returns it.

I told her I loved her, because it was an honest admission I found self-evident. It was true. Sometimes I think we forget that recognition of feelings is separate from how we act upon those feelings. I wasn't saying it hoping to carve out more of a relationship or to encourage or persuade her to do something she didn't want to do. The feelings I felt were ones that bubbled to the surface, dormant for years. She was a special person in my life, a good person, who deserved to be told she was loved. I wanted her to hear it. Frankly, we all need to hear it.

From the park, I drive straight home. As I pass through the streets of Renton, thoughts of the morning and what it means keep my mind and my emotions busy. Yet, I am not sad at our parting. I know we both are going the directions we need to go in life. We both want to respect where we are, yet also want to recognize the feelings for what they are: rich, powerful, warm. Maybe being friends would be too hard on both of us, yet shouldn't we try? I know I don't want to enter a physical relationship with her until we are clear of our responsibilities, but does that mean we can't be friends? I just don't know how to define this relationship I have, or want to have, with her. This is tougher than I thought it would be.

I arrive at home and jump onto my computer and send an email with the subject line, "Just One More Email":

> June 7, 2011 – 12:48 PM
>
> *Virginia-*
>
> *I love you and always will. You truly are someone I could trust to hand my heart to and keep it safe. That really is a big step for me personally, just to know how it feels, again. Truthfully, whether as a friend or something more in the future, I will always have strong feelings for someone as wonderful as you.*
>
> *Love Dave.*

She answers quickly:

> June 7, 2011 – 1:00 PM
>
> *Dave-*
>
> *I just have to see you again. Tomorrow, 10am, Water Tower Park.*
>
> *Virginia*

I reply:

> June 7, 2011 – 1:11 PM
>
> *Virginia- I will be there. :-)*

She responds with a joke:

> June 7, 2011 – 1:33 PM
>
> *Dave- That's two more emails . . . and a smarty pants answer from me. Yes, tomorrow.*

Later, she follows up with another email:

June 7, 2011 – 4:00 PM

Dave-

Now I cannot stop thinking about you. How I want you to kiss me passionately. How I want you to touch me.

I wanted to say "I love you" and now I will, to your face. I am on fire for you. I cannot avoid it; I am burning for you. Did you drive away wanting me at least that much? I was and am in a haze. I hope I do not chicken out about tomorrow for fear of further unlocking my desire for you.

Maybe I will inspire you to write your book(s) and you may dedicate one to your "femme", private as it is to just us.

You make me weak and very weak in the knees. I want to fall into your arms as soon as I see you. I was suppressing more than I realized.

I am planning on holding your neck in my hands and kissing you there until you cannot stand it any longer. I have been thinking of all the incredible things we could do with each other, driven by the need for intimacy and satisfaction. My thoughts are intertwined with my body in a raging fire. I must sign off. I am driving myself crazy.

Thank you for telling me you love me, I cherish this as you have always cherished my letter and photos. I cannot hear that enough from you. I am melting into your arms in my mind at every moment of this day until I see you.

Signed with a sensual kiss, until tomorrow,

Virginia

I write back:

June 7, 2011 – 5:02 PM

Virginia-

As we hugged I could feel you letting go and melting into me. Trust that I understand exactly how you feel. I wanted to kiss you badly at the park and almost did. Just holding your hand was tremendously passionate. The thing I find most exciting about you is the emotional intimacy I feel with you and how much deeper the possibilities are in that realm.

I will be there tomorrow.

Dave

She explains more:

June 7, 2011 – 5:30 PM

Dave-

I should not have shared so much, but you deserve it for opening up and finding me.

I felt you holding my hand in a very intimate way. I can still feel it. See you in the morning. I will try to be early 9:45. You will likely hit traffic, I am sorry for that. Otherwise we would not have enough time to see each other.

Love, Virginia

The last few responses I had typed using my phone. Now, finally at my computer, I answer her more fully.

June 7, 2011 – 7:44 PM

Virginia-

I can still smell you on me. I've been smelling my clothes all afternoon. It reminds me that you were in my arms. It reminds me of the noises you made as we hugged, so deeply honest about how you felt. I couldn't tell you if you were saying "Oh my God" or "I love you" or "You need new deodorant". Honestly, I didn't even need to ask; I knew you loved me. I already knew.

If I'm emotionally deep with you, it's because you make it easy. It is as natural as breathing.

I've spent years moving around looking for my place in the world. Where can I be happy has been the question? I really always thought it would be a place. This is the first time I've ever thought it could be a person. And, it's not that I need a person to be happy, but that it would be a person and not a place that would ultimately ground me. You enrich my life and that's what I always wanted out of another. That's a pretty big realization, as I'm a pretty independent guy.

It will be difficult not to spend my entire time thinking of you. But then, I've been thinking about you every day since that first day we talked.

- Dave

Her last email of the evening explains what she whispered:

June 7, 2011 – 8:30 PM

Dave-

Thank you for this heartfelt response. I am tired now and will check these later and/or see you in the morning. I was saying "Oh my God".

V

Oh my God. Those were my feelings too. Oh my God our connection is strong. Oh my God we need to be careful. Oh my God we can't do this. Oh my God I don't want to hurt her again. Oh my God I don't want to have an affair, even if I plan to be single very shortly. So many feelings whirl through me as I think about our short time together.

Not able to think clearly, I decide to grab a late dinner. I drive over to Pho Hut, a favorite pho restaurant in the Fairwood Shopping Center. It is a family run place that consistently serves soup with a rich broth and plenty of meat for a reasonable price. I have never had a bad meal there.

As a frequent customer, I walk straight to the register to order my number 19—beef soup with rice noodles, tripe, tendon, flank, and beef—before sitting down. I find a table, sit, and wait as they prepare my soup. I quickly receive a large glass of water and sip it, slowly.

I'm trying to piece together how late August and September of 1986 unfolded; what I was thinking and doing when Virginia left after her second visit.

I remember writing her a letter soon after she drove away. I remember the days shortening quickly as August turned into September and Labor Day weekend. As the end of the barbeque neared, I remember Grant and Reaf offering me a full-time position on the dinner line that would last until early October, after which they wouldn't need me again until spring.

Despite sifting through those memories, I still couldn't remember how I felt about not receiving a response from Virginia. Instead, by far the clearest memory I have of the time period between Virginia leaving in August and me receiving her letter in late September was a jeep trip Cullen and me took over the Naches Trail: my favorite all-time adventure.

23. EARLY SEPTEMBER 1986: SUMMER'S END JEEP TRIP

It only took a few boneheaded moves for me to land in this spot: pointed uphill in my jeep, a forty-foot cliff twenty-feet behind me, the battery dead, the engine dead, my foot shaking on the brake, stuck in the middle of the Cascade Mountain Range far from any phones or help. Actually, I did have help, as my co-pilot on this adventure was Cullen. He had already pulled the winch cable toward a tree and wrapped the cable around it. Then, he had run back to the jeep and wound the loose cable around the bumper, until it was as tight as he could make it. At that point, I removed my shaking foot from the brake, as my emergency brake—a future enhancement—had yet to be installed, causing me to drift slowly backward for a distance of a foot until the winch cable tightened, anchoring the jeep to the tree.

We found ourselves in this predicament far from where we began on San Juan Island. With summer over, we'd wanted to celebrate with a few days of fun, so we decided to go jeeping on the mainland. Since Cullen had never been jeeping, except for some short island excursions, he was excited to give it a try. I suggested we explore a trail I knew: the Naches Trail.

We'd started our trip at my parents' house in Renton, two days earlier. Packing the jeep with a winch, rope, tools, a heavy chain, a shovel, a pulley, and camping gear, our destination was the Cascade Mountains. Though we had no map, I did have a general sense of where to go.

Initially, we drove to the town of Enumclaw, which sits at the foothills of the Cascades. Along the way, of all things, a bee stung me as we entered the city limits. Cullen was driving, while I sat in the passenger seat, the air whipping through the open jeep, when I suddenly felt a sharp pain on my arm. Pulling off my jacket, I saw the bee momentarily before the wind sucked it away. Thankfully, this was a minor irritation rather than a medical emergency, because I'm not allergic to bees.

We left Enumclaw driving east on Hwy 410 and passed a place called Greenwater. A few miles later, a train trestle I hoped to see came and went, increasing my confidence we were heading the right direction. After passing a few remote gravel roads that disappeared into the landscape, I spotted a forest service road that I thought looked correct. Unsure if this was the right one, we turned onto the logging road and drove toward deep green mountains. I figured if we were going the wrong way, we could always come back down.

Once on the dirt and gravel road, wide enough in some spots for two vehicles and in others for just one, we still had to locate the jeep trail. At the very least, we had to drive a few miles into the interior of the valley before it started. I remembered that the jeep trail went straight up a hill, while this logging road zigzagging up it. Eventually, I calculated, the jeep trail would cross the weaving logging road, assuming this logging road was the correct one.

The hill steepened and the road wove back and forth with greater frequency. Soon, we spotted the Naches Trail veering off to our right, up a sidehill. We stopped, jumped out, and turned the front hubs to four-wheel drive (no auto-four wheel drive hubs in older jeeps). I also shifted the transfercase into four-wheel drive, low range.

Only one last detail left. After a quick discussion, we decided to remove the windshield and tie it to the back of the rollcage. Without the windshield the visibility improved. Also, driving without the windshield was fun, go-kart like. Having nothing but the nose of the jeep in front and the wind coming directly at us improved our connection to the forest.

Since the jeep's birth, dropping the windshield has been a time-honored way to travel.

Cullen and I are about to explore the Naches Trail in September 1986. With the windshield tied to the back, we are ready to head up the hill.

But, I couldn't drop my windshield, because my fiberglass hood had a rise on its top, due to the custom intake manifold I had on my Buick V6 motor. Therefore, removing it was the next best thing. Once we secured the windshield to the back of the rollcage in a makeshift manner, Cullen and I were ready to crawl up the trail and disappear from the main road and our hectic summer.

• • • •

What I remembered as an all day drive over the Naches Pass, took a mere four hours as we came to the end of the trail, crossing the little Naches River, the dirty tires parting the low late-summer stream. I was disappointed the trail was so short; what I'd thought would be a great adventure was merely an afternoon drive on this day. Maybe the road was smoother than in past years or I didn't pay close enough attention as a teen, but we'd finished with the Naches Trail and had to decide where to go next. I'd like to say we had some grand discussion where we weighed all our options, deciding to pick the best direction based on some worthy goal.

No, instead, after crossing the Naches, we spotted a mud pit called the Rabbit Hole and, because we now suffered from temporary delusions of grandeur, decided to drive through it. We had just jeeped for four hours, traversing varying terrain and obstacles. We figured a forty-yard mud pit couldn't be all that difficult.

Turns out, it can be *really* difficult!

As I approached the mud hole, I did so slowly. I wasn't the type to hit a mud hole at high speed. Instead, I carefully entered, thinking the tires would part the mud like they had the water in the stream, grab the bottom and pull me through.

But, that's not what happened. Not even close. I made it all of two feet before getting stuck. In those two feet I felt like I turned from jeeping expert to jeeping goat. I knew better than to attempt a mud hole with only one jeep, but I guess my twenty-one-year-old cockiness got the better of me. Possibly, my lust for adventure was so great that I needed to take a risk. I would pay a muddy toll for making such a bad decision.

With the jeep stuck and my ego bruised, Cullen and I jumped out and surveyed the situation. The problem, we concluded, was that the hole was deeper than my deluded brain had imagined. I wished we had realized that *before* entering the hole. Fortunately, I had a solution: my trusty Warn winch would save the day.

I stepped onto the front bumper and pulled out the winch so I could hand it to Cullen, who was standing on the bank. He then walked forward, pulling the winch cable until he found a big enough tree to wrap the cable around. With the winch rigged, all that remained was to hit the winch button. Simple, right?

Wrong, again. Boy, I was on a mental tear. The mud was so thick the winch couldn't drag the jeep through it. Even worse, the winch was draining the electrical system, despite my attempts to increase the engine speed.

The jeep is stuck in a mud pit and help is far far away.

Without an alternative, I put the jeep in first gear so the tires could chew through the mud while the winch pulled me. In theory this was a good idea. In practice, this was a very muddy idea, because, as the wheels began to turn, cold thick mud flew, mostly onto me. Worse, to keep the winch working correctly, I increased the engine speed, which improved the performance of the winch, but also increased the tire speed, causing mud to spray everywhere.

The spinning wheels helped immensely and I began to slog forward. But with every inch of travel inside the trench, mud flew, covering me, the jeep, the seats, the camera bag, and everything else in the jeep. Slowly, very slowly I made it through, the winch working hard to wind up the cable. Meanwhile, Cullen was laughing hysterically, keeping his distance so he stayed clean. I couldn't blame him, because this was mostly — ok completely — my dumb idea.

By the time I escaped the Rabbit Hole, inches of mud caked everything. I started the hole with a blue jeep and ended with a brown one. I felt pretty stupid and very mad at myself for entering the mud in the first place, but not as dumb or mad as I would have been if we'd had to walk out of the forest for help. Still, I was humbled by the experience. Nature has a way of doing that to a person.

The jeep and I are pelted with mud as I try to keep the wheels spinning to keep the winch winching. I avoided mud pits after this experience.

After that, we spotted a perfect camping spot, nestled along the river just fifty feet away. So, Cullen jumped onto the back bumper of the muddy vehicle and we idled over to it. While he unpacked the jeep and began the tedious process of cleaning everything that had been in it, I stripped off my muddy clothes and jumped into the Little Naches River for a very cold bath. Then I washed off the jeep.

Luckily, I'd brought Dad's collapsible canvas bucket, which I used to fetch water from the river. At first I poured water all over the jeep, both inside and out. Then, I turned my dirty t-shirt into a washcloth, scrubbing away any mud that stuck to the body. This was a good time to have a poor paint job, because I didn't have to worry about scratching or damaging paint.

By the time we finished cleaning, the sun was going down. We made a small fire, cooked some dinner, and relaxed, happy we had conquered all our obstacles so far. We were all alone, with the forest to ourselves, enjoying our great adventure.

On Wednesday morning we awoke to a beautiful day with a cool edge, a reminder that summer was waning and fall was near. We packed our tent and sleeping bags, ready for more excitement. Even with our adventures, and my questionable decision-making so far, Cullen continued to be a willing participant, open to my suggestions as well as making his own. Sometimes I can't help but wonder if he was questioning my sanity or, maybe, his own. Perhaps, more truthfully, he was having as much fun leaving sanity behind and taking on each adventure as it came.

It was good his outlook was upbeat, because it didn't take long before we found ourselves faced with an even bigger problem than the one we overcame the day before. From our previous night's location at the Little Naches, we jeeped half an hour before we arrived at an odd turn in the trail. The path we followed to this point was a standard double-track trail, parallel bare paths worn by tires over the years and separated by dry grass.

To our left was a grassy slope. Fifty yards up the hill was a stand of trees, which hid the ridge beyond. In front of us was a river gorge, perhaps forty feet below the trail, which veered toward us, intersected the trail in front of us, and then flowed off to the right. To avoid the river, the trail turned left up a relatively steep hill, becoming a single-track trail.

The trail confused me. Something was wrong. I stopped the jeep, jumped out, and checked it. Sure enough, the trail led toward the river, then did a ninety-degree turn up the hill and disappeared into the trees. However, not only was the trail up the hill a single track, it was also much newer. Yet, there was nowhere else to go, except uphill.

Looking up the slope I could see plenty of space through the trees to drive. So, without inspecting further (which I should have) I hopped back into the jeep and put it into gear. Following the trail, we crawled in low range toward the riverbank, turned uphill, and drove another twenty feet when the engine unexpectedly died. I'm not certain why the engine chose that spot to die, but I suspect it wanted to teach me a lesson for driving it through the Rabbit Hole the day before.

Assuming the carburetor flooded, I pushed in the clutch with my left foot, pressed on the brake with the top of my right foot while simultaneously pressing the gas pedal with the bottom of my right foot. It's a dance I had to do anytime I stopped on a hill. I quickly twisted the key, hoping I could overcome a flooded carb and make the engine fire up, but after trying to start it a few times the battery died. Damn, now we were in trouble!

There were a few things about my jeep that were undependable, such as the electrical system, but the engine had always proven dependable (at least until nine months later when it blew apart). This time, the engine let me down.

So, there we were, stuck on a hill, with no emergency brake, not daring to back up, no way to go forward, my foot shaking while I held down the brake, wondering what I should do next. Looking back, I realized that of all the things that went through my mind, my father's crashing roll down the hill wasn't one of them. Shades of his experience never haunted me, because the forty-foot cliff behind me, and the river below it, kept my mind focused on the immediacy of my predicament.

Stabilize the situation was the first thing that came to mind. That is why I had Cullen wrap the winch cable around both the bumper and the tree. We would anchor the jeep off a big pine tree until we decided what to do.

Duly hung, I jumped out of the jeep. We walked up the hill to take a closer look at the trail. Only then did we understand there was no trail, as even the single-track motorcycle trail disappeared. We explored more, eventually finding the other side of the trail. That is when we discovered why nothing made sense. At the point where we veered up the hill, the trail should have gone straight, but an enormous portion of the trail and hillside had been undercut and washed away by the river. This was obvious from the other side the trail, but not so obvious from where we'd come from.

We had a problem and needed a solution. Without battery power (so no winch) and without the ability to start the motor, how could we move the jeep uphill twenty feet and around a large pine tree? Because, if we could do that, we could traverse the side of the hill, compression-start the engine, and continue onward.

Fortunately, I had compression-started the jeep in a ferry line and on a ferry itself (with the help of the boat's crew), on trails, in my parents' driveway, and backward in the limestone quarry of Roche Harbor. I could compression start my jeep anywhere, anytime. If we could make a short runway and generate enough speed, I could get the jeep started again, assuming the engine would fire.

With a general plan in place, we explored specific options.

Believe it or not, this was when I had a flashback to all the physics courses I ever took. My thought process went like this: we needed to create enough force to move the jeep forward. I pondered the forces at our disposal and ways to make them strong enough to move the jeep. I decided we had two options.

> **Option 1.** Chop down a tree. We could run the winch cable to a pulley chained to a tree, thread the cable through the pulley, and then run the cable downhill securing the cable to a sacrificial tree. Then, we'd chop down the sacrificial tree with the cable attached to it using the axe. The tree would fall, pulling the jeep up the hill. The problem was, the jeep was about five feet out of place for that to happen. We needed it further uphill before the angles were right.
>
> **Option 2.** Push down on the winch cable. If the winch cable was stretched long enough between the jeep and a tree, we could step on

it, forcing the cable down. If we used a big enough tree and tied the cable to the base of the tree, the only thing that would give would be the jeep, assuming the cable didn't stretch. Therefore, the jeep should move ahead, even if it is just inches at a time.

Since the jeep was already anchored to a tree by thirty feet of winch cable, Option 2 was an easy plan to test. I told Cullen to jump in the driver's seat, press on the brake, and shift the transmission into neutral. I ran to a point half between the tree and jeep, stepped on the cable and told him to take his foot off the brake. As the cable, with me on it, dropped to the ground, the jeep moved forward slightly. When the cable could drop no farther, the jeep stopped.

At that point Cullen stepped on the brake and I stepped off the cable. I ran down to the jeep and wound the newly loosened cable around the bumper once. Then, I ran back to the middle of the cable and stepped back on it so we could repeat the process. Amazing enough, this desperate plan actually worked! It allowed us to move the jeep forward five feet, before it stopped working.

But that was okay, because now we could execute Option 1, the chopping of the tree. Our goal was to move the jeep an additional ten feet up the hill. From that point, we could round a large tree and then traverse down the hill at an angle, rolling along a sidehill until we gained the speed necessary to compression-start the jeep.

To execute Option 1, we selected a tree to fall, one leaning downhill and large enough to move the jeep, but not so large we risked our lives chopping it down. Next, we snagged the heavy-duty pulley from the back of the jeep and chained it as high as we could to a massive tree twenty feet in front of the jeep, running the winch cable through the pulley. Finally, we tied the end of the cable to our sacrificial tree, leaving some slack so the tree could start to fall and build momentum before the cable tightened.

We double-checked the wind, which was very light this day, a non-issue, before making our first cut. Taking turns, we chopped a wedge out of it in the direction we wanted the tree to fall. When completed, we made a second cut higher than the first, but on the opposite side of the tree.

Sometimes, no matter how good an idea is, an elementary mistake thoroughly mucks up the execution. Case-in-point, just as we planned, the tree fell downhill. Also, the falling tree caused the cable to tighten, tugging at the jeep via the chained block and tackle. Unfortunately, I was so concerned about the direction the tree would fall and whether the plan would work, that I forgot one little detail: to shift the jeep out of gear so it could roll forward.

Ugghhhh . . . Because of my mistake, the jeep remained in gear, acting like a brake, so the falling tree jolted the jeep forward only a few inches.

Admittedly, and fairly, Cullen was a bit miffed at me (as was I). Shifting the jeep into neutral was my responsibility. But my frustration turned to laughter as Cullen grumbled over and over again, "You *forgot* to shift it into neutral. Of Course! *Why do that?*"

With options 1 and 2 spent, it was time to hatch a new plan. We talked through a few ideas, but believed only one would work. The downside was that it was too dangerous to drive part of it. So, we decided to take a risk and send the jeep on an unmanned expedition in what we called Option 3.

Option 3: Tie a heavy chain from the driver's side rollcage bar to a tree and send the jeep down a hill too dangerous to drive. The jeep would pivot around the tree, yet not roll because it was held upright by the tree via the chain. We hoped this would leave the jeep positioned for the last remaining route we could take. We were really reaching with this plan.

First, we had to move the jeep a little farther uphill to skirt a giant pine. Turning back to Option 2, we tried the winch-cable-between-tree-and-bumper strategy, but this time with a twist, literally. Using the tree we were supposed to skirt minutes earlier, we wrapped the winch cable around the tree, then around the jeep bumper, back to the tree, and back to the bumper. Then I took the axe, slipped it between the back-and-forth winch cable, halfway between the bumper and the tree, and started twirling the axe handle.

Twirling the winch cable together wound and tightened it. With the jeep in neutral (see, I can learn), each twist slowly pulled the jeep forward. With patience, time and rewinds of the cable, we maneuvered the jeep a few feet up and around a large spruce, pointing it toward a short, steep, and awkward sidehill. This was the foolhardy part of our plan.

Since we couldn't be sure this would work, I owned and executed this idea myself. I wrapped one side of a long, heavy chain around the driver's side of the roll cage. I connected the other end to a tree. I reached into the jeep and shifted it into neutral. We gave it a push and down the hill it rolled, driverless. As the chain tightened, the jeep was forced to turn, rotating around the tree. The tires fought to go down the hill, while the chain pivoted the jeep around the tree, keeping the jeep upright while forcing it to rotate the tree and navigate the difficult sidehill. After completing the trickiest part successfully, the jeep traveled a little farther than planned. Just as the chained ran out of slack, stopping it abruptly, the passenger side fender hit a tree, damaging it badly.

Ok, so it didn't go exactly as planned, but it was close enough to call it a success. After all, what's a broken fender? I could patch that in minutes with some fiberglass and resin after the trip was over.

With the jeep successfully down the difficult hill, we put it into gear, undid the chain, and chopped down the tree the jeep had hit, because the small tree was blocking our path. Now, we had one more thing left to do before we compression-started the jeep: the tree we had chopped down as part of Option 1 had fallen right across our new escape route; so, we had to chop a large enough section out of the fallen tree to drive through it.

I retrieved our trusty, but even duller, axe and we commenced chopping the felled tree into three sections. An hour later, we removed the middle portion of the tree and shoved it downhill.

Now we had an escape route, though it was hardly perfect. Our exit out of this mess was still a sidehill, the hill sloping to our right. This meant Cullen had to hang off the jeep to improve the chances we would make it out safely.

I climbed into the driver's seat. Cullen jumped onto the driver's side, his feet planted on a piece of rollbar that paralleled the bottom of the jeep body and his hands holding onto the driver's side of the rollcage. He stuck his butt outward as far as possible, like sailors hiking out to keep a boat upright when they are trying to go fast. With Cullen in position, we were ready; this plan *had* to work, because we only had enough distance for one shot at compression-starting the jeep.

Our adrenaline pumping, I pushed in the clutch and the jeep began to move forward. It sluggishly gained speed as it rolled over dirt and pine needles. We slowly passed through our fallen and chopped tree, happy to have it behind us, our speed improving. I willed us forward, hoping we didn't roll sideways and wishing we were moving more swiftly. Cullen hung to the side, but stared forward, ready for me to drop the clutch. We bumped along, faster and faster. The other side of the original trail was coming into view and our sidehill was flattening. We weren't going to go any faster; instead, we would start slowing soon.

It was now or never.

I yelled to Cullen to hang on as I let off of the clutch, causing the pressure plate of the motor to grab the clutch, spinning the motor's crankshaft (a starter effectively does the same thing) forcing the crankshaft to turn.

The jeep lurched, then slowed temporarily as the engine sputtered. At the same instant, Cullen was jerked violently forward, hitting the cowl and the side of the windshield. Yet, he held fast and the jeep remained on all four wheels.

The lurch, the speed and pressure of the drive train forced the engine to turn enough times that it fired. I pressed the gas pedal, persuading the engine to keep firing. As we coasted onto a flat area, the engine sputtered again. Cullen hung on as I massaged the engine to life with the gas pedal.

To our relief, the motor was humming smoothly. We both felt proud. We had survived. Nothing nature could throw at us (or we at ourselves) could stop us. Slow us, yes, but stop us, no!

We were not without injury, however. The jeep had suffered a broken fender and was low on battery power. We could rectify the latter by running for a few hours, but the former would have to wait. Cullen was also injured. He'd twisted his wrist, while hanging off the jeep, but his survival seemed likely, so he hopped into the passenger seat and off we went. The question was, would we be dumb enough to head right back into the hills or smart enough to head home?

Given our recent success against overwhelming odds and our renewed faith in ourselves, we elected to keep jeeping. So, onward we went until we came to a trail that disappeared into the trees on our left. We took it, venturing into the great unknown.

Ok, maybe the great unknown is an exaggeration, as there were several things I did know. First, I knew that we were heading roughly east. As long as we kept heading east we had to hit I-90, because it angled southeastward as it descended from Snoqualmie Pass into Ellensburg, a distance of roughly fifty miles, making the interstate a pretty big target.

Also, as I understood it, there weren't that many four-wheel drive roads over the Manashtash Ridge, the main ridge that separated the Little Naches river valley (where we were) from the Cle Elum river valley (the area we wanted to reach). So, given that we'd already found a four wheel drive road, I felt confident that we would summit the ridge on this trail and that it would end at a set of logging roads on the other side of the ridge. Once we found the logging roads, we could follow the roads down until we got to a paved road. With roughly seven hours of sunlight left, our goal, as usual, was to get as far as we wanted, hopefully all the way to the town of Cle Elum.

So, up the Manashtash Ridge we drove. The wariness I felt about the jeep just a few hours earlier drifted away with each bump and hill, as my trusty vehicle ascended the ridge without issue. The engine was back to its old self.

After a couple hours of trail climbing I began to see areas of familiarity. One was the climb over a long, sloping rock field with a barely visible trail of rocks polished by passing tires. Another was Tripod Flats where the club had camped under a wood shelter one year, everyone spread out in sleeping bags. Finally, there was a familiar spur trail that ended at an overlook of Mt. Rainier to the south.

By four o'clock, we'd reached the eastside of Manashtash Ridge. We emerged from the trail at a gravel logging road. Decision time. Left or right. Left or right. These logging roads were pretty deep into the woods and still on top of the ridge. Neither direction seemed more right than that other. So, guided by instinct, left we went.

Somehow, we picked the correct direction. The gravel logging road allowed us to increase our speed to 25mph, which felt fast after crawling through the forest all day. And, except for the occasional washboard, which is irritatingly bumpy, we enjoyed a smooth winding drive out of the mountains. We drifted and turned with the road and landscape, slowing down for switchbacks and washboards, speeding up for straight sections, and keeping a look out for any signs directing us to civilization, the absence of which wasn't much of a shock.

Our first sign of civilization was a summer cabin, then a small farm, and then acres of farms. Soon, the Ellensburg basin opened before us. Minutes later, we were approaching the onramps to I-90, halfway between Ellensburg and Cle Elum.

It was five o'clock. We'd only burned an hour coming down the hill. We still had today and Thursday to kill before catching the Friday morning ferry. Decision time again. Do we turn left and head back home to the island or right toward more adventure? Of course, right it was. We drove east to the Beverly Sand Dunes.

The Great Escape looking rough at the Beverly Sand Dunes. The fiberglass grille broke in half. We duct taped it back together for the remainder of the trip.

• • • •

It was twilight when we arrived at the sand dunes. No matter where dunes are located, twilight is a beautiful time of day and it was especially beautiful on this day. We had the entire dunes to ourselves, since it was a Wednesday after the Labor Day Weekend. Because we were all alone, I thought, just this once, why not camp in the middle of the dunes and let the sand cushion our sleep. So, we found a low, remote spot out of the wind, where we fell into a deep sleep after a long adventurous day.

In the morning, I coaxed Cullen into heading to Idaho to visit my grandmother Eilers, who I hadn't seen in a couple years. So, from the Beverly Sand Dunes, we drove east to Coeur d'Alene, arriving late in the afternoon. When I arrived, I learned that Grandma had been moved from the Hayden Lake house to an apartment with assisted living. Parkinson's disease coupled with a series of small strokes was robbing her of her voice and expression.

I have always been glad I made the decision to see her, because that was the final time my grandmother talked with me. One year later, during the fall of 1987, my father and I saw her alive one last time. By then she was fully trapped inside her body, able to do nothing for herself, yet she appeared to be completely cognitive. Dad was with me on that visit, but her poor condition left him speechless. He never said it, but he was devastated. Realizing he was unsure how to interact with her, I did my best to entertain her, talking non-stop about my adventures at Roche. Able to move her eyes, it seemed she badly wanted to interact and respond, but she couldn't. Instead, near the end of our visit, she shed one long tear that broke my heart. For such a beautiful person, it was an ugly way for her to exist. Though sad, I was also relieved when she died a few months later.

• • • •

After we visited Grandma, we traveled westward to the islands, driving all night to catch the 6am ferry in Anacortes on Friday. Despite broken body parts on the jeep and Cullen's sore hand, we'd survived.

Upon our return to the islands, I checked the mail, disappointed to discover I had no mail. Virginia still hadn't written me. My assumption was that she had forgotten about me, didn't receive my letter, or was too busy to write. Meanwhile, my summer was winding down. The mornings were colder and the resort slower, because the tourists were back in school or at work and, thus, no longer visiting in droves. My job as a cook at Roche Harbor for the 1986 season would end soon and though I had no plans for the future, Reaf had invited me to return in April to cook again.

• • • •

Two weeks after the trip to the Naches, Cullen, David and I took a weekend trip to Vancouver, BC, to see the 1986 World Exposition. The trip included sleeping in a tent on an empty lot in the middle of the city. It turns out cars get very noise very early in the morning in the middle of a city, so we didn't sleep well. Of course, there was also the concern of being accosted by the police for camping illegally that didn't help.

Following our trip to Vancouver, we returned to Roche Harbor in late September with a plan for the winter. We had decided that Cullen and I would travel around Washington State starting in mid-October for two weeks. Then we would then meet up with David at his home in Oregon. From there all three of us would drive down to California for fun and sun.

Meanwhile, weeks had passed since I wrote Virginia. Having already made plans for the winter and assuming I wouldn't hear back from her, I finally received *the card and pictures* from Virginia. Given all that transpired over the previous month and my new plans to travel, I believe my youthful twenty-one-year-old-self misinterpreted her letter as a goodbye-letter rather than a come-visit-me-letter. And, from that time forward, I viewed the card that way.

However, now, after meeting her again and taking a fresh look at the card through the eyes of my mature-self, I could easily see I misread it.

24. JUNE 8TH, 2011

Just like we did yesterday, Virginia and I meet again at Water Tower Park. She is early, as am I. We say hello with a quick congenial hug. We walk up the hill, disappearing into "our park".

As we approach the bench we sat on the day before, I stop her. I turn her to face me, put my arms around her, and we hug again. Unlike first one, this was a deep, more intimate hug. As we move apart, I put my hands behind her neck, and bring her lips close to mine. Her conscience resists the move, but her passion relishes the kiss, just as I do. The is warm, but brief, sensual not erotic. Our lips part. We smile, awkwardly, unsure what to do next.

Instead of sitting on the bench, we cross the grass toward the bushes at the western edge of the park. I look out at Lake Washington and downtown Seattle, but she isn't looking at the view. Instead, she examines the bushes and mentions how pretty they are. She says the color is heliotrope. I don't see heliotrope; I see blueberry.

Suddenly, I realize her view of the world must be more colorful and beautiful than mine. What I wouldn't give to look through her eyes, to see how vivid and intense her world is. My world is a geometric, practical world. I see shapes and mechanics; she sees colors, contrasts, and beauty in ways I am sure I don't.

I grab her hand and we walk back toward the bench, stepping onto the path that circles around the water tower. She stops momentarily and looks through a chain link fence at a house with a nice pool in the backyard.

"You know, I love to swim. I used to swim everyday. The one thing I never had was a pool in my backyard. I always wanted one," she says, staring longingly at it. Then she adds, "I need to start swimming again."

She falls silent. I can tell there is much she wants that she doesn't have.

Something about her comment about the pool simmers inside me. She wants a pool. I could imagine how a pool could make her happy for years. The fixer in me wants to fix this for her. I want to figure out a solution, but how?

Right there, a seed was planted. If I could write my story, and her story, and our story, would anyone care to read it? I've rarely shied from risk. I enjoy throwing caution to the wind, watching it float away like balloons at a celebration. So, to me, writing a book would be another new adventure. Yet, I wonder if I can do this . . .

We continue walking on a trail that takes us outside the park and around the block. Part way through our walk, I turn and stop her.

"I need to tell you something, " I start. "I love you deeply and I will love you forever. There is no question in my mind about it. I'm not sure I understand it. There are lots of things I don't know in this world. But, I do know that my love for you is strong. Whether we are together or not, I will always love and care deeply about you."

She says nothing, but reading her eyes I can she loves me back. After that, we don't say much. We know there is nothing else to say.

• • • •

The next day, feeling inspired, I write her a note from a teashop on Queen Anne Hill in Seattle:

June 9th, 2011 – 12:45 PM

Virginia,

Teacup: A World of World Class Tea. Now serving, at my table, Golden Sun Assam Tea, a bold yet smooth tea (according to the store manager). I'm atop Queen Anne hill, at the corner of Boston and Queen Anne Ave. The teashop is housed in a very earthy feeling space, with baby blue walls, light woods, glass and stainless. The clientele is mixed; two older ladies are either pretending to crochet and talking or pretending to talk and crocheting. I truly can't tell which.

My table is simple, round and all too small. The table strains to accommodate both my computer and my tea tray. Soon, the tea 'barista' (Tearista perhaps?) brought me a flowery tray, with only colors you could identify, though now versed in heliotrope, I can say with confidence that no heliotrope exists. On the tray is my white teapot, in which sat my Golden Sun Assam loose tea within a strainer. Next to the teapot sits a rather pedestrian, small plastic cup used to hold the teapot lid. The lid remains in the cup until the tea properly steeps. Next to the plastic container is my teacup saucer, upon which sits my cup. Both saucer and cup have a blue asian motif; perhaps heliotrope is the proper description of the color, but I'll define the colors as blueberry and white? Finally, and most importantly, on the tray sits a stainless timer filled with a 'sand' that appears to be more like a red, no more like strawberry, colored sugar. I say sugar because the grains look a little larger than sand.

I have to say I was shocked when the Tearista delivered the tray. I expected nothing more than a paper cup. So, I'm feeling pretty uptown about now. When my maitre'de delivered the tray, he told me that once the strawberry colored sugar completed it's journey from up to down within the old fashion glass timer, my tea would be ready. It was all very exciting, watching and waiting for the sugar to drop. Once finished, I immediately poured my tea. Indeed, as claimed, the tea seems bold at the front and smooth at the end. I would order it again on my next trip, as this won't be my last here.

Changing subjects . . .

The movie has changed. It is no longer the "Parent Trap". It is the "Notebook". Perhaps the better title is 'the letter'. I loved the movie the "Notebook", but I never expected to live it myself. However, rather than a combination of explosive personalities, it's a combination of caring, selfless personalities. It's a story I must write. A book I must write. I'm just not sure how quite to end it. I guess the best ending isn't the ending itself, but the lessons I can teach my kids, especially the one that demonstrates how to love someone selflessly and how to be loved back in the same way.

I'm truly at peace right now, in this moment. I know what I want to do. I know where I want to be.

Love D

She responds:

$$\text{June } 9^{th}, 2011 - 1:10 \text{ PM}$$

D-

You are a beautiful writer and the heart to go with it. You should write. I never saw "The Notebook". I started it and for various reasons did not complete it. I know I want to enjoy each day, not sit at the end of my life and regret unexplored opportunities. I want to be loved every day not just from afar.

Thank you for your thoughtful words to me as we walked.

I am so glad that you made sure we kissed, by your choice. I was trembling. Now I know the expression "trembling with desire". I did not know how I would react in person. I wanted you to kiss me badly and I wanted to kiss you back. What we shared was an almost paralyzed Virginia. I wanted to let go and kiss you passionately. I wanted to kiss your neck, as I said yesterday, until you had to kiss me with all your feelings.

I just froze and was shaking.

We could try again tomorrow. I do not work until the afternoon. You and I will not have a chance while the kids are all out of school, so it may be a long time. Why? Why am I torturing us by proliferating our intimacy? I just must have a good long time kissing you just once, before we let go. I had my chance today and I blew it.

A special love, Virginia

She is right. I should not feel so settled, but I do. I found what I want to do. I want to write. I have always wanted to write. My website is an excuse to write. What differs now is I can visualize a book I am capable of writing. In fact, I don't need to write the story; several stories have unfolded on their own. I simply need to capture and share them. There is the story of my father, of Virginia, and of me. It is a story of love, love lost, of youthful passion and dying. And there are jeeps. Who doesn't love a story about jeeps! (Ok, maybe that last one is a stretch.)

However, I also note she wrote, "before we let go", near the end of her email. Perhaps she is trying to tell me something, even accidentally, with that phrase. The wording suggests more than goodbye; with it can she be saying we need to create a safe distance between us? Or, perhaps, I am reading too much into it. Unsure, I decide not to address the issue.

With those thoughts in mind, I answer Virginia's email promptly:

June 9th, 2011 – 2:14 PM

Virginia,

Yes, of course I can meet tomorrow. As you have the tight schedule, you name the time and place and I will be there.

By peaceful, I mean I have a direction. Is everything in my life just how I want it? Not yet. But I see a path; I haven't seen a path in four years. There are bumps and rocks ahead, but that's all part of the adventure ahead of me (and us in however that might play out). No one wants to love from afar, but just feeling again — hope, love, kindness — helps me.

So, that's why I'm at peace. I kissed you for myself, because it was something I really wanted to do.

What I hope you can take with you is a sense of how love and intimacy should feel. You've given me that feeling. I just didn't have enough experience the first time we met to understand how special it was. I get it now.

Love D

Her email is short:

June 9th, 2011 – 2:43 PM

Dave,

I love that last line. I had a great letter written to respond to it and lost it. Same time, same place. We will pick another spot another time.

- V

• • • •

But, the next visit doesn't happen. Our planned encounter was derailed by an emergency appointment, so she had to cancel. I got the message while driving to our rendezvous. So, instead of meeting her, I went to a coffee shop and sent her an email. At this point, I was bursting to write:

June 10th, 2011 – 10:43 AM

Virginia,

I'm at the Cafe Felipe at the Renton Landing again. It has an open, very high ceiling, hanging lights, and a semi-industrial feel due to exposed ductwork. The open ceiling magically causes the seven simultaneous conversations to morph into background noise, reminding me that people are here, but background pieces of my own story, as I am a silent background in theirs (I think I play the roll of the good looking, silent type, dressed in black, typing quietly away . . .).

I will try to describe the wall colors, but it may just result in another epic color failure on my part; nonetheless, here it goes: A light green color is what jumps to mind, but it surely isn't that. Perhaps it is muted, or a gray/green. I thought it was white until I actually looked. Maybe it is a white, yearning to be a green, but only made it halfway. Yet, it isn't as sickly as that combo would be. It contrasts well with the dark brown accents (that might even be tope, but no one with my skill level, or lack there of, should be armed and allowed to use a description as advanced as tope . . . Yikes! I've just figured out TOPE is spelled TAUPE! See, I have no business using that word).

The otherworldly green walls do contrast well with the darkly stained (black-oakey-kind-of-sort-of-looking) tables and chairs. Overall it is a perfectly satisfactory place to hang out. The Teacup was a far better place though, as their tea choices were much more imaginative. Now that I've beaten this description to death, I hope, however briefly, you have been distracted from your difficult morning.

- Dave

I sent the email certain our emailing and interactions to continue, expecting we would have some type of friendship as we worked through our feelings. Her answer was short and brief.

June 10th, 2011 – 11:59 AM

David,

Thank you for your note and thoughts. Sorry so short. V.

• • • •

That same day, June 10th, my dad came home from the hospital. In the evening the visiting nurse arrived at my parents' home to teach us how deliver the twice daily, six-week antibiotic. The medicine was injected into a picc, or catheter, in his arm that led to a tube reaching all the way to his heart, that great big muscle that just keeps on ticking.

• • • •

I sent additional emails to Virginia over the succeeding days; I heard nothing back. Uncertain why her communication had ceased, and with my kids arriving soon for their scheduled summer visit, my emails to her tapered to zero. I eventually decided to wait until she contacted me before writing again. I was neither sad nor happy about the situation, but perplexed. Our interaction had been a series of tumultuous, unexpected events. But then, that's been my life over the past decade: thoroughly unpredictable and rocky.

I had to marvel at the turn of events during the preceding three weeks. My father was back home, feeling better, and ready to fight his way to eighty years of age. Meanwhile, after finding Virginia, I seem to be losing her for the second time in twenty-five years.

Yet, no matter our situations, I will never completely lose her. Once again she has entered my life and I have entered hers, powerfully. For me, in finding and losing Virginia, I've found myself again. The gift she has given me is an open heart.

In exchange for what Virginia gave to me, I hope she received an answer she sought. Being a very spiritual person and frustrated with life, in early May she prayed to God, asking if she had made a difference in anyone's life. I hope this book reminds her that the answer to that question is a huge, YES! Twice she has made a huge difference in my life!

EPILOGUE: AUGUST 30TH, 2011

On June 30th, I drove down to Boise and broke up with my girlfriend, moving out the next day. With the Boise house on the market under the HAFA program, she no longer needed my help to make payments on the house, because she was making no payments. I felt like I'd met my responsibilities in that area. Moreover, I had no interest in maintaining a romantic relationship with my girlfriend, as I no longer had the feelings for her I once had. In fact, I'd felt cruel prolonging it as long as I had. The whole thing felt cruel, but life just isn't easy at times. Decisions aren't black and white. There are many shades of gray. I hope she remains a friend and will always wish her the best in life.

I also felt it was time to be near Mom and Dad. I could, at least for the summer, be around to help out with Dad and fix some things at the house. Also, in Seattle I would have time to write.

Importantly, I did not move to Seattle to start a love affair with Virginia. This wasn't the right time for us.

• • • •

I wrote this epilogue in late August after living in Seattle for two months. During that time I began writing this book, while keeping eWillys up-to-date. But, all my work and life changes made me question whether I could really finish the book and maintain eWillys effectively, because, especially while the kids were with me during the summer, I made almost no progress on it. So, I wrote and posted this on eWillys in mid July:

> *My mother tells me the month of July in Seattle is on pace to be one of the coolest on record. Fortunately, I didn't move here for*

the heat! As I took a relaxing walk this morning dodging tourists through bustling Pike Place Market, with new female friend in tow, to the Seattle Art Museum in the drizzle that defines Seattle, I rather relished it. I relished the cool rainy July day, weather I ran away from back in June of 1992 as fast as the moving van would travel on a journey that seems otherworldly at this point.

So, nineteen years later, here I am walking only a few blocks from the very spot from which I moved, an apartment in Lower Queen Anne. As I walked down 1st Ave toward the SAM, I realized I'm older, yes; I'm grayer, slightly; I'm richer, financially no, experientially yes; I'm wiser, maybe; more introspective, absolutely! I sold my jeep to finance the move in 1992 and now arrive back in Seattle with a nicer one. Maybe that was worth the entire adventure?

I guess I can't help but be introspective at this time. A heady move followed by a delightful time with my kids, which after their summer stays, I'm always simultaneously proud at who they have become and disappointed that their time with me is up for another summer.

And, of course, there was the added element of my father, whose dignity we fight to preserve as time weighs heavily on his formerly stout constitution. The truth is Dad is a little south of odd for the kids to understand, because they did not know him the way I did. I wanted to show the kids he is facing his mortality head on, despite infirmities and incontinence, and fighting for his end goal, to live to the age of eighty. Will he make it? If he has any say about it, he will.

With all my recent changes, eWillys has suffered a little. When life gets in the way of the website, I wonder if I have run out of time and energy to keep it running.

Yet, at times like these some far-flung reader I have never heard from sends me an email. In this case, the reader's name was Joe who hails from the Nashville area:

> He writes, "Ewillys has refueled my passion for old flatfenders. I never knew much about them growing up, other than I wanted one and they were cool as all get out in all the old black and white war movies. I have wanted one ever since I was a kid. Two years ago I finally got a 46 cj2a. I traded a Harley for it, straight up. Figured both were about 3000.
>
> I put 2000 miles on it in the first year and I am currently replacing the motor and catching up on some long over due maintenance. I will send a pic or two.
>
> I took my mom for a ride in it last winter through the snow and it was 21 degrees out side, no heater. I have created a monster of her now. This past November she called me and told me that she wanted an "old" jeep. I figured a cj5 so she could get around and go fishing. She said, "I want one like yours!" She wanted a flatty! After searching all over the craigslist and ewillys we finally found her a beautiful 48 cj3a in GA. She drives it everywhere! I will send you pics of it as well. Now my son is 5 and I have created a jeep nut of him as well.
>
> I bought a parts 2a and it had a title. So my son and I have tinkered with it and after getting his hands greasy he's hooked. He can see the corner of a hood behind something and he will shout, "JEEP DADDY!" He is also convinced that they don't make "real" jeeps anymore and he loves cj's. We plan on building from the ground up(with a lot of help) the parts 2a into a daily driver. When he turns 16 I will sign it over to him.
>
> My father and I never had a project like this and its been great and created an even larger bond with my son. He will sit with me in the recliner and look through eWillys and give me full commentary on all the jeeps. My father

> is now retired and has run out of projects around his house……until now. We have disassembled my 2a and replaced the motor and are working on the body. My family is now 3 generations deep in jeep and I hope it continues. So a BIG THANK YOU for ewillys! I hope there is many more years of it.

I shared that letter with my kids and they thought it was pretty cool. So did Mom.

After my introspection, with the kids gone, back to Salt Lake, and my life sort of re-orienting to normal, with Joe's passionate call for another few years of eWillys, updates will commence on a more regular schedule starting tomorrow.

Until tomorrow's updates, I am happy to report, for the record, that four paddle tires will fit inside a BMW 540i. Matt, who specializes in early Dana axle rebuilds, sold me a set at a great price. Thanks Matt!

Once again, a reader re-ignites my passion to keep the site going. It seems the project I launched to help others and to heal my own wounds, has returned the favor, making my life not only better, but giving me good friends throughout the world and a greater purpose in life.

Perhaps now, having read this book, readers will better understand why I started eWillys and continue to run it.

• • • •

As for Virginia: On June 25th she sent me a single message from a work account, saying her cat knocked her coffee onto her laptop, frying the board on her personal computer, which is why she stopped sending emails. She asked that I call her and leave my phone number on her phone. She wanted to make sure we never lost contact.

In July we shared a single phone call as travel and family filled her summer, while life changes, eWillys and writing filled mine. I initiated the

July call to let her know I was living in Seattle on a permanent basis and of the life changes I had made. As we spoke on the phone, I reminded her that if she needed a friend, I would be there for her.

She will always be a special person in my life, whether we spend time together or not. I am happy I could tell her she was special to me. And, I hope she will always feel the same. Truly, how many people get to share such feelings with a lost love, let alone reconnect in such a powerful way?

We ended that July phone call, not as potential lovers, but as two friends who cared deeply for the other. At least, that was the way it felt to me. She ended the call telling me that she'd call soon.

Well, 'soon' lasted until the end of August, when she called me, apologizing taking so long to return the call. That's when I told her I was writing a book that included her. I said she had to read it and, I hoped, would approve it, because I had included some of our private conversations in the book. I knew this was a lot to ask of her.

While flattered to the point of being overwhelmed, she was also fearful about it. She was afraid her family and friends would know it was her. So, I faked her name and made other changes to her background to protect her identity. The emails between us had to be slightly altered to reflect the fake background, but otherwise are the words we shared.

However, the experiences between us at Roche Harbor in 1986 happened as truthfully and faithfully as I could remember them. The Gene Coulon Park and the Water Tower Park meetings occurred at those locations just as I describe. The dates and times of our meetings and emails are accurate as well; this entire story unfolded as I explained it in May and June of 2011. My personal stories, family history, the drives from Boise to Seattle to Spokane, and the descriptions of my jeeping and sailing adventures are also all true.

• • • •

So, I find myself back to the beginning, concerned over Dad's health. As of this writing, he continues to suffer from incontinence and has lost some weight. His balance has gotten a little worse, his stride is decidedly smaller, and his confusion comes and goes. I think his biggest fear is that he will end up like his own mother, trapped inside a stroke-ridden body.

I am living at my parents' house, which is something I never expected, but then I never expected to live in the Seattle area again. Unfortunately, many people of my generation have been forced to move back in with relatives, so I am not alone. Perhaps it is all a blessing in disguise. My generation can get to know their relatives in a way they probably wouldn't have otherwise.

For me, staying with my parents seems like just another way-stop on my journey of life. It has been a wonderful opportunity to reconnect, deeply, with my mother and father, laughing with and cooking for them, debating politics, and fixing things around the house, even if the arrangement might dampen my social life.

We've even developed our own rhythms and habits. For example, I eat eggs and bacon most mornings for breakfast. Now, both Mom and Dad *expect* slices cooked for them, too, with Mom always wanting just one and Dad always requesting two. It has become a morning routine.

So, life goes forward. eWillys keeps growing, my jeep is with me, my family loves me, my hunt for family history continues, and my lust for adventure remains. I hope I can build a Museum one day. Maybe I will even leave the cracks and become a functioning person in society again.

Until that time where I feel like a real person again, life will continue to be a bit of a struggle and unpredictable. Therefore, the words from "Paint Your Wagon" continue to feel relevant:

> *Where I'm going.*
> *I don't know.*
> *Where I'm I headed,*
> *I ain't certain.*
> *Alls I know is I am, still, on my way.*

APPENDICIES

APPENDIX I: MORE JEEP HISTORY

This is a post I posted a couple years back. So many of the histories of the jeep are dry that I thought I would spice it up a bit.

As already noted, the first jeep, that is to say the first quarter ton four wheel drive reconnaissance car, was built from scratch by the American Bantam Car Company and delivered to Camp Holabird in Maryland on September 23, 1940 (with only 5 minutes to spare!). With a gestation period of only 49 days, this truly was a quick birth and quite an accomplishment, especially since American Bantam teetered on the edge of financial collapse and banked that the jeep would hit a home run.

Of course, the army's test drivers from Camp Holabird couldn't wait to test the jeep once they saw it. Naturally, boys being boys, the first test was, would it attract females? Reports are sketchy, but one unnamed source verified that the backseat was neither as padded as the new 1940 Studebaker Coupe nor as springy and luxurious as the 1939 Cadillac DeVille. None-the-less, the ever determined testers discovered that 4WD solved this problem, because they could more easily get to remote spots where they didn't have to remain in the back of the vehicle; instead, they could jump out, spread blankets on the grass, and do what soldiers and young ladies enjoy doing — have a picnic of course! Yes, the amazing Bantam Reconnaissance Car (aka the BRC, the Pilot Model, Number One) was an instant hit with the men and women.

Unfortunately for those early testers, that very first BRC only lasted 19 days before it died from overuse. Officially, the army testers drove it over rugged terrain for more than three thousand miles during those nineteen days, repairing it until the frame broke in two different places.

But, true researchers know that sometimes the whole truth isn't told in official reports. No, my sources confided to me that what really happened was some of the boys tried to sneak all the girls from the Phi Kappa Gamma sorority back to the barracks for a party while the officers were away one night. With the girls squished together on the hood, and every other part of the vehicle, even the mighty Bantam eventually gave out when the driver tried to navigate up a set of steps to avoid the normal entrance gate to Holabird. This might explain why Bantam's next invention was the Bantam 4wd Party Bus.

Despite only nineteen days of use, the soldiers believed this uniquely American vehicle could be an asset for both fighting future engagements with other countries and procuring future engagements from the ladies (which seemed to work for many soldiers in Europe). So, the Army Quartermaster was convinced to up-the-ante and purchase fifteen hundred vehicles from three different car companies, Bantam, Ford and Willys, to test different designs. The actual final numbers produced varied for several reasons to esoteric to discuss here.

Over the next eight months, Bantam Ford and Willys produced the following models:

>**American Bantam Car Company:** After the BRC (aka the very first jeep), Bantam produced the BRC-60 and then the BRC-40. Yes, the 60 was produced before the 40 and, no, I never understood why they numbered them backward.

>**Ford Motor Company:** First came the Pygmy, then the Ford Buddy (never submitted for testing) and finally the **GP** (remember that initialism – **G** for government and **P** for eighty inch wheel base).

Willys Overland Motors: First came the Willys Quad, then the Willys **MA** (Willys **M**odel **A**).

After testing all the designs and navigating some corporate and governmental politics, on June 30, 1941, Willys Overland was awarded the contract to design the final standardized jeep. Of course, anyone who knows the history of the jeep also knows it wasn't quite that easy, but I'll leave those specifics for other books, except to say that Ford used its connections to act as a second source for the final jeep that Willys designed (hence the Ford GPW).

Finally, in Mid-November of 1941, the standardized World War II jeep that we all love, cherish, restore, modify, maintain, repair, swear at, and enjoy was approved by the Army. Again, as usual, it was not the final, final version of the WWII jeep, because as the war moved forward, the Willys model, which most jeepnuts generally refer to as the "Willys MB" (for Willys Model B), and the second-sourced Ford model, which most jeepnuts refer to as the "Ford GPW", both of which have unique production aspects, because the Army, Willys and Ford would tweak and make changes until production ceased in mid 1945.

While producing the Willys MB, Willys Overland was also busy altering the MB into a civilian farm vehicle over several years, starting with the original CJ-1 and then CJ-2s, before beginning official production of the initial civilian model, the CJ-2A, in July of 1945. The history of civilian jeeps (CJs, Trucks, Wagons, Jeepsters and foreign licensed vehicles) becomes so complex so quickly, that I won't try to cover that here.

APPENDIX II: THE JEEP CREATION MYTH

> *"The Internet may be culturally important, just as the automobile was culturally more important in the '50s than the '20s, as we got suburbia and built the Interstate Highway System. But the last successful car company started in the US was Jeep in 1941."*
>
> Peter Thiel, Wired Magazine, January 25th, 2010

While writing an early draft of my book, I did a full chapter on my birth (subsequently I deleted most of it). I sent it to my mom for corrections, since the history in my head about my birth and first few days was likely part myth and part reality. I just didn't know what parts were real and what parts weren't. It turns out I was right when writing about my parents' delay in naming me and I was wrong that my father was out playing golf during my entire birth; instead, he was there in the hospital during my birth, visited me for ten minutes and *then* went to play golf. Thus, I had to correct my own creation myth for reality's sake.

This leads me to the creation myth of the jeep vs. the reality. Since you have already read my tongue-in-cheek history of the jeep, paralleled by the real history, you would think the history of the jeep isn't a complicated topic. However, it seems people just make up the history whenever convenient, which has complicated understanding the actual history. I guess some people don't want facts get in the way of a good story. The following is a perfect example of how people obfuscate the jeep's history for their own motives. To understand the confusing creation myths of the jeep, I think we'll start with Facebook.

I got thinking about this because last night I watched the movie The Social Network. If you are unfamiliar with the movie, it is a docudrama that now defines the creation myth for Facebook, and coincidently, into which Peter Thiel, quoted at the beginning of this essay, invested an early round of Venture Capital. I say docudrama because along the continuum between documentary and fiction, the movie's adherence to history is likely somewhere in the middle, probably more toward the latter than the former. The creators of the movie hoped to reflect enough of the truth to compel us, the audience, to watch it, obviously to make money. Given the people's love of Facebook, with over 500 gazillion users, making a movie about it seemed destined.

For those who haven't seen the movie, it begins with a nice piece of dialogue between the eventual co-founder and CEO of Facebook, Mark Zuckerberg, and his girlfriend. Also, **SPOILER ALERT**, the movie ends with Mark attempting to "friend" this same woman through Facebook. In my mind, one clear message of the movie is that the motivation for Mark's drive to make Facebook a success can be attributed to Mark's passion for a woman, to prove himself to her. Whether fact or fiction, true or not, I don't think many viewers can walk away without that imagery in their mind. And thus, I believe, no matter what the true history of Facebook is, the movie now defines the creation myth of FaceBook.

This is a good example of a creation myth born by an absence of information. In this case without the information Mark could have detailed, at least as I understand it he didn't participate in the development of the movie, the writers have to create the story. Creation stories are also born of mistakes; of ignorance of the truth, or by the absence of history (as in the truth is lost to history). Nature abhors a vacuum and so do humans, so myths tend to fill the void and are only exposed as myths when passionate researchers jump in and ask the tough questions about how something really came to be.

The history of the jeep, as noted earlier, also has its share of creation myths. In fact, I thought I knew all of the creations myths, until I ran across a new one in Wired Magazine in 2010.

You see, on and off for many years I've been a subscriber to Wired magazine. For those not familiar with Wired, it is a high gloss, semi-geeky look at humanity, science and technology that is pretty approachable for non-techies. I find some of their articles interesting and short enough that it's great bathroom reading material. One day, after reading an article that I couldn't complete in the bathroom, I took it to bed to finish. Pretty soon I was glancing through the other pages. That's when I innocently read an article with questions for and answers by Peter Thiel called "*Utopian Pessimist Calls on Radical Tech to Save Economy*".

I often read before going to sleep. The risk of reading before sleeping is that sometimes I find some reference that gets my mind spinning, which means I can't sleep. But life is a risk, something I fear Americans forget. So, I forged bravely forward with my night reading. As I read through the Thiel article, I was expecting to be put to sleep and enjoy a night of slumber. Instead, the article shook me awake, because I read, to my surprise, that Thiel seemed to think he knew something about the history of jeeps and, even worse, he had it completely wrong.

Well, I couldn't let this inaccuracy go unrecognized, so I leapt from my bed and headed to my computer to write the Wired Editor a letter. After all, there were innocent tech heads out there that might seriously believe what Thiel had to say, with the jeep example a key piece of evidence in his theory. Since I and other jeep authors, bloggers, et all, when discussing some of the histories of the jeep, have to continually re-educate people about the history of the jeep because the early history is complex, it was important to me to send the email as quickly as possible, or at least that's how it seemed to me at one o'clock in the morning.

So, I typed out the following to the author of Thiel's article, Gary Wolf:

> *I read through your article last night titled "The Utopian Pessimist". I just wanted to note that, while I generally agree with Peter's assumption about the slowdown of wildly successful companies following booms in industries, I had to point out how wildly inaccurate Peter's assertion was that a company named Jeep was launched in 1941.*
>
> *First of all, no company was created to build the jeep in 1941. Instead, 3 companies competed to obtain the 1/4 ton contract from the military. The first, American Austin (called Bantam later), was launched in 1929. The second, Willys Overland, was originally called Overland and launched in 1903. The third, Ford, was launched in 1903. Two companies would eventually build the jeep for the American government: Ford and Willys. Willys was allowed to control the rights to build and license jeeps for civilians following the war, but that wasn't until 1945. Finally, no company was called Jeep (with a big J) until 1962 when Kaiser became Kaiser-Jeep.*
>
> *David Eilers*

As you can imagine, my letter hardly shook the venerable and virtual halls of Wired Magazine. While Gary politely thanked me for my "interesting correction" and noted that he forwarded my information to the letters' editor, to the best of my knowledge the correction never appeared in print and, as best I can tell, never saw the light of internet on the web. Of course, this hardly surprised me as I'm sure Wired does not want to correct Peter Thiel, a celebrated Venture Capitalist, Entrepreneur and Silicon Valley Insider.

No, I suspect my email has been entered, recorded and stored in an electronic vault the size of an Indiana Jones governmental warehouse, never to be seen again (well, until now). But that's ok, because even my letter doesn't tell the whole story of the jeep, because I was more worried about being mostly accurate, for brevity sake and to improve the chance that my correction would get published, than entirely accurate.

APPENDIX III: WILLYS VS. JEEP, WHICH IS WHICH?

****** WARNING ******

Now, consider yourself forewarned, because here I attempt to explain the difference between willys & jeep & Jeep, during which I might just thoroughly confuse you and then, after your eyes cross, you will leave knowing that I call most every ¼ ton produced by Willys Overland a jeep (lower case J). Also, if you are listening to this via book-on-tape and you fall asleep and crash, consider this a legal disclaimer against potential lawsuits for said crashes!

****** WARNING ******

Okay, if you have made it this far, you probably have an interest in jeeps, or a morbid curiosity about me, or simply have nothing else particularly interesting to do. Well then one thing to know for sure is that by the time you get done reading this you will be rewarded, for you will know what makes a jeep a jeep . . . maybe. Oh sure, I refer to jeeps, Willys, Willys jeeps, ¼ tons, WWII jeeps, with an occasional Bantam and Ford thrown in for spice and accuracy throughout the book and throughout eWillys.com. But, when is a jeep a jeep vs. a Willys? To be honest, it is confusing.

So if I, the great God of eWillys, the master of his domain, Darth Willys, doesn't know what makes a jeep, a jeep, or a Willys a jeep, who does? I mean, I have more than 30,000 images of jeeps . . . errr Willys . . . errr . . . four wheel drive vehicles . . . on the website. If I can't use that sample size to accurately determine what a jeep is, well then, I must not be very good at what I do . . . Can someone explain exactly what I do again? . . . Clearly, it must take someone more knowledgeable than I. Perhaps finding someone isn't that difficult? Well, until you find someone smarter, you are stuck with me, so let us proceed.

With all the different styles — round fenders and flat fenders and high hoods and forward controls and more — with all the different models — MBs, GPWs, CJ-2As, CJ-3As, FC-150s, and more — and all the different manufacturing and trade names — Willys, Jeep, Ford (yes, there are Ford jeeps) — it is no wonder people get confused about jeeps. In fact, I ran eWillys for two years before I sat down one day to unravel why I was so confused about what defined a jeep (the noun), what defined a Jeep (big J trademark) and what defined a Willys.

Just to make it worse, even the dictionaries have it wrong. For example, here are two random entries for the definition of jeep.

> JEEP — *a small, sturdy motor vehicle with four-wheel drive, especially one used by the military. ORIGIN:* World War II: from the initials GP, standing for general purpose.
> *Oxford Dictionary*

> JEEP — a small general-purpose motor vehicle with 80-inch wheelbase, $\frac{1}{4}$-ton capacity, and four-wheel drive used by the United States Army in World War II; also : a similar but larger and more powerful United States army vehicle.   *Miriam-Webster Dictionary*

The Oxford Dictionary maintains, falsely, that the initialism GP stands for General Purpose (note that an initialism differs from an acronym — acronyms can be spoken as a word, like NASA, ICE, ABBA (formed from letters in each singer's name), while initialisms are sounded out by letters, like CIA, BBC, or FBI). Miriam-Webster's definition ignores the fact that post war vehicles were/are also called jeeps. So, what is right?

To start, let's define GP. GP was Ford's designation for one of their prototype jeeps, with the G describing the vehicle as a "Government"

Vehicle, and the P defined as a vehicle with an eighty-inch wheelbase. Through most of WWII, Ford made a jeep described by the model designation of GPW, with the G and P referring to the info above and the W defining the model as a Willys-type model. So, that's the definition of GP and, regardless of what oxford claims, it never had anything to do with how a GP or GPW became a 'jeep'.

Now the Miriam Webster claims that a jeep is a four-wheel drive vehicle. Yet, there are ¼ ton vehicles, specifically DJ-3As (along with DJ-3A Surreys, the pink jeeps with frilly tops) made from 1956 to 1965 that are two wheel drive vehicles called jeeps. There are also two wheel drive DJ-5s and DJ-6 jeeps. In addition, two-wheel drive Wagons and Trucks were labeled 'Jeep Trucks' and 'Jeep Wagons' by Willys Overland. Finally, for several years Willys Overland manufactures Jeepsters, which are two-wheel drive vehicles that some consider jeeps. So, this evidence suggests the Miriam Webster definition isn't quite right either.

So, in an attempt to learn more I will now define (1) where the term jeep originated, (2) how it was applied to what we now call a jeep, (3) when it was applied, (4) Trucks and Wagons & (5) Pronouncing Willys. After reading this information, I think you understand why people are so confused and why I am confused.

(1) **Where the term jeep originated:** To put it succinctly, no one seems to know for sure. However, if you need to know more then that, read onward. Lots of people conjecture (or simply re tell what their cousin's uncle told them) about the history of the name.
    a. Various vehicles in the Army were called jeeps before 1940. So, some soldiers simply repurposed the name for the jeep.
        b. A cartoon character was called jeep prior to 1940.
        c. The Curtis AT-9 airplane was called a jeep by the USAAF.
        d. The letters GP, which never stood for General Purpose, despite what the Oxford Dictionary claims, and was never blurred together into the term jeep, is still an origination myth for the term jeep on some websites.
        e. The Egyptian God for off-road driving was called a jeep.
        f. Aliens named it. (Ok, I made up e & f).

As you can guess, no one is one hundred percent sure where the term jeep originates. Now at this point I could do something creative and search the Oxford English Dictionary (a resource different from the Oxford Dictionary above), the gold standard of English language history. But I would have to subscribe and I am too damn cheap to do that (though I did check Wikipedia and the site echoes the GP=JEEP misinformation). Even with the internets, I can't break through the Fort Knox security that surrounds the robust OED storage servers. It is ironic, given the fact that the OED was constructed from volunteer help, not unlike Wikipedia, that this resource is unusable by most people online.

What I *can tell you* is that the term jeep is one of twenty-nine *verbs* in the English language that all have the same monomorphemic sound, in other words, being spelled with eep or eap. My favorite has to be the term 'leep', which means to 'wash with cow-dung and water'. So perhaps the term jeep morphed from the verb 'leep' and comes from the idea of traveling through cow-dung and water. It's too perfect not to love it!

(2) **How 'jeeps' transformed into 'Willys jeeps':** If you think that history was complex, how the name jeep is applied is even more complex. Personally, I buy into the theory that various soldiers at Camp Holabird, Maryland, the original testing location for the very first 'jeep' are credited with early use of the name. However, technically this wasn't a jeep or a Willys; it was actually a ¼ ton four-wheel drive Bantam, made by American Bantam.

Once established, all parties adopted the use of the term jeep quickly. Whether made by Bantam, or Ford Motors, or Willys Overland, which all developed early quarter ton prototype four wheel drive reconnaissance cars, these vehicles were all categorized under the umbrella of a jeep. There was the Bantam jeep, Ford jeep (or Ford GPW), and the Willys Overland jeep (shortened to Willys jeep or Willys MB). Out of those three carmakers, Willys Overland would win the rights to manufacture the jeep for the Army.

Willys Overland also realized the jeep trademark could be a killer trademark and, in fact, the very first prototype civilian jeeps (the CJ-

2) in 1944/45 of which there were under one hundred made, actually were printed with JEEP on the hood and other places. Ford countered that Willys didn't have the rights to that name so a pissing contest . . . errrr . . . legal battle ensued . . . over the Jeep trademark. Even with the inconvenience of the legal battle, Willys Overland advertising continued to include "Jeep" phrases, such as "The Sun Never Sets on the Mighty Jeep".

Eventually the legal issue forced Willys Overland to choose an alternative trademark for the jeep for a few years. They chose the shortened form of Willys Overland, or 'Willys', for some of their four-wheel vehicles. Hence, their civilian jeeps became 'Willys jeeps'. However, many people didn't recognize this distinction throughout the 1940s or even later on and still referred to a Willys Overland four-wheel-drive vehicle as a jeep (just as Willys-Overland advertising did). A perfect example of this is that even the earliest jeep clubs were called jeep clubs (or jeep associations) and not Willys clubs. So, Willys was the trade name for the jeep while jeep became a noun to describe a four-wheel drive quarter ton vehicle.

(3) **When is it a Willys and when is it a jeep?** As we have learned, initially the prototypes, and then the World War II vehicles, despite being built by both Ford and Willys Overland (and Bantam), were all called jeeps (and I could bring up the fact that the Brits actually called jeeps 'Bantams', but let's not go there). When Willys Overland launched the civilian jeeps in 1945, the same year World War II ended, they stamped the bodies with 'Willys'. When Willys Overland launched their trucks and their wagons in 1946 they affixed labels such as "Jeep Trucks" and "Jeep Station Wagons". They weren't even four-wheel-drive originally (confused yet, given both definitions at the beginning of this chapter explicitly state 4wd?).

Even with the fact that Willys Overland was not supposed to use the term jeep as a trademark, Willys Overland imprinted the name Jeep onto their civilian Willys (on the tool box compartment – strangely sneaky), on Jeep trucks, Jeep wagons, Jeep firetrucks (which is ironic in that this was a quarter ton civilian Willys with fire stuff on it) and more. So by 1950, when Willys Overland actually did receive the trademark "Jeep" (one wonders how the IP folks could award that trademark based on all the aforementioned confusion and 'nounizing' of the term jeep), Willy's Overland had successfully, for better or for worse, confused and conflated the term jeep with the trademark Willys.

Even worse, after obtaining the trademark in 1955, Willys Motors, having taken over the Willys Overland company a few years earlier, was making both a Willys labeled quarter ton (CJ-3B) vehicle, while simultaneously producing a quarter ton CJ-5 (the first civilian 'round fender' jeep), whose body was stamped Jeep (big J) and whose tailgate was stamped Willys. So, is it a Willys or a jeep? You make the call!!! The name Willys continued to be used at least through 1968 on the CJ-3B, while other Kasier Jeep (the company which bought Willys Motors) vehicles had begun using Jeep without any sign of Willys (such as the Forward Control four wheel drive jeep trucks). So if you're confused about what you should call a jeep and what you should call a Willys, even the manufacturer couldn't decide!!

(4) **Trucks and Wagon:** Since we learned that Willys Overland labeled their trucks and wagons, at the very beginning, as 'Jeep Truck' and 'Jeep Wagon', you might assume that the common vernacular amongst hobbyists might be those terms, but you'd be wrong. 'Willys Trucks' and 'Willys Wagons' are almost universally used. And, usually, the word 'old' is added as well, as in 'Old Willys Truck' or 'Old Willys Wagon'.

(5) **Pronunciation:** Finally, I pronounce 'Willys' as Willies or Willeez. That's the way I learned to pronounce it and never heard anything different until my recent research led me to read that some people felt the 'proper' pronunciation was 'Willis' similar to the way actor Bruce Willis' name is pronounced. Now, I really do my best to be accurate, but in this I cannot change. I will not. I must take a stand! You will have to pry such a pronunciation from my cold, dead lips, while pressing on my expired chest, because it just sounds wrong to me. It's not unlike the issue I had with vietnamese pho noodle soup (which I love, love, love, especially with the tendon, tripe and anything else interesting). It just seems that "pho" should be pronounced "FOE", but someone told me is actually pronounced "FOO" or "FU". However, that just doesn't sound right to me. So, I'm sticking to my position on Willeez . . . And "FOE".

So now that you, dear reader, have that fifty thousand foot view of the situation, don't you feel better? No?

You might wonder how I navigate this mess? Easy, sort of. I call any ¼ ton vehicles made by Willy's Overland, Willy's Motors, Kaiser Jeep, or their assignees, a jeep (lower case). Or, I refer specifically to the model, such as a CJ-3B or a FC-170, etc. If I refer to the brand, I use Jeep®, capitalized, after all Jeep/Chrysler/AMC® has registered and paid for that right. Also part of the jeep family are any Ford or Bantam four-wheel-drive vehicles made during or before World War II. Finally, I have one small addition. I call any custom vehicles made to look like, but not manufactured by Willy's Overland — like a flatfendered old-style jeep out of fiberglass or stainless steel or aluminum, or any other jeep-ish design, such as a stretched 2wd sand drag jeep — jeeps as well.

If I discuss Wagons or Trucks, I nearly exclusively call them Willys Trucks or Willys Wagons, simply because everyone else I encounter refers to them in the same manner.

Equally important, when I say jeep I am not talking about an International Harvester Scout, a Ford Bronco, a Toyota Land Cruiser, a Land Rover, or a variety of other extremely capable, completely valid, four-wheel drive vehicles. In fact, many owners of those vehicles are offended if you do call their vehicles jeeps. So tread carefully with this newfound knowledge.

Regardless of how I approach the name of the jeep, my intent is not to convert any others to my way of thinking. Instead, I'm only hoping to point out a pretty confusing situation.

APPENDIX IV: A FEW EWILLYS STORIES

There are four stories here, which reflect some of the feature stories I share on eWillys. I wrote the first two stories and readers shared the latter two with me.

Wolf Creek Pass

Yesterday I played basketball, like I do most days of the week. Before we got started, one of my basketball chums asks me if I've had any major injuries from basketball, which is normally a segue for the other person to tell me about their injuries. Fortunately, he's a likeable guy and I knew he'd have a couple good stories.

So, I told him that when I was twenty I had a major sprain on my left foot and when I was forty I had a major sprain on my right foot. Otherwise, I've had the normal jammed fingers and such, but nothing else major . . . I've been pretty lucky I tell him.

After he gives me the complete run down on his major scars and basketball-related deformities, he asks how old I am. I tell him forty-four. He says, that I don't look that old. That statement didn't surprise me, because I get that a lot. And, it's working out well now, but when I was younger, say twenty, I looked about eleven. That wasn't so good.

I bring up my age because, back in the day, we used to have these vinyl things we called records. Now, this was before iTunes, before iPods, before CDs, before boom boxes and even before Sony Walkmans.

It is true, I actually remember the day my cousin, for his sixteenth birthday (I was sixteen at the time too) got a Sony Walkman II for his birthday. It was 1981. Those were high-end, expensive devices.

It was soooo cool! You could put a cassette tape in it and listen to music through high quality earphones. The sound was amazing! I wouldn't say I was green with envy or jealous beyond reason, but I sure wanted one of those myself. Anyway, I digress . . .

I bring all this up because Gerald emailed me this morning, asking me if I remembered a singer named C.W. McCall and his album Wolf Creek Pass? He asked me this because he had just ran across some Youtube videos of Wolf Creek Pass, which aren't videos so much as they are audios.

You see, this was before MTV, too. And, despite whatever propaganda you might have heard, God didn't create MTV on the seventh day. No, I might be old, but I'm not so old that I remember hearing a Big Bang, yet am old enough to remember the launch of MTV, which might not have been a big bang, but was accompanied by a lot of noise.

That was when they used to play music videos on MTV, all day and every day, 24/7. This was when we skipped the occasional high school class or two to go watch MTV — yes truly rebels without a cause. Ok, as you have probably already guessed, I never ran with the Lost Boy crowd or anything close to it.

Now, I speak of all these music references as if I'm some kind of audiophile; but, I confess to never have been cool or hip enough to own much music. When records were cool, I only owned a few. When cassette tapes were all the rage, I was still listening to Dad's eight-track John Denver albums (all two of them) — and that was only on trips to Idaho, as the only eight-track tape player was in our motorhome. Well, there was also the "Paint Your Wagon" eight-track tape as well, which I memorized and can still sing pretty well to this day.

Of course, now that eight-track tapes might actually be cool again, I no longer have any eight-track tapes; I no longer own any cassette tapes; I might have a total of ten CDs. In fact, my fifteen-year-old son not only owns, but knows more about eighties music now that I ever did. But, I still own one record, one piece of vinyl, carefully stored at my parents' house — C.W. McCall's "Wolf Creek Pass" in its original Cover.

I remember the evening Dad brought it home. It was the first, and last, music Dad ever brought home for me. If I remember correctly, he didn't even buy it, but rather won it somehow. I'd never heard of the album nor C.W., but Dad said there was a song about four-wheel drive on it, about jeeps. I put it on the record player and, sure enough, it was as close to a jeep song as I was likely going to get. I played that album more times than it deserved, because, no offense to Mr. McCall, but it wasn't really very good. No matter, though, I enjoyed it — as did Gerald, who played the title song "Wolf Creek Pass" at his wedding. Perhaps only then did Gerald's wife really understand what she was in for!!

• • • •

Always Check Your Nuts

It all seemed simple enough. I'd pull off the front driver's side tire, pull off the front brake drum, adjust the brakes (The front right was pulling some when braking, so I needed to adjust the front left), and put everything back together ... easy enough, yes?

Well, that was last night. This morning, I hopped in the jeep and drove down to the local gas station to get some gas, before heading to the local home/garden shop (Zamzows) in Boise.

As I exited the gas station, my pedal suddenly dropped to the floor. Hmm ... not good. I jumped out, lifted the hood, and, sure enough my accelerator cable connector had come loose. I re-attached the cable and drove back home to more permanently fix the solution.

After fixing the problem, I was back on the road, heading to Zamzows again. Life was good. I drove about two miles and started hearing a tinging. *An odd sound*, I thought to myself . . . I listened more closely . . . *That is coming from the front left side.*

And then it hit me. *Had I tightened the lug nuts from my brake work the night before?* Crap, I couldn't remember.

At just that moment, when a grip of dread descending upon me that I might have forgotten to tighten the nuts, I was looking down at the driver's tire, driving about 35mph, when a silver bullet shot from the wheel and landed in the grass divider (never did find it). Holy shit! That was a lug nut! I pulled over into the median (it's a rural road with a grass median) and checked out the situation.

After doing some accounting (yes, that MBA of mine really came in handy about now), I concluded the situation was not good. One lug nut missing. Two lug nuts loose. Two lug nuts holding on the rim. No tools . . . and one idiot standing there (yes, that would be me).

What to do? Head back home very slowly. Every quarter-mile or so I stopped, jumped out, hand tightened the lug nuts, got back in, and kept going. Drive another quarter- mile & repeat. You get the idea!

I finally did make it home, tightened everything back up, PACKED MY TOOLS, and took off again. No more problems the rest of the day . . . whew!

However, to add insult to injury, my brake adjustments still didn't fix the pull to the right I have! Just know that I won't be forgetting to double-check my lug nuts in the future!!

• • • •

Gremlins in the Gas Tank

A reader named Sam called me today. He told me he had a great story to share. Hopefully, I've remembered most of it correctly.

For a little background, Sam is retired after a lifetime of building hotrods, drag racing and owning a shop in Sacramento, but now operates a small flattie-oriented shop in Arvada, Colorado, where he fixes, modifies and maintains Willys (and probably a few other vehicles) for fun. I'll be explaining more about in a future post, but for now you have enough information to understand why a jeep owner, in some distress, had his jeep towed to Sam's shop to investigate a problem.

And now to Sam's story . . . The owner of this willys had tried to drive his jeep to work, but the jeep stopped working while driving down the road. So, the owner pulled to the side of the road, waited a moment, and started it up again. Sure enough, it fired up and the owner drove onward.

Another few miles down the road the jeep shutoff again. So, the owner repeated the process: pull over, restart, and continue onward.

At some point, this re-occurring process became too much for the owner to bear, so he called a towing company and had his jeep towed to Sam's.

So, Sam looks the jeep over. He starts it up and, sure enough, after a little while it shuts down. He knows it has an electric fuel pump and suspects that could be causing a problem, so he unhooks the hose from the carb and points it into a gas can. Then, he turns on the fuel pump. Sure enough, after a little while, the fuel dribbles to a stop, yet he can hear pump still pumping . . . hmmmm, Sam thinks to himself.

He decides to try an experiment. He knows the owner only fills the tank to half full, because if the tank gets too full gas leaches out of somewhere (I can't remember where Sam said it leaked).

Sam decides to fill up the tank all the way, because he suspects there might be something in the tank. Sure enough, he fills up the tank and out pops not one, not two, but three ping pong balls.

As Sam explains it, the sucking power of the fuel pump was pulling the ping-pong balls to the outlet area of the tank (where the fuel line connects), stopping the fuel from exiting the tank, which shut down the jeep.

How'd the ping-pong balls get there? Well, that still remains a mystery... So, the moral of this story is that even the mightiest jeep can be humbled by an even mightier ping-pong ball. And, a side moral, is that buying a locking gas cap is a pretty good idea sometimes.

• • • •

John Drives at age 2

Hi Dave, this is my story. At the age of two-years-ten-months, I was put behind the steering wheel of a 1946 CJ-2A (this was in 1955). My Dad had me with him one sunny fall day sowing wheat in the north forty. It was the field with a half-mile lane to it. In the back of the willys were wheat seed bags.

As Dad would run out of wheat in the grain drill, he would walk back & bring the Willys to the drill fill it up and continue on. I got to nap on the seed bags, lying in the sun. As I napped, Dad could watch me as he would make his rounds with the drill.

As Dad finished up the field we were on the opposite end from the gate out of the field. So, here comes my first Willys drive. Dad stood me up on the seat, put it in low range, pointed the jeep to the gate, and away I went. He drove along side me till we got to the gate, where he stopped me, and said, "Move over I'll get you through the gate!"

He said I made a fuss about moving over, but, after he got the Willys through the gate, he turned me loose again for the half-mile drive up the lane. Dad said I would lie on the steering wheel and let it roll me around.

My love of Willys jeeps is deeply rooted and this story is special as it was told to me by Dad only a month before he passed away. Mom said if she had known this back then, I would never have gotten to go out with Dad again.

Finding Virginia

David Eilers

PICTURE CREDITS

Page 7:   Picture of Lost Biscuit with David and his kids, 2011 – Brenda Ann Ritt
Page 16:   Tesh and David at the Burgerworks, 1985 – David' Eilers Photo
Page 51:   David on a Ferry in 2011 – Brenda Ann Ritt
Page 57:   The Yellow Brick Road at Roche, 2011 – Brenda Ann Ritt
Page 59:   Roche Harbor Resort, 2011 – Brenda Ann Ritt
Page 73:   David and Karl at Milk Lake, 1981 – WWJC Scrapbook
Page 75:   Wandering Willys Jeep Club Logo – WWJC Scrapbook
Page 77:   Gypsy B piled with club members – WWJC Scrapbook
Page 78a: Marge and Kim balancing the jeep – WWJC Scrapbook
Page 78b: Jeep in a tire pit – WWJC Scrapbook
Page 79:   Potato stab event – WWJC Scrapbook
Page 90a: Karl's CJ-5 from the front – WWJC Scrapbook
Page 90b: Karl's Dad's CJ-5 from the back – WWJC Scrapbook
Page 102:   David at the telephone booth at Roche Harbor, 1986 – Virginia
Page 103:   David at the Roche Harbor Restaurant, 1986 – Virginia
Page 125:   Paul's Stainless Steel M-38 – Paul Bierman
Page 127:   The Eilers' 'temporary' barn – David Eilers
Page 142:   The front of the 'Great Escape', 1984 – David Eilers
Page 143:   The rear of the 'Great Escape', 1984 – David Eilers
Page 146:   The 'Great Escape' in the pasture, 1984 – Kimberly Eilers
Page 147:   David testing his first jeep in the pasture, 1985 – David Eilers Photo
Page 156:   David and Aunt Marilyn at Roche Harbor, 1987 – David Eilers Photo
Page 158:   Towing a Hobie Cat with my jeep, 1987 – David Eilers
Page 175:   Looking north toward Spieden Island, 2011 – Brenda Ann Ritt
Page 181:   David at the old barbeque area, 2011 – Brenda Ann Ritt
Page 193:   Three generations of Eilers, 1908 – Eilers Family Photo
Page 196:   Anton Eilers, photograph from the Memorial Book – Eilers Family Photo
Page 199:   Dan Van Wormer's jeep before and after, 2011 – Dan Van Wormer
Page 201:   Two Girls in the Forest, a painting by Emma Eilers, 2011 – Brenda Ann Ritt
Page 233:   Karl, B.B., and Tony Eilers, 1942 – Eilers Family Photo
Page 250:   The mausoleum entrance, 2011 – Brenda Ann Ritt
Page 251:   David behind the broken column at the mausoleum, 2011 -- Brenda Ann Ritt
Page 254:   Karl and Kimberly, 2011 – David Eilers
Page 256:   Karl's brain, 2011 – Eilers Family Photo
Page 275:   The jeep at the start of the Naches Trail, 1986 – David Eilers
Page 277:   The jeep stuck in the mud, 1986 – David Eilers
Page 278:   David driving through the mud, 1986 – Cullen Finley
Page 288:   The jeep at the Beverly HIlls Sand Dunes, 1986 – David Eilers
Page 333:   David – Brenda Ann Ritt

David Eilers

ABOUT THE AUTHOR

A blogger, web developer and entrepreneur, author David Eilers is a Lindbergh High School graduate from Renton, Washington. He earned a Bachelor's Degree from the University of Puget Sound and a MBA Degree from the University of Utah.

David is passionate about jeeps, evidenced by this book. When not writing or playing with jeeps, he can often be found dribbling a basketball, cooking in the kitchen, building websites, playing a guitar, spending time getting beat by his children at video games, or reading and researching something passionately.

Always willing to try something new, David has rebuilt transmissions, delivered newspapers, cooked in restaurants, run a kids bike camp, acted as a substitute computer teacher, painted homes, rebuilt houses, written bank financial analyses, created business plans, developed financial pro-formas, raised capital, sold stock, directed software teams, installed phone systems, founded companies, developed websites and much more. To that list he can now add, written a book. "Finding Virginia" is his first.

David Eilers

Made in the USA
Charleston, SC
08 February 2012